"A fascinating account of a celebrated nineteenth-century woman who was a nun, a mother, and, possibly, a saint."

Jubilee

" . . . unsentimental, often most amusing, uncommonly well written and based on research. . . . That (Mrs. Connelly) was a most remarkable woman is proved by this fine account of her career."

The Sunday Times (London)

"Cornelia Connelly's story is stranger than fiction. Such a life belongs solely to the realm of fact; that one woman in a lifetime should play so many parts defies the imagination. . . . This excellent biography has been deftly done by Juliana Wadham, who was herself educated by the nuns of the Society of the Holy Child Jesus. . . . Mrs. Wadham . . . has not allowed her feelings to influence her objectivity nor her objectivity to diminish her profound understanding of her subject."

Messenger of the Sacred Heart

"Mrs. Wadham writes with passion, power and scholarship. She has succeeded in that most difficult of undertakings—the baring of a human heart and soul that was transformed by suffering to an image of Christ."

Catholic Book Club Newsletter

"In spite of Mrs. Wadham's beautiful job of restraint and dispassionate respect in relating the details of Cornelia Connelly's life, the events of that life are so fantastic that the book cannot be read with any attitude other than that of the detective story fan who cannot put his book down no matter how late the hour."

Baton Rouge Advocate

"No stretch of the imagination could produce a fiction as strange as the true story of *The Case of Cornelia Connelly*."

Ave Maria

"A fascinating account of a ... and ... a whole ..."

—*The Sunday Times* (London)

—*Publishers Weekly*

—*The New York Times Book Review*

—*Chicago Tribune*

—*Booklist*

THE CASE OF CORNELIA CONNELLY

JULIANA WADHAM

Courage, Confidence—and Simplicity
CORNELIA CONNELLY

IMAGE BOOKS
A DIVISION OF DOUBLEDAY & COMPANY, INC.
GARDEN CITY, NEW YORK

IMAGE BOOKS EDITION 1960
by special arrangement with Pantheon Books Inc.

Image Books edition published September, 1960
1st printing .... August, 1960

Nihil obstat: Carolus E. Diviney
Imprimatur: Eduardus P. Hoar, LL.D.
           Vicarius Capitularis Bruklyniensis
           Bruklynii
           Die xx Decembris, 1956.

COVER BY SHIRLEY SMITH
TYPOGRAPHY BY JOSEPH P. ASCHERL

TO
ANOTHER CORNELIA

ACKNOWLEDGMENTS

I would like, above all, to thank the nuns of the Society of the Holy Child Jesus who have made this book possible. Although they had no influence upon my desire to write it, and it in no way reflects their opinion, this life of Cornelia Connelly could not have been written without their consent. They have put no restrictions in the way of my research, have made no attempt to impose their views, and have been most generous in their help over original documents and letters.

I would also like to thank my mother, Mr. Mark Bonham Carter, Mr. Adrian House, and Mrs. Janet Ward for their extremely helpful and constructive criticisms, and the Hon. George Hardinge for reading and correcting the finished manuscript.

My thanks are also due to Fr. Gervase Mathew, Professor Denis Gwynn, and Professor Michael Lewis for answering questions about historical background, and to Princess Marina Borghese for allowing me to use the photographs she has so kindly lent and for describing her memories of her father and grandfather to me.

And last, but not least, I would like to thank my husband, without whose unfailing and invigorating discouragement this book would never have been written.

CONTENTS

PREFACE

THERE IS, I have always suspected, a desire in most of us to bring down a saint—to see how he flies and how, if he is, he is different. But the opportunity so seldom presents itself, for saints, as they come down to us, are creatures of legend, so often removed from one's understanding by years of tradition or from one's sympathy by the sentimentality or prejudice of their close supporters. They appear, like the pillars in the allegory, either pure granite or pure mist.

In Cornelia Connelly I thought I had found the perfect opportunity to study a saint at close quarters. Not only was she a candidate for beatification but her attitude of mind was both modern and fearless and her life, at least in its second half, closely documented. I had been fascinated by her predicament ever since, as a child, I was at one of her schools and found myself unable to make up my mind on which side of the argument I would have come down in her lifetime. The success of her order* and her convents was altogether in her favor; her children and their happiness were not.

At first sight she appears a curious candidate. The first part of her life she lived always at one remove from God; her choices were her husband's, her advisers', her guardians'—spiritual and temporal—even the choice of her religion was

---

* Strictly speaking, "order" is not the correct term for the Holy Child nuns, who have taken *simple* and not *solemn* vows. But then, strictly speaking, and for the same reason, they are not nuns. They should be referred to as "a congregation" or "society" and their collective title should be "religious" or "sisters." But, in the interests of simplicity, I have used the more familiar terms throughout this book except when quoting, directly or indirectly, from original sources.

dictated to her. The second is a headline for the sensational press in any age—a nun sued in court, the most Protestant court in Europe, for the restitution of conjugal rights by her husband, a priest. And the third is a series of worldly successes achieved only by endless litigation and apparent failure; of domestic tragedy that by so many might be interpreted as a sign that, even from God's point of view, the wrong decision was made; and of personal and public rebukes, disappointments, and distrusts so great that on her death her successor refused to allow her name to be mentioned and hid all the private papers she could find so that her memory should not destroy her works. Yet through all these runs a firm thread of continuity—a resolute love of God that begins tentatively and soon consumes her, and which is bought at a greater human cost than is asked of many saints.

In writing this book I have tried, wherever it is possible, to follow her story chronologically, so that it appears, in order of choice and events, as it must have appeared to her. And it is impossible, I think, to escape from the fact that whatever her faults—and, like all saints, she had them—Cornelia was a woman of outstanding spiritual graces and capacities. Her courage, her self-discipline, her gaiety, and, perhaps most attractive of all, her humor were all brought to bear upon the one huge task of interpreting God's will.

It is sometimes difficult for an outsider to appreciate this task. Unconsciously, perhaps, we glow with warm appreciation when a saint's weaker moments and more fallible decisions are betrayed because they are so much more humanly attractive, and forgive them for their stoical efforts on God's behalf only because they are, after all, saints. This is inevitable because sanctity is a supernatural state. It has little natural appeal, and in order to understand or judge it we have mentally to put on the same desire to please God that the lover puts on to satisfy his beloved. But having done so, having accepted the unfamiliar motives and behavior of those who desire perfection and the realization of God's love for them, it is possible to relax in one's attitude toward the saint as well as to fear him, to see his successes with God as successes indeed; to realize his failures not as stronger attractions than his successes but as real failures.

This is not to keep one's critical faculties at bay but to train them to follow the right scent and not bark up the wrong tree; to hunt not merely the saint in pursuit of his sanctity but the saint in pursuit of his God. Then only can one begin to decide if a candidate for sainthood is, in fact, a saint.

It is difficult for us, as it must have been for her, to decide how near Cornelia came to realizing God's will for her. For unlike human ambition, with its hurdles to be crossed and its clearly defined crises, there is no certain horizon of achievement, no permanent certainty of success, with the ambition of the soul. But however one decides in her regard, from the facts—and throughout I have tried to let them speak for themselves and, in situations where it is impossible to reconcile two opposing opinions, or to decide upon which is the more likely, to give them both as accurately as I can—one thing must, I think, be clear. This is no case of hysterical piety or hypocritical attainment. It is a case of human personality surviving such cruel pressures of circumstance as to become, if not a saint in the sense of canonization, then a saint in the sense of complete identification with the will of God. Whether or not Cornelia Connelly is a saint in the first and popular sense I do not know. That, more than the trial which is the climax to the first half of her life, provides THE CASE OF CORNELIA CONNELLY.

Part One

Chapter 1

THE AMERICAN DIVINE

IN 1790 Philadelphia could look forward to the future as complacently as she looked back upon her past. She was the cultural capital of America without rival from any other city. All foreigners came first to Philadelphia, with her enthusiasm for the fine arts, her publishing and playhouses which stocked the Continent, her hostesses who kept religiously abreast of English fashion in letters as in dress, her lively disputatious politicians, and her merchants whose fortunes were as great as was their daring in land speculation. With the establishment of the second Bank of the United States, Philadelphia took over the financial lead as well, receiving and disbursing the money of the Government and attracting outside funds for investment. There seemed no limit to her influence.

But by 1830 the picture was sadly changed. The seat of federal government had been moved to Washington in 1800 and with it the hub of the glittering wheel. There was another, more formidable, obstacle to slow down the revolutions. Philadelphia was to fall an unwilling victim to topography. Between her and the inland empire lay the Appalachian mountain range. And mountains were a serious barrier to cheap transport. In effect, Philadelphia was deprived of her hinterland, and as she also suffered from the disadvantage of being upriver, with a harbor that could not handle the largest ships, the rise of more luckily situated New York finally ensured her decline.

But in 1809 she still easily held her own, unaware of how much she was to lose. The years that followed were still pleasant years—the same interests and fashions prevailed and society was not to be deterred by the prospects of backwaterdom. And in 1809 Cornelia Augusta Peacock was born.

The youngest of six children by her mother's second marriage (there were two by her first), Cornelia's heritage was still a fortunate one. Her mother, whose maiden name was Swope, and whose forebears of only two generations back were to be found in the Palatinate, had first married a wealthy sugar planter in Jamaica called Bowen. She was, therefore, an extremely rich widow when she met Ralph Peacock, Cornelia's father, an Englishman of yeoman Yorkshire stock interested in marble quarries and in buying up American land patents. To the attractiveness of wealth and widowhood were added a dark handsomeness which was often attributed to Spanish blood and, less often, to Jewish ancestry. They met, according to the somewhat hazy recorded recollection of a grandniece, when Mrs. Bowen was out riding in her carriage. The romantic encounter soon led to matrimony and, according to Cornelia herself, to a most happy, uneventful domesticity.

But this was not to last. When Cornelia was nine her father died, and by then it was no longer possible to disguise the fact that he had managed to carve his way through most of his wife's fortune.

She was left, with those of her children who were not already married, in comparative poverty, for the income from the plantation had passed by inheritance to John and Isabel Bowen, the children of her first marriage. Of her Peacock children three were fortunately stalwart sons, and her eldest daughter, Adeline, was not to remain a burden long. She was of marriageable age and soon became engaged, in the most pleasant circumstances, to Lewis Duval, an attractive young man and the son of an importer, James Seraphim Duval, who proved at his death to be the second-richest man in Philadelphia.

When Cornelia was fourteen her mother died. It is curious that she seldom writes or speaks of her mother. Her memory does not seem to throw back naturally to her early childhood at all, and when she is asked about it she can only remember its happiness and schoolroom freedom. Perhaps—like so many children brought up in the comfortable remote nurseries of the time, she saw little of her parents and that little, though pleasant, was not enough to impress her with definite memories.

They must, in any case, have been uneventful years compared with those that followed. For on her mother's death Cornelia went to live with her half-sister, Isabel, now Mrs. Montgomery. Mrs. Montgomery's wealth was not diminished by matrimony, nor were her social ambitions. She was a formidable person and, judging from the marble-fronted house she built in 1829 (the only one in the street), a successful one. There is nothing to suggest whether the nickname "Montgomery's Folly" was inspired by envy, contempt, or grudging admiration. She certainly did her duty by her half-sister, though one questions with what end in view. Cornelia was educated at home by the best tutors and governesses. She learned what her contemporaries in England were learning: drawing, sewing, music, French, and Italian. But she learned more than these, perhaps because Philadelphia was her home and men more often than not were her teachers. She was thoroughly grounded in grammar, mathematics, history, and geography.

There is little known about her at this time except, from the same source as before, that she was pretty, charming and gay, and sometimes self-willed. Her gaiety owed nothing to wit. It was a natural buoyancy of spirit which rose to the surface at every occasion, and lasted all her life.

Cornelia left the schoolroom to lead the conventional life of a debutante of her day—not only from Mrs. Montgomery's house but from Adeline Duval's as well. And Adeline was no dowager awaiting results. She was a young, very beautiful woman whose husband's wealth and position put her at the head of Philadelphia society.

We do not know what Cornelia felt and thought at this time. There is only one souvenir of these years—a poem, or rather a translation of a poem, written when she was nineteen in her sister Adeline's scrapbook. It is a freely adapted jingle from Metastasio, and the sentiments are not surprising in a girl of nineteen. In fact, their very appropriateness makes one suspect a conventional cause. The verse has survived the weight of its sentiments with remarkable lightheartedness, except in the melancholy bump with which the rhyme is abandoned and the poem ends—or has a later undiscerning hand substituted "heart" for "breast"?

> *If everyone's internal care*
> *Were written on his brow*
> *How many would our pity share*
> *Who raise our envy now.*
>
> *The fatal secret when revealed*
> *Of every aching heart*
> *Would prove that only when concealed*
> *Their lot appears the best.*

It was to prove an ironic prophecy, not of the immediate future but for the many years ahead.

Three years later, when she was twenty-two, Cornelia announced her engagement to a young man called Pierce Connelly. How or when they met we do not know. It is unlikely that they did so through the normal channels of social intercourse because Pierce was not acceptable to families like the Peacocks and Montgomerys. For the Connellys were in trade —the furniture trade, with its aura of dusty rooms, shuttered windows, and sunlight filtering slowly across silent piles of unused wood and upholstery. Behind lurked an even more sinister implication. A large proportion of the Irish immigrants who stole across the Atlantic to find their vocation in the land of promise came as indentured servants. There is, of course, no suggestion of the Connellys' having arrived in such a way, other than the combination of their name and occupation. But to Mrs. Montgomery the threat must have been a very real one.

It did not, however, deter Cornelia. She was swept off her feet like many others by Pierce's charm, which lay halfway between his humor and his zest. He loved to tease, to startle into appreciation with a laugh. And he loved exploring the new and exciting in ideas and in fact. There was something peculiarly flattering in his appreciation. It was so obviously real and uncynical. He had a fascinating ability to stimulate and amuse as well as to warm his acquaintances. He could listen and talk, and his quick wits picked their way neatly between arguments and discussions so that they seemed to interpret more exactly all that others wished to say, to offer them the better phrase, the more exact account, as if he had just borrowed it from them and was giving it back. He had, in fact, that delightful gift of making others feel more intelligent, more important, than they were, because he was himself entranced with their cleverness and their power and had talent enough to make his savoring seem worth while.

As a suitor he was irresistible, and the fact that a number of the young ladies of Cornelia's acquaintance were rivalling each other for his attentions added to his attraction. Pierce had trained for the Episcopal ministry and was now a curate. Socially, it was a mark in his favor and the reason why, perhaps, Cornelia and her friends knew of him. She sang, it is said, with her sweet soprano voice trained meticulously for evening parties, in the choir of his church.

The scene was all set for a stock romance: the young clergyman with his eloquence and his sincerity accompanied, it seemed to those who knew him at the time, by a becoming modesty; the beautiful ward forbidden to see or speak to him by her guardian—for Mrs. Montgomery was not slow to act upon her apprehensions—and the background of church music and high-flown sentiments. It was an exciting, dramatic situation pregnant with whispered consultations, forbidden letters, and secret encounters.

Throughout, Cornelia had the support of her sister Adeline. She needed it. Mrs. Montgomery was not a woman to be trifled with. She forbade Pierce the house and refused her consent to the marriage.

Cornelia, however, could be as firm as she. With composure, and we presume with tact, for Mrs. Montgomery's affections were only temporarily alienated, she left the marble-fronted house in Walnut Street and went to join her other unmarried sister, Mary, who was already living with Adeline Duval. From Adeline's, on December 1, 1831, she was married to the Reverend Pierce Connelly.

Looking back on Cornelia's adventurousness in the matter, it is easy to assume it typical. She could on occasion be strong-willed, and towards the end of her life she was to become so, in God's service, again. But at this time, and for the next fifteen years, there is little to suggest that she relied more on her own initiative than another's. There is much to suggest the opposite. Her inspiration and decisions seem to have come to her always through others, predigested and predirected. Her boldness in marrying Pierce was exceptional. It was a strong, decisive gesture, but Cornelia had fallen very much in love and Pierce's powers of persuasion were capable of turning stronger heads than hers. It was her last original decision for many years, although evidence of a characteristic they both shared to an astonishing degree, that of immediately translating their convictions into vigorous action. For the moment, however, her convictions were at his disposal. It was, besides, the age of gentleness and wifely submission, qualities of which Pierce warmly approved: "hierarchical subordination, whether in Church or State, in a kingdom or in a family, I still consider [1853] the only basis for a community to be built upon, the tranquillity of order, the only tranquillity that deserves the name."

A painting done of Cornelia in 1832, when she was twenty-three, even allowing for contemporary fashion, shows her sitting in a position of unusual docility. Her eyes are as dark, her features as delicate, as when they caused so much admiration a few years later in Rome, but there is as yet little character stamped upon her prettiness. Her mouth is uncertain, her chin weak. The striking thing about her is her relaxation. Even mediocre craftsmanship and hesitant watercoloring cannot disguise the amazing tranquillity of the sitter —no superimposed placidity but a real calm.

If she was for the moment content with interpreting Pierce's will as perfectly as she could she had ample reason for supposing herself safe in doing so. For Pierce's abilities found other, more impressive, audiences than the young women of his parish. It was generally agreed that at twenty-seven he was a young man with a future. In addition to his considerable powers in the pulpit and his personal charm he had had a good university education and put it to good account. He engaged in the religious controversies of the day that caught his attention and showed himself, to his bishops as well as to his parishioners, a sincere as well as a forceful enthusiast.

An address delivered at the anniversary meeting of the managers of the Female Orphan Asylum in March, 1833, caused so much stir that the secretary wrote "respectfully to solicit a copy of it for publication." It was an effective plea for the stray and the homeless founded, in a way that Rousseau would have disliked, on the assumption that "with the noblest faculties, with celestial aspirations, with an immortal destiny, man is the most helpless and the most self-depraving of beings." Beneath the rhetoric and carefully chosen phrase there is a strength of feeling and a sureness of touch which, with very little alteration, would make a convincing appeal for funds today. It also reveals a knowledge of human nature founded more upon observation than upon cant. "Dependent wholly for his virtues and his happiness, [man] can only boast within himself passions which, unrestrained, still lead to vice and sensibilities which, unsanctified, only bring upon him unhappiness." It, too, was a prophecy.

All through his life Pierce was to exercise the most extraordinary powers of persuasion over men far his superior in intellect, will, and character, men like Wiseman, Flaget, and Alberto Cappellari, and to do so in a very short time and to momentous effect. Soon after his marriage he began blazing the trail of his changing beliefs. The conviction with which he carried through each successive change was due, perhaps, as much to the fact that he was seldom in one place, or among one set of people, long enough for his personality to pall as to his vivid, infectious enthusiasm.

There are, unfortunately, no portraits of him as a young man. Those that exist were done in his middle fifties or old age. A painting by his son, Frank, in 1859 shows an intense, hollow-cheeked intelligence, a thin-lipped indwelling on private grief. But in 1859 Frank was only eighteen and he was accustomed to seeing his father in the same role. His impressions are not altogether shared by the camera some years later. For here, in these soft, faded prints, one can see in caricature the qualities which cannot be dismissed in the phrase "A tall thin plausible Yankee" with which, in 1849, Lord Shrewsbury's agent sought to dismiss them. He is looking directly at the camera as if to subdue his audience as effectively through one dimension as in three. He is deliberately posed and deliberately at ease—wily, assured, amused. The humor round his eyes and under the thick heavy eyebrows, and the intelligence of his thin pointed face with its craggy nose and enormous ears, seem undeterred by the specious air of sanctimony that surrounds him. But the humor lies round, not in, his eyes and the years have tightened the corners of his mouth.

In 1835, however, he was still at peace, devoted to his wife and to his new parish. Immediately after his wedding he had been offered, and had accepted, the rectorship of Trinity Church in Natchez, Mississippi. Natchez was very different from Philadelphia—a provincial town many miles away and reached only by several weeks' journey through the Allegheny Mountains in the slow rumbling wagons of the time and then by boat from Pittsburgh down the Ohio River to the Mississippi.

Natchez had been the head of its state until 1802, and Trinity Church itself was an imposing building with a classical façade of six fluted Ionic pillars supporting an unbroken pediment; beside it, oddly alien in its native brick and rustic informality, was a campanile. There was something altogether Italianate and unexpected about the church as well as about the campanile. It was evidently as much the center of every sort of activity as it would have been in any Italian town or village.

Here the Connellys lived for four years. In 1832, on December 7, their son Mercer was born and, in 1835, on March 6, a daughter, Adeline, called after her aunt to whom Cornelia wrote often and affectionately. She always loved getting letters and there was so much to write about as well—Pierce's goodness and consideration, Pierce's eloquence and inspiration, Mercer's first words, Ady's first steps and her growing likeness to her namesake. They were the gay happy trivialities that presumed upon the same loving curiosities. It was the comparison and contrast of their lives and families which, across more than a thousand miles, were of such absorbing interest. They were letters that sprang on both sides from happiness and confidence.

But perhaps after all the confidence was not complete. Cornelia urged Pierce's perfections too emphatically and too often to suggest perfect agreement from Adeline, and Adeline did not come to visit.

It was Mary, the younger sister, who came to stay and added her voice to the chorus of praise for Pierce. Pierce had been advising her to buy land to sell at a profit. She hoped from the sale of 650 acres to realize twenty dollars an acre, "which will make me comfortable for the rest of my life. But that I do not anticipate and shall be very grateful if I realize five dollars an acre." On Pierce's advice she had retained some stock. She was "ready to follow his advice in everything. He has been so remarkably fortunate in all his investments." Even his slaves were turned to good account. "For his man Abraham, for whom he gave 750 dollars a year ago he now expects to get 1,500. For Jenny, who cost him about 150 dollars, he is offered 800." (His slave dealing, in all fairness, was not speculative. It coincided with the selling of his property in 1835.) Everything was a cause for satisfaction. Pierce was "always entertaining much company and living so generously." The "great lands in Arkansas" are rich and fertile, the occupants delightful. One family in particular, the Wilkinses, "surrounded by every luxury that wealth can give them," are an "intelligent, accomplished, refined family, of Catharine the eldest you have frequently heard me speak. There is scarcely a young lady in ten thousand who has a mind and abilities equal to her. Ann, the second one, is very smart, and Maria, a sweet, pretty little affectionate creature. Oh, how much I wish our dear boys [her brothers George, Lawrence, and Ralph] were here to try their chance. I feel certain it would be very good. There is such a great dearth of gentlemen, though plenty of pretenders to that title."

Unfortunately, the boys, "particularly R," were never given the opportunity to meet and win the charming Miss Wilkins. For, on September 1st, 1835, Cornelia wrote to Adeline and broke the news.

DEAREST ADY,

I have put off writing to you for several days past from my unwillingness to tell you what I know will give you great trouble. Pierce has resigned his parish—he has laid aside the active duties of his ministry to examine at leisure and with care the distinctive doctrines of the Roman Catholic religion. The attacks upon the Catholics have led him into a laborious study of the controversy, and he begins to doubt whether they are not more near the truth than we. His health is considerably injured by his late labors and he is now suffering with a constant pain in his breast. His parish show great regret at his resignation and give him stronger proofs than ever of their confidence and affection —are very anxious for him to live amongst them at any rate. They are going to have a gold cup made to be presented to him. I need scarcely point out to you, dear Ady, the importance of the step he takes . . . the great sacrifice of feeling as well as of interest that he makes—his salary is 1,500 dollars, fees within the last eight months 580 dollars, and presents to the family, during that time, I have estimated at 700 dollars.

But, dear Ady, what are these things? He must do his duty. . . . He intends preaching his farewell sermon next Sunday and then taking the first boat for St. Louis to see Bishop Rosati. Of course he will not take any further step without long and careful deliberation. As our future movements are uncertain we determined it was better he should leave us here—he will return as soon as possible. Our property will probably be sold in five or six weeks—we may possibly go to Europe, but everything is at present uncertain —2,000 or 3,000 dollars spent there will give him the opportunity and leisure to pursue the studies he desires—will be of great service to his health and will still leave us about 8,000 dollars from the sale of our little property, every single investment of which God seems most mercifully to have helped.

Do not be unhappy about me, dear Ady, and do not be too anxious. I have perfect confidence in the piety, integrity, and learning of my dear husband, and if you mistrust my judgment recollect that he has the increased confidence and esteem of the first men of his parish.

May God bless you, dear Ady, and lead us all into the truth for His dear Son's sake. . . . Keep perfectly quiet about all I have told you. You will before long hear it from other quarters—but at all events the least said about it the better, at present. We are looking anxiously for letters from you, dear Ady. I have so much to say to you that I can scarcely stop writing—but have no more time to spare.

Believe me,
Your affectionate
CORNELIA

But the letters did not come, for a while at any rate. Perhaps the shock was too unexpected for immediate reaction or Cornelia's businesslike acceptance of such revolution too singleminded. Or perhaps Adeline's opinion of Pierce, clearly from Cornelia's letters not as appreciative as her own, was too strong to put on paper. There is, however, evidence, from what Lewis Duval wrote to his brothers-in-law later, that eight or ten letters were written by various members of the family, including Adeline, before October 10. At all events, it was Mary, who was staying and must have listened to many anxious discussions before and after Pierce's departure for St. Louis, who took up the pen on their behalf. On October 13 she began lengthily and fussily to Adeline: "I have deferred writing to you from week to week, that Pierce's plans might be determined on and that I might give you some certain information. . . . He has now returned from St. Louis after a most delightful trip, his health much improved, and has decided to go to Italy. He will take a vessel at New Orleans for Marseille, there a steam packet for Rome, and will be off as soon as their passports arrive from Washington, which will be about the last of November.

"You will, therefore, dearest Ady, if you write immediately, be enabled to give them the happiness of hearing from you before they go. I shall be much grieved if anything should occur to prevent it, as they are already so greatly disturbed at not seeing you. Oh, dearest Ady, why did you not come out?"

The letter wanders on through many pages of Pierce's "noble and disinterested course" and his "submissiveness to God's will," where "lies the great secret of his happy and cheerful disposition"—not, one suspects, entirely uninfluenced by the prospect of raising seventeen thousand dollars from his estate.

Their letters must have crossed, for in those days letters took several weeks to travel between Natchez and Philadelphia. On the morning of October 17, Cornelia received a distraught letter from Adeline which no longer exists. She replied, rather coldly, the same day:

DEAREST ADY,

We have this morning received seven letters from Lewis, two from your own dear self and one from mother [Mrs. Montgomery]. There is not the least cause for all the trouble and distress you have suffered. Pierce is not a Catholic nor could he be a Catholic priest if he desired while I live.

Ady's prophetic perspicacity is strange. It far outdistanced Cornelia's. Did she guess, from her knowledge of Pierce, that his was the sort of vocation that must speak from a pulpit, that found its natural expression in some form of religious interpretation—rather like that of Richard Waldo Sibthorp, his English contemporary, who, with evident sincerity, changed his faith five times in all and died a Catholic priest possibly contemplating a sixth, for the Book of Common Prayer was found upon his knee.

It is probable that Ady's letter was, as its successors were to be, a surprisingly well-argued case for Episcopalianism. The Peacocks had clearly shared a profound knowledge of their religion, with a quick ability to express it, as well as a passion for dancing and parties. Cornelia answered her attack point by point. Pierce's mind is "as sound as ever and as capable as ever to support his family." He has "meddled with controversy" (Ady's objection) "to find out the truth, and as one who professes to teach nothing but the truth, he is bound to cease preaching the moment he doubts." She defends Catholicism on the grounds of its unity, universality, and continuity; on its Petrine claim and interpretation of the Scriptures. She insists that its "forms and ceremonies help to lead the heart."

She argues briskly but without wishing to disturb Ady's peace of mind, for "it is a very different thing with you and with one who teaches or is thrown into the way of examination by the force of circumstances."

Her letter, just recently discovered, contradicts the traditional belief about her conversion—that she was the first to become attracted to Catholicism, through watching a Catholic convent near her house, and then excited Pierce's interest in it. In fact what had first stimulated Pierce's interest was the success of the Negro Catholic Mission across the river from where his own church had failed miserably. He was, too, dismayed by the "restless spirit of democracy in Church and State" and, eager to find a haven in authority and institution, "I gave myself up to the Church which I hoped was to save the world from anarchy and disbelief." It was a curious, instinctive shelter for such an individualist.

Cornelia makes this order clear in her letter. Her own former attitude to the Faith would have done justice to Maria Edgeworth: "I am proud to say that, against my prejudices and in spite of the horrors which I have always nurtured for the Catholic faith, I am ready at once to submit to whatever my loved husband believes to be the path of duty." But the path of duty is never easy and, in spite of her convictions, she confessed to Ady: "How Our Saviour should have allowed His Church to remain in the hands of the Devil 1,500 years and be spread in the miraculous manner it was, while under diabolical influence and that too from the time of his Ascension until the days of Martin Luther, a degraded priest, who allowed bigamy and was notoriously unmoral, I don't pretend to explain. You must remember, dearest Ady, I once thought *all* Catholic priests instruments of the Devil, if not the Devil himself, and believed all Hume's falsehoods about monastic ignorance and superstition, etc., and entertained a thousand other prejudices. We have seen Miss Read's *Six Months in a Convent*, De Ricci's *Secrets*, etc., etc., etc., and sundry periodicals, so you see we cannot be much in the dark respecting all that can be urged against Catholicism."

Ady professed herself above such propaganda: "I never entertained the violent prejudices against Catholic priests that you did," and insisted she had never read *Six Months in a Convent*; her position was argued solely from intellectual conviction. But her distress about the Connellys' conversion was somewhat mollified by Cornelia's letter. She warmly accepted the idea of reconciliation. "However we may differ upon these points, my dear, dear Nelie, I feel confident that we enjoy the warmest affection for each other. While life lasts I shall feel the deepest interest for you, my darling sister, and for all those sacred ties that bind you so far from me." Yet she sent Cornelia's letter to her brothers, George and Ralph, and made quite clear, in a covering note, what she presumed were Cornelia's motives for changing: "I am not at all surprised at the effects of Pierce's influence over her mind—nor would I for a moment wish her to differ with her kind husband. No indeed . . . the path of duty will lead her to think as he does—and she ought certainly to view things as he does for their mutual happiness."

The Bishops and public generally did not share Adeline's, or the parishioners', understanding of the change. They were startled and upset; although Bishop Otey, when he was first told, wrote to Pierce: "I am amazed, overwhelmed, confounded [sentiments that were to be heard frequently during Pierce's lifetime]. How shall I give you up? I have loved with an affection that I want words to express. I still love you with an undying affection." It was Pierce's publication of his letter to Bishop Otey and his farewell sermon that gave real cause for alarm. "If Pierce has not become a Catholic," wrote Adeline, "how imprudent to publish his letter to Bishop Otey and his farewell sermon! And what service do they render to the cause of true religion?"

Pierce's action was typical. His decision was made. He must immediately make it impossible to retract. He sold his property, with the exception of a small house kept against an emergency, and made a public announcement at once. He had cut the ground from beneath his feet and there was nothing to do but go. It is a reflex action that always accompanies his gestures of renunciation and sacrifice—to put between him and a possible change of heart an overwhelming barrier and the ridicule of public recantation.

On this occasion his plans went slightly awry. He took Cornelia and the children to New Orleans but the sailing of the boat in which their berths were booked was postponed for several weeks. They did not sail for Europe until the middle of December, 1835.

In the meanwhile Pierce's brother, Harry, told Lewis Duval that he had for several years suspected Pierce of being a Catholic at heart. Duval, to calm the female agitation with which he was surrounded, and the attacks of his brothers-in-law, wrote soothingly to them that "We live in a strange world, my dear boys . . . things may look much better in a short time. . . . It is not as serious an affair as you might perhaps imagine, and is already giving way to some new Nine Days' Wonder."

So much for public scandal. Meanwhile at New Orleans, for the first time Cornelia took the initiative from Pierce. She would not wait for Rome to be received into the Church. Her determination is curious, considering how superficial her introduction to Catholicism seems to have been. Perhaps it is from here, the unwelcome break in their well-planned itinerary, that her own conviction really dates. If Catholicism is the right faith then there is no point in remaining outside it; no point in remaining cut off from the sacraments and the means of grace. Perhaps she was thinking, too, of the long, uncertain voyage ahead and did not wish to face death in a state of spiritual neutrality. At all events she presented herself to Bishop Blanc of New Orleans, who, after satisfying himself that her disposition and knowledge were genuine, allowed her to make her first Communion.

Pierce was there but he was not persuaded by the fervor of her acceptance. He would wait for the impressiveness of Rome, for abjuration with full pontificals in the Eternal City.

Chapter 2

ROME

ROME was not reached in a day—it took a month to reach Marseille. From there Pierce wrote to his mother: "The children are quite well and have both grown a little in length and a great deal in breadth. Nelie is better than she has been since her marriage. I am so fat I can scarcely wear the clothes I brought with me." A picture that was certainly colored, for when they did reach Rome at the end of February, Pierce, writing outside his family, described the horrors of the voyage: "Fifty-seven days at sea with the poor good creature procured for us as nurse worse than useless . . . Mrs. Connelly suffered sadly, each of the children in turn was also sick."

But it was a journey that could soon be forgotten, for they were in Rome. And they had introductions from American Bishops that would take them to the papal levees, where they would meet not only the Princes of the Church but the Princes of Europe.

They stood at the entrance to an unknown world. The vast, complex, entrancing world of European privilege. At the center, a Venetian nobleman, Bartolommeo Alberto Cappellari, Pope Gregory XVI, the last great papal patron of the arts. The Pope who could protect scholars and poets, commission huge architectural projects and plan the execution of engineering ingenuities with superb indifference to expediency, his own financial embarrassments, and the indecent poverty of his subjects. The same Pope, a man of great personal austerity, who, undisturbed, held back the onslaught of progress wherever it threatened his frontiers, condemning the building of railways, issuing bulls against the liberty of the press and the translation of the Scriptures into the vulgar tongue, refuting the clamors for reform with exile and prison and quelling Italian rebels with Austrian troops.

He upheld the past at the cost of the future—but he upheld it magnificently.

No wonder that to two Americans who were, as well, fervent converts to the Faith he represented, the prospect was dazzling. Nor was it exclusively Roman. Four years before the tricolor had flown over Bologna. It was the first gap in the wall and through it climbed the leaders of Europe to negotiate a reform of the Papal States. The influx of priests was as great as ever, and the argument between the Ultramontanes and the Gallicans within their ranks brought the giants among them to the papal arena. Roman society was as cosmopolitan, as political, as affected, as malicious as in any other capital of Europe. Lady Arundell of Wardour, wife of the tenth Baron and daughter of the first Marquess of Buckingham, paints the scene vividly in a letter to her sister-in-law a few years previously. "The new occupants of the French Embassy, the Chateaubriands, I am very intimate with. He is very agreeable and with her I revel in hearing the St. Germain news, and we go together to every convent within the bills of mortality. I go to her quietly of an evening when she is alone *et souffrante*, which poor thing she almost always is, and we set in for *haute dévotion* and arrange devout excursions for the morning . . . the Shrewsburys we go to at least once a week, and I am anxious to keep on close terms with them and to cement the friendship between Lord A and Lord S. With her I make progress for she is good and good-humored and anxious to be intimate with me, and if she had less gossip and talked less in general and less of what others did and said, I should be more intimate but we are not suited. She likes diamonds and going out and great dinners and driving with her four horses on the Pincio, instead of enjoying the beauties of Rome. . . . Then Lady S has no *esprit de corps*, which vexes me, no wish to patronize popery, will not visit half the papists here because they are not fine enough, throws away all her dinners and balls on heretics . . . her great aim is intimacy with the great, and to please and court them her occupation."

Lady Arundell and the Chateaubriands had gone by 1836.

But Lady Shrewsbury had not. Her eldest daughter, Gwendoline, was already married to Marcantonio, Prince Sulmona, shortly to become Prince Borghese; her second daughter was to marry Prince Doria Pamphili. Lady Arundell commented caustically on Lady Shrewsbury's ambitions: "If Roman Princes can make happiness what a happy mother she must be, but as the Borghese did not make that I wonder at her ambitioning another. Though poor Massimo would never, I think, make his wife unhappy or fail in temper." But whatever Prince Borghese's deficiencies as a husband, and Gwendoline's diaries do not hint at them, his wife became a fable in Rome, with her beauty, her goodness, and her charity. She brought with her from England the serious breath of social reform. The spirit that, in England, instigated the abolition of slavery and the Factory Act of 1832, and was striving towards Lord Shaftesbury's Mines Act and the First Public Health Act, made of the gentle Princess a legendary figure of kindness. She started soup kitchens and charity stalls. She tried with her private wealth to fight the ghastly poverty of Rome which went uncovered in the streets, assailing the nostrils and offending the sight. But above all she gave herself to the wretched, unloved populace. She looked after the sick and helped the poor, and she did so in the midst of her life of "great dinners," which Marcantonio wanted her to lead, without condescension and without restraint. The people loved her and they did not forget her as they did so many of the young Roman wives who found it amusing to imitate her and become, for a time, fashionably concerned with charity.

It is not surprising that the Connellys loved Rome. It is surprising that Rome loved the Connellys—that this enormous and complicated hierarchy should have absorbed them as it did. They were, of course, a novelty, two earnest, handsome Americans converted in a foreign land and from a foreign faith—but they must have been a very attractive novelty to achieve what they did.

They had soon moved from their original apartments in the Via della Croce to an apartment in the Palazzo Simonetti. They found themselves enthralled by the parties and buildings, by the churches with their separate aspects of the Faith, by the excitement and the peace. On Palm Sunday, March 27, 1836, Pierce made his abjuration, Lord Shrewsbury standing sponsor for him, and, on March 31, husband and wife received the sacrament of confirmation.

Pierce was delighted with the way Cornelia delighted Rome. "We have enjoyed the society of some of the most distinguished and delightful people that can be found and received the kindest of attention from all the first people. Cornelia has indeed been a universal favorite and has received flattery enough to turn even her head. The President of St. Luke (the oldest academy of arts in the world whose organization suggested to Sir Joshua Reynolds his plan for the English Royal Academy) said before her that her profile was more beautiful than the Grecian models, but I know her Christian feelings are too strong for her ever to be carried away with love of admiration or love of society." Pierce was in love with it all. It would be hard not to be.

They saw a lot of the Borgheses—although they did not accept an invitation to live in apartments at the Villa Borghese as this would mean too great a loss of their independence— and their portraits were executed in crayon by the Princess Sciarra Colonna. In August, Pierce accepted an invitation from Lord Shrewsbury to stay some weeks in England.

He stayed at Alton Towers, the fabulous Gothic palace that Pugin had built for him and which Disraeli described in *Coningsby* as the Abbey of St. Geneviève, "a pile of modern buildings built of a white and glittering stone. Its striking situation, its brilliant color, its great extent, a gathering as it seemed of galleries and halls and chapels, mullioned windows, portals of clustered columns and groups of airy pinnacles and fretwork spires . . . with its . . . chapel in which art had exhausted all its invention and wealth offered all its resources." He was introduced to all the old Catholic families and toasted by the Jesuits as a celebrity. "Through his great kindness I have found some valuable acquaintances and have spent my time as delightfully as I could anywhere away from dear Nelie and the children . . . I miss them dreadfully."

It is not surprising that he was dazzled by his own good fortune in being accounted great among so much grandeur. Already, he was suffering from the temptation to trade upon those virtuous sentiments which, in this particular setting in this particular age, were the ones most likely to have brought him so far. Already, he was feeling secure enough to discern and discriminate. "I have not been able to accept all the invitations I have had from great people." It poured out of him to his family—the proud display, the boisterous naïve affection. But it is warm and spontaneous, and one suffers with him the stern rebuke to his vanity, the earnest enjoinders against snobbishness which his brothers were not slow to administer. He was curiously dependent upon his family—more so than Cornelia upon hers. He wrote to them continuously, long affectionate letters that were as eager for every detail of their lives as they were generous in revealing his own. He was upset by their mistrust and when, later, he learned of his mother's death he was hurt, too, because she had never loved him as he wished, though "love even of parents does not always depend upon merit, yet perhaps if I had deserved more love I should have had it."

While Pierce was in England Cornelia lived with her children in Rome, and took her lessons in painting and singing and read the lives of St. Ignatius, St. Francis of Sales, and St. Francis of Assisi, who impressed her so much. And then, in the spring of 1837, cholera broke out in Rome. The heat and dirt, the sluggish unmoving Tiber, the stinking overcrowded poor could no longer remain unnoticed. They erupted suddenly and frighteningly into a summer plague. Thousands suffered and died. The Pope himself, slippered and on foot, carried the "Madonna di San Luca," a miraculous picture attributed to St. Luke and always invoked by the Romans against disease, through the streets of Rome.

The great Romans retired discreetly to their villas on the surrounding hills. To one of these, the Villa Aldobrandini at Frascati, Cornelia was invited with her children. In this great house built high above Frascati, on which it looks down across flights of terraced steps that emphasize its height and thence across the vast deep bowl which contains Rome, she spent the following months.

There is no evidence that she helped Gwendoline Borghese

and the few other Roman ladies in their fight for the plague-stricken. There are many reasons why she could not. She was expecting another child, she had the sole responsibility for Mercer and Adeline while Pierce was away in England, she was a foreigner in a strange land, and, having accepted the chance of safety at Frascati for her children, she could not endanger her hosts with a risk of infection.

All the same, her reticence about the plague is strange. There are no allusions to it now or later in letters or in memories. But then there are no allusions in her, or Pierce's, letters to the state of the poor. They remain curiously detached from circumstances that Gwendoline found insupportable. But Pierce was already living in a world of make-believe, and Cornelia's reticence about events and situations outside her own sphere of action is often astounding. She was not at heart a missionary, she did not burn with zeal for the poor (although later she took many practical steps to help them), nor did she subscribe to the violent devotion to social reform which was already stirring England. She had in fact never visited England. And in America slavery was still taken for granted by a large number of her fellow countrymen. Publication of *Uncle Tom's Cabin* did not begin until 1851.

In England the last few years had already provided the Abolition of Slavery Act, the Great Reform Bill, the First Factory Act, the Municipal Reform Bill, and movements towards many more. The country's conscience was tender and the tender-hearted interpreted it scrupulously. In Rome Gwendoline's generosity was only one expression of what in some cases was becoming constant practice. In England William Charlton, according to his wife's diary, "was straining at the leash, yearning for roads, workhouses, poor laws, and paupers much as the Israelites craved the fleshpots of Egypt." His yearnings were echoed everywhere, even in the Royal household. They were to achieve practical demonstration in the Great Exhibition of 1851 with the Prince Consort's exhibit of a model house for the laboring classes consisting of four dwellings each containing a general sitting room and kitchen, two small bedrooms (one for boys, another for girls), and a large bedroom for parents and babies, with cupboards, scullery, water closet, and water supply at a rental of 3s. 6d. a week and an estimated building cost of £440 for the block. The Catholic Churchmen were not behind in fighting for their particular causes—orphanages, foundling hospitals, poor schools, asylums. Men like Manning, Vaughan, and Wiseman wrote and fought continually in the years to come. Newman alone remained remote and owned dryly that he had never asked himself the question whether the number of public houses in England was excessive.

But this is anticipating. And however one explains Cornelia's attitude it leaves one with a slight emptiness, a sense of unease. It may not have been her vocation to serve the poor, there may have been far too many enthusiasts already hot in pursuit of their welfare, but the fact remains that she showed a lack of heart in the circumstances, circumstances which would have no connection with the mission on which Wiseman ultimately sent her.

Nicholas Wiseman was in England, on his first long visit since his Rectorship of the English College in Rome, when the Connellys arrived in Rome. There is no record of their meeting when he returned. But it is probable that he and Cornelia met while Pierce was still at Alton for, among his other capacities, from 1829 to 1837 Wiseman was acting as agent for the American Bishops, some of whom had given the Connellys their introduction to Roman society. She must certainly have heard of this extraordinary, versatile young man who, at the age of twenty-six, when he first became Rector of the English College, was already Professor of Oriental Languages in the Roman University; author of the *Horae Syriacae*, whose principles and methods of textual criticism earned him universal fame as a philologist and scholar; member of the Royal Asiatic Society and honorary member of the Royal Society of Literature; a connoisseur of old china and stained glass; a music critic and a practical musician.

He had arrived in Rome, according to Barbara Charlton, "a thin, delicate-looking youth," and the time he spent over the Syrian manuscripts in the Vatican Library, pursuing his Oriental studies, and planning his sermons and lectures had done little to improve his physique. He suffered intermittently

from severe attacks of ill-health which had their moral counterpart in moods of morbid depression. He was always to be
subject to moments of intense elation alternating with moments of despair and dejection.

He was in part an enigma. Erudite, shy, militantly devoted
to Catholicism and Rome, to begin with his life seemed safely
directed towards scholarly achievement "under the very
shadow of the Apostolic Chair." But the contradictions were
already there. Already his facility was exciting the usual don-
nish prejudices. "He can speak with readiness and point in
half a dozen languages without being detected for a foreigner
in any of them," wrote Newman, and they included Arabic
and Persian as well as the languages of contemporary Europe.
But worse still, he enjoyed his own facility—he even boasted
of it. For this learned man, whose mind combined an exhaus-
tive imagination with an incisive intellect, was as conceited
about his own feats of memory and tricks of improvisation as
he was humble about his private intentions and more profound abilities.

He returned from England in September, 1836, a far fitter
man. He was thirty-four, six foot two inches high, and already
beginning to get plump—this "ruddy, strapping Divine," as
Macaulay called him in 1838. His physical improvement gave
him an impetus towards a new life. The flamboyance apparent in his tastes became more apparent in his actions. He
loved pageantry and ritual and his retinue showed it. He no
longer spent hours in concentrated study but, drawing upon
the acquired knowledge of his youth to convince and entertain, he flung himself with energy and delight into the social
life of Rome. In conversation he discovered the same stimula-
tion and enjoyment that he had found previously in writing
and debate. And he did not abandon the latter.

His smooth, pink cheeks, his urbanity, as he leans a little
forward to catch better what is being said, and to appreciate
it perhaps more carefully, remind one inevitably of the successful head boy who has just left school and achieved the
entrée to his mother's drawing room. There is a lot that is
boyish: his humor, his pleasure in his friends and his own
success, his love of display. But underneath his charm and

small superficial complacencies there lies one of the most powerful personalities of his age.

If Cornelia did not actually meet him she must have seen him across the rooms of her Roman friends, moving his beautiful hands in explanation, as he used the Italian gestures whose significance he has so wittily and shrewdly interpreted in his *Recollections*.

She was beginning to know Rome from within, to take it for granted as well as enjoy it, when Pierce returned from England. He came back full of enjoyment and excitement. Money had not yet begun to worry him. He was still living comfortably off the landed property he shared with his brothers as well as from the capital he had made from the sale of his property in Natchez. It was his anxiety over the plague which caused him to begin thinking of their return to America. They would return at their leisure, more especially as Cornelia was expecting another child.

Early in May they started for Venice, spending several days at Terni, Perugia, Florence, Bologna, and Ferrara. They left Venice for Vienna, where Adeline had measles, and Pierce, leaving Cornelia, now heavily *enceinte*, for a few hours, took up an introduction from Lambruschini, Cardinal Secretary of State at Rome, and visited Prince Metternich, whom he was thrilled to find "extremely gracious, slightly stiff but not in the smallest degree preoccupied, *gêné* or awkward; a countenance noble and intelligent but strikingly quiet, which indeed is a word quite characteristic of the great man, who may be said for forty years to have controlled the diplomacy of Europe."

It is interesting that this meeting, anticipating another, "blossomed into a delightful intimacy" in the years to come. Although there is no record of Pierce's ever meeting Metternich again, he makes the astonishing claim twenty years later, when Metternich is safely dead, that "in 1837 so wise a statesman as Metternich did me the honor to invite me to enter the Austrian Diplomacy" and "in the first [presumably because the only] interview I ever had the honor to have with Prince Metternich the subject of his most minute inquiries was the religious development of America politically considered, the relative numbers of the different sects and their distinctive doctrines and disciplines. Upon my remarking one day in his private cabinet the admirable *American Almanac* for the current year, he playfully boasted that I would find few in Europe better acquainted with my native country than himself, but it was ever, even in that new Empire, its religion that was his chief interest, that which he considered the preponderant interest of the state. The experience of Europe during the last four years, it would seem, should be enough to make all men think it so in every commonwealth."

This is a very different picture from the one he drew at the time in his letter home to his brother, dated May 15, 1837, where he says: "The day after I reached here I had the honor of being received by Prince Metternich. Four years ago I should almost as soon have expected to see Cardinal Wolsey for the one seemed already to belong as much to history as the other." He goes on to describe the awe and excitement he felt in this interview, obtained for him by Metternich's beloved counsellor at the Vatican, Lambruschini. It lasted exactly twenty minutes, since Pierce, too shy to prolong it, asked leave to retire without the customary permission to do so.

From such slender shoots the story spread. But it is an interesting example of how Pierce's imagination works. With time his impressions become exaggerated and confused with his motives and desires. It is a more dangerous imagination than that of adolescence, the dream fulfillment not of what might happen in the future but of what has happened in the past. In 1837 it was no more than a tendency to dramatize, but it is a habit that is to grow on him more strongly. It is curious that wherever possible he avoids the lie direct. The conversation he relates with Metternich is, in essentials, what one would expect from a formal interview such as he describes. As always he gets his effect by omission, suggestion, and emphasis.

For the moment, however, he remained content with Vienna. Cornelia's pregnancy, which was very near its end, and Adeline's measles made it imperative to settle down somewhere for several weeks, and Vienna seemed the best place.

They found a good hotel, and there, on June 22, their second son, John Henry, was born. It was comfortable and pleasant, Adeline's measles were gone, and Cornelia was well. They decided to stay until the baby was old enough to travel with them to Paris.

When Pierce left Rome for Vienna he had good accounts of his American property. But both in Vienna and in Paris those that followed him grew steadily worse. His brothers wrote to say that unforeseen circumstances and losses had seriously reduced the income from their joint estate and it was necessary for him to return at once.

Without a job or the prospects of one, and after the luxuries of the past two years, Pierce's responsibility seemed suddenly acute. He wrote anxiously to his brother for "some clerkship in a bank or drivership in a plantation or mastership in a school. In fine, any place whatsoever that will bring in annually a sum somewhat proportionate to our desires as well as our necessities"—an idea of the status proper to him as extreme as it was unlike the life they had been leading. He was full of foreboding and desperation, though Cornelia was "dancing with delight at the thought of being so soon back in our own home." "An angel of consolation," she was "more rejoiced than I can say over a return to our peaceful quiet home life though at the same time she can bravely look ahead to coming—I must not say storms—but times when we may find ourselves without a home wherein to live."

They arrived in New Orleans on January 7, 1838, after an exhausting voyage of sixty-one days, and returned to Natchez. Their reception was cool, and the months that followed were difficult ones owing to their new position in the parish, and the polite disapprobation and, worse, the incomprehension of their friends; their financial situation, which turned out to be extremely serious, seemed harsher than it had before. Through it all Cornelia acted with her curious combination of placidity and gaiety—in spite of the fact that she was again expecting a child. Mary's words to Adeline three years before were still true: "They are, and always have been, the happiest couple that ever breathed." Cornelia regarded adversity only as a superficial test of their good faith and of what Mary described as Pierce's "great mind and the generous, affectionate qualities of his heart."

For five months they worried over what they should do while Pierce enthusiastically explained his conversion to those willing to hear and tried his best to persuade them to his own course.

And then, in June, 1838, they were offered a post. They were asked, by the Rector of the College of St. Charles at Grand Coteau in Louisiana, to come and teach. He needed a professor of English and he had heard of the Connellys through the Sacred Heart Convent there. They would live in a bungalow in the convent grounds. Pierce gratefully accepted the offer. Perhaps nostalgically, perhaps as a gesture of renunciation for the Europe they had left behind, he named the house Gracemere. Was he thinking of the Gothic extravagance of Grace Dieu which Ambrose Lisle Phillipps, Disraeli's Eustace Lyle, had commissioned Pugin to build for him not long before in Leicestershire, or, less specifically, was he trying to recapture in this new uncharted territory the exultant Arthurianism of his friends?

Whatever the motive, they lived there very happily, enjoying their children and allowing them as much freedom as possible. Cornelia thought that it was easy to be good when one was happy. Not only did she supervise her family. The nuns, knowing their history, and probably wishing to help as tactfully as possible, asked her if she would take on pupils for singing, piano, and the guitar. She was extremely glad to accept.

As we see them settle down, with their three children, to what must have seemed an assured if circumscribed future, with no thought of change or prospect of promotion, it is only fair to measure their sacrifice. They had abandoned the Episcopal Church, to which they had been accustomed by tradition and environment, and in which preferment was assured, and in doing so they had disgusted their family and disappointed their friends. They had tasted the excitement of a glittering world and had turned their backs upon it without regret. They had followed their convictions at the cost of their prosperity and they had done so, considering their circumstances and their age, with little fuss and some humor. It is

not possible to judge them by the future, to suspect character-
istics and anticipate motives from the safe haven of retrospect.
At the time they were willingly embarking upon a course of action which they must have assumed was going to last forever.

Chapter 3

VOCATION

THE CONNELLYS arrived at Grand Coteau on June 24, 1839. A month later, on July 22, their second daughter and fourth child, Mary Magdalen, was born.

She was eleven months younger than John Henry, who had been born in Vienna the previous year, and not much allowance had been made for her. Her mother had been on a long sea voyage in the first three months of her pregnancy, travelling in a steamship where life, stuffy and confined even in the passenger class, was led mainly between decks. Although the Philadelphian Line, by which they crossed, provided fresh meat twice a week, eggs from the hens carried aboard, and bread newly baked each day, there were few vegetables, the water grew stale, and anxiety for the children and the discomforts of the crossing, among them seasickness from which Cornelia and the two children suffered, were great. The strain of their arrival in America allowed no relaxation and the journey from Natchez to Grand Coteau, which they undertook five weeks before the baby was born, meant an exhausting week by steamboat and train. Whatever the reason, Mary Magdalen was a weak and ailing baby. She died when she was a few weeks old, leaving Cornelia in a state of mental and physical depression which is the commonplace of a great many happy births and must have seemed overwhelming in a tragic one.

But her resilience was always amazing. Her recovery was swift. There was, besides, too much to do. She ran her house with one maid, she made her children's clothes and taught and played with them as well as preparing and giving her lessons in the convent.

Grand Coteau was a strange, exciting place that lay upon a long low ridge of land whose sides fell down to meet the small tributaries of the Mississippi which, in the rains, swelled and slipped their banks in vain imitation of the great river in which they ended. The convent grounds were thickly wooded, and wild grape vines trailed over the walnut, copal, and cottonwood trees, in which the mockingbirds kept up their sweet high song when they were not imitating the cry of a child or cat, or the harsher-throated call of a distant bird.

The children were completely happy. Mercer went every morning to school at St. Charles, where Pierce taught. Adeline and John Henry, too young to go to school, played continually with the younger children from the convent, one of whom, Odiède Mouton, spent nearly all day with the Connellys as she was only five. She remembered them as among "the brightest memories of my life," and was so attracted to Cornelia that many years later she wrote: "Young as I was then I can never forget her lovely face, and still lovelier manner." Cornelia never patronized children; she accepted their sense of equality, and for this they did not easily forget her.

The days passed quickly and in peace. Gradually, with Pierce away all day, Cornelia fell more into the quiet, meticulous routine of the nuns under their Reverend Mother, Madame Cutts, who had been installed by the founder of the Sacred Heart Convent at Grand Coteau, Blessed Philippine Duchesne, in 1821.

So far Cornelia's spiritual life had seemed remote. She had been introduced to a new, unwelcome religion as a sacrifice to her husband's belief, and straightaway she had been taken to its center, Rome, where the pulse that beat so strongly was smothered beneath the finely piled sophistications of fashion and the *haut monde*. But here, in this quiet country convent, she became slowly and thoroughly acquainted with the practice and precepts of her Faith, and was fascinated by them both. Initiation was made all the easier because Pierce, in his days at the college, was as strongly attracted as she. Together, they began the first laborious steps in their search for personal sanctity.

Cornelia was enchanted with the bold, clear strokes of St. Ignatius and surprised her spiritual directors by embracing what he called "the third degree of humility"—the voluntary preference for suffering, hardship, and humility whenever possible. In fact, so deeply did the exercises of St. Ignatius impress her that after reading them for three days she felt unable to understand how anyone could do the same and not give themselves wholeheartedly to God. She was held entranced and had to be restrained from penance by her confessor. The enthusiasm she learned at the convent was echoed at home, for when Pierce returned in the evenings "we read together," as he wrote, "always ending up with a chapter of the Imitation of Christ." Many years later, Cornelia told her nuns that her actual conversion dated from a retreat she made at Grand Coteau in December, 1839. She had been a Catholic for four years but this was the first time that the fact held any reality for her.

Both the Connellys astounded the Jesuits with their sincerity and their progress. The scene was, for a time, a happy one—his "hidden life" as Pierce, in unattractive parody, later called it. But there was nothing of the recluse in Cornelia. She loved gaiety and celebration. She did not have to drive herself to social activity as Gwendoline Borghese had done in Rome. She could not have written, as Princess Borghese wrote in November, 1836, "I dislike the prospect of the coming winter's many gaieties; I am almost sorry to have to dance. It will be an exertion to enter the world's vortex. I am almost a misanthrope, but am too young to give up society. . . . I have merely fallen into a habitual routine, troublesome to change, nothing more."

Now that the freedom of choice had become so important to her Cornelia could no longer bear the thought of any human being deprived of it. She adopted her young Negro slave girl, Sarah Goff, and finally freed her. She also converted her.

The number of the Connellys' converts during the years at Grand Coteau was, in fact, impressive. The year 1840 claimed Cornelia's sister Mary, who was followed, not much later, by Adeline. Eighteen forty-one added George Peacock and John Connelly to the list—to be followed a year later by John's wife, Angelica, or Geckla as she was affectionately known to Cornelia, who came to stay with the Connellys a Protestant and left, after six months, a Catholic. John Connelly, whose feelings for Pierce were always reserved, became on this visit a great admirer of Cornelia's, and "it was then and there the strong attachment grew up between us which lasted, I hope, till her death."

Pierce had always been devoted to his brothers, and Cornelia was glad to find that the coolness her own family had shown towards her since 1835 had faded into a tolerance which was soon to quicken into an active acceptance of her beliefs. Her only regret was that her favorite brother, her "sweetest and dearest old Ralpho," showed no signs of following their example—an attitude he maintained with adamant good humor until the day of his death.

In spite of her growing awareness of God, Cornelia had no idea of what the future held. Indeed, she was secretly rejoiced, as she wrote at the time, that she "cannot be a nun" and that such a sacrifice would never be asked of her, "for had I been a girl . . . I should always have felt that I must have given all —my very best—to God."

The irony was unconscious. She had no idea that already Pierce was becoming restless. Institutions did not become him. He was not good at being one among many. And here he was an amateur among professionals, a layman among priests. His sentiments were still sincere, his piety impressive, but he was restricted and limited. He had no one to convince, no one to sustain. To his credit he tried. He willed himself to accept their deprivations and his own dejection. But the backwash of wistful discontent flowed through the gaps. "Our solitude," he wrote to Bishop Purcell in 1840, "has been more of a solitude than ever and it seems doubly hard that the loss of dear Father Point [their special director at the College who had been sent to the Rocky Mountains to convert the Indians] should have been one of the reasons of our not having yourself among us." And, some months later: "More than a long year since the few days you spent among us, a long year that has not run idly for us here in our solitude any more than for the great crowded world that we hear little of and that we are not the worse for hearing little of." It was all the harder because the Connellys still preserved their contact with "the great crowded world." Letters from Lord Shrewsbury were fairly frequent, and he was anxious to find Pierce a post with greater scope for his ability in England. The unrest was barely apparent, even to Cornelia. From her presumption of their mutual good will it must have seemed unimportant, the natural companion and temptation to their spiritual progress. And there are too many sensible men as witnesses to the strength of their progress to doubt its sincerity. They were firmly supervised and tightly shepherded.

If Christ uses the metaphor of the shepherd often it is, perhaps, because it illustrates so many points so well. And yet the herdsman, protecting his flock and searching for the stray lamb, is not the only guardian of the soul. His dog, who nudges a frightened sheep away from its fellows huddled together in the fold, may sometimes perform the same task. For the soul does not always strive towards its individual salvation —it will run deliberately with the flock, afraid of being alone because, in the loneliness, it might hear a voice that it does not wish to hear—a voice it fears as strangely as its own response. Instinctively it seeks the anonymity as well as the protection of the flock; instinctively it will try to double back when it finds the sheep dog at its heels to single it out; instinctively it will kick against the pain of the iron which brands it as its master's.

Cornelia was too happy at Grand Coteau. She had her three children, Mercer, Ady, and Pretty Boy (John Henry), whose nickname accounted only for his good looks and not for his love of fun and sweetness of temper. He was the darling of the family, adventurous, lighthearted, and gay. He had his mother's dark eyes and she loved him dearly. When the new year began in 1840 he was just two and a half years old.

It was January when Cornelia, as she has told us since, was standing one day in the garden watching him. Suddenly, it seemed to her that she was too fortunate, that her love for God had meant no proper sacrifice, had brought with it no special demands. In a moment of generosity, familiar to us when we have enjoyed great happiness or a unique experience, she asked God to ask of her any sacrifice He chose. It is not often that the casual uplifting of one's heart is taken so

literally. But the offer was genuine; the time had come for
Cornelia to be marked out from the flock.

Twenty-four hours later her little son lay dying.

He had run into the garden in the keen morning air with a
huge Newfoundland dog. They had played together and somehow, between the large good-natured clumsiness of the dog
and the young, inexpert limbs of the child, he had climbed up
and fallen, or been pushed, into a sugar boiler which was used
outside the house for converting the raw maple juice into
sugar. He took a long time to die. For forty-three hours,
scalded and in agony, he lay in his mother's arms.

There is no need to contemplate her feelings as she waited
for him to die. There was no question of her love for him and
here, in his tormented movements, was the embodiment of
her prayer. She must have asked both of herself and God that
night whether such fearful suffering meted upon an innocent
was the best answer to her prayer for sacrifice; whether so
terrible a measure was necessary to pull out the stops of her
own capacity for grief. She was a woman, passionate and devoted. She was allowed not even the reprieve of a short introduction to pain. The night was protracted, interminable. But
there was no bitterness, no recantation. On the following
morning, as she later wrote, "at early dawn on the feast of the
Purification he was taken into the temple of the Lord."

Her diary is the only witness. Three words record the night.
There is little to show whether they are resigned or rebellious,
given involuntarily or wrung from her by insupportable pressure—only the reiteration, like the beating of a closed fist upon
the page, "Sacrifice! Sacrifice! Sacrifice!"

Cornelia's spiritual notes at this time are very different
from those of her age. It was an age of note-taking, of resolu-
tions and counsels, of long, careful introspection. Not only
priests and clergymen kept lengthy accounts of their spiritual
progress, and of the maxims and counsels that guided them
best, but soldiers and politicians, schoolmasters and house-
wives did the same with almost the same intensity and certainly the same diligence. The notes of Miss Beale, who
founded the Cheltenham Ladies' College, were written with
as much scrupulous attention to failure and distrust of mo-

tives and success as if they were the works of a monk. But Cornelia's are different. They are haphazard jottings in a neat script, sometimes one line on a page, sometimes several pages carefully filled, sometimes several pages left empty; sometimes in English, sometimes French, and often decorated in what one can only call atrocious taste with little Gallic designs. They are contained in small fat books with mother-of-pearl or leather bindings. The entries are often undated with nothing to suggest when they were entered beyond the comprehensive dates on the flyleaf and the position, beginning, middle, or end, that they occupy in it. They are haphazardly entered but profoundly considered. Where they are largely different from their age is that they are short and practical, a shorthand of experience and contemplation jotted down, one feels, for practical reference and consolation, rather than as a record of personal analysis or for use in meditation. Saints, to distinguish between their motives, must be analytical, but Cornelia seldom commits her analysis to paper. At moments of crisis she is usually as impersonal as she is in moments of generalization.

At this time she was writing: "Practice and God will give the possession of virtue"; "Abandon the possession of any virtue to God and content myself with the practice"; "Ourselves the worst enemies to those we love naturally, because we do not help them to mortify themselves," and the advice of her spiritual predecessors: "The two feet by which we walk to perfection are mortification and the love of God, the first is the right foot, the latter the left" (St. Ignatius) or "One single 'Blessed be God' in adversity is of more avail than a thousand thanksgivings in a day of prosperity" (St. Theresa of Ávila). The way was clearly not easy, and pitifully near the day of John Henry's death she wrote: "O my God trim Thy vine; cut it to the quick, but in Thy great mercy root it not yet up. May God help me in my great weakness; help me, help me in trial to serve Thee with new fervor."

John Henry had died on February 2. In August she was again expecting a child. In October Pierce, who never believed in postponement for his enthusiasms, and in this particular instance seems to have shown even less consideration for circumstances and his wife's feelings than usual, told her, without preliminary, that he wanted to be a priest.

They were walking home from Mass on October 13 when he opened the subject, presumably the cause for endless meditation. It is strange that she had no foreboding, no suspicion of any kind. He had been worried and anxious, but that might have been due to a number of things: the death of their son, their poverty, his sense of frustrated ability. His reticence is inconsistent and, in spite of the selfishness of its ending, it hints strongly of sincerity. A conviction that was strong enough to stand up against his wife's affection and has to preserve the secret of their intentions for another two years, is a conviction that contrasts remarkably with the public maneuverings of his other, equally fervent conversions.

It implied, too, a very real deprivation. They could no longer live together. The Church, only in very rare cases gives the permission Pierce sought, admitted two alternatives: that the parties should separate, one becoming a priest and the other a nun, or that the man should become a priest and his wife should make a public vow of chastity, continuing, for the sake of their children, to live under the same roof or separately, but not in a convent. The alternatives exist in their own and similar cases in theory only. The practical solution, if propriety is to be observed and scandal avoided, is that both parties should take religious vows. All this must have been put to Cornelia on their walk home as well as the suggestion that, since such causes move slowly, they should live together as brother and sister for a time in order to test his vocation and their endurance. If they felt confident that it was God's will for them they could then pursue their cause with Rome.

This was no thrilling call to sacrifice, no romantic crusade, but a sober frightening demand. The responsibility was a double one. If Cornelia refused him she might be standing in the way of his proper vocation as well as in the way of his decision. She was stricken and disbelieving.

The hierarchy was against her. They were sure that Pierce was a man cut out for great things, a man apart. Among the spiritual directors who urged her most strongly and there were several, including Father McCloskey, later to become the first

American Cardinal, was Bishop Flaget, their friend and admirer for many years. An exile from the French Revolution, Flaget, when he came to America, was from necessity, a missionary, pioneer, and executive. Yet he had lived all his life with the burning desire to become a Trappist monk. He was a man dangerously ready to sympathize with frustration of the spirit and to promote its goal. To him, and to the others, the special vocation was a delicate important call that must be heard. They assured her, in spite of, on one occasion, her tears, that tragic as the situation was, and rarely as the Church allowed it, they were convinced that both Pierce and she were specially called, that anyone "that hath left house or brethren or sisters or father or mother *or wife or children* or lands for My Name's Sake shall receive an hundredfold and shall possess life everlasting."

Fourteen years later Pierce attributed his priesthood entirely to Flaget's intervention: "It is twelve years since I began my ordeal—preparation for Holy Orders in the Church at a supposed supernatural intimation given to a dear and venerated, but deluded, prelate who rejected a Cardinal's hat and an European Archbishopric to live and die with his first flock." In fact, this was not quite the case. The idea was solely Pierce's, as he was only too anxious to insist in the early years. Yet Flaget's support, which was great, and which was brought to bear heavily upon Cornelia, played a large part in getting it past the early stages.

Cornelia agreed. She had to. There were too many arguments against her and, in the argument of the heart, suffering as well. There is a stage in dilemma where, if the intention is to discover and act upon the right thing, the right thing seems identifiable only with what demands most sacrifice. It was so in Cornelia's case.

Her acceptance was the hardest thing ever asked of her, against which her instincts and reason rebelled. Years later, she said that the Society of the Holy Child Jesus was founded on that day, October 13, when Pierce told her he wanted to become a priest, and that it was founded on a broken heart.

In January of 1841 she went into retreat with the nuns.

The notes she made have been torn out of her spiritual note-book. She believed that suffering should be private.

In March her youngest son, Frank, was born. She must have found relief in the normal demanding affections of a baby. For the moment it stopped the criticisms that she was living an unnatural life, in exaggerated imitation of the nuns.

Pierce himself was preserving his contact with the "great crowded world" not only through his correspondence with Lord Shrewsbury but through the English Catholic periodicals to which he subscribed. His interest in England is the zeal of the proselyte. He saw her ripe for conversion, a country deprived of her religious inheritance for two hundred years and eager to be reinstated. An exciting prospect. On September 16, 1841, he wrote to the Bishop of New Orleans: "I had a letter from Mr. Spencer of as late a date as the 28th July. [Father Ignatius Spencer, brother of Lord Spencer, had been ordained at the English College in Rome in 1830. He had been a gay young man who was converted to thoughts of salvation by a performance of *Don Giovanni* in which the last act, where Giovanni is seized in the midst of a licentious career and hurried down to hell, was particularly vivid. Becoming a Catholic, and then a priest, he had given away all his possessions and devoted himself to the gospel of the poor. He had recently been gripped with the idea of converting England and was urging Wiseman and everyone else in England and abroad to join him in praying and working for this.] He tells me the progress of Catholic feeling among the High Church is astonishing. They insist upon it they are priests and the Church of England is not Protestant. They have their directors and go to confession regularly and have, moreover, printed the whole *Regina* breviary (with the *Salve Regina* and all the antiphons to the Blessed Virgin) though they have not yet published it, and *many of the C. of E. as well as among Catholics begin to look forward to the return of the whole of the established Church as no impossible event.*" The italics are not Pierce's. They represent what it is tempting to assume is the chief contributive cause of his desire for priesthood.

On September 17, the day after this letter was written and the Feast of the Stigmata of St. Francis, Cornelia went into retreat again to consider her vocation. Three hundred years before, St. Theresa of Ávila was undergoing the same exhausting strain upon the spirit. "When I was in the midst of worldly pleasures, I was distressed by the remembrance of what I owed to God. When I was with God I grew restless because of worldly affection." She, too, had become a nun with little inclination, in her own words from "servile fear," but though "I would not incline my will to being a nun I saw that this was the best and safest state and so, little by little, I determined to force myself to embrace it." She was twenty-one, Cornelia was thirty-two. The transition was greater and later but, strangely enough, their lives as foundresses were not unlike.

Some short jerky notes in one of Cornelia's spiritual diaries are all that remain of the struggle that went on within her. In one place arguing with herself she writes under "Pros": "It is for the glory of God that we should save our souls. If we can save our souls more surely in that way, and help others to do so too, this is fulfilling God's designs upon us and procuring His glory." Under "Cons" she answers back: "We are very weak. Those who are very weak are not fit for so perfect a state, and not more sure of saving their souls in that state, therefore not for the glory of God. We do not know ourselves and cannot judge whether we are weak or strong." A little later she thinks aloud again: "It is not presumption to think one is called to perfection, but it is presumption to think there is no fear of ourselves. It is not presumption to have hope and joy and confidence in God's grace. What one is called to do, one is called to do with all one's strength."

"O my God," she prayed, "bless us and fill us with Thy Spirit that we may come out of this retreat dead to ourselves and living only for Thee." The prayer was answered. With a brevity and a briskness that is, later, to become typical, she writes: "Examined vocation. Decided. Simplicity—confidence." The suffering was not less but it was made supportable by decision. Borrowing the prayer of Pierre de la Colombière, she writes: "I cast all upon Thee, all my anxieties, all my scruples. . . . O my God *in te domine speravi non confundam in aeternum.* I know the temptation, I have seen the stars of Heaven fall, but this will not alarm me—I hope in my confidence in Thee my God"; and again in her own words: "I abandon without reserve all to Thy will." There is a luxury in abandonment in religion as well as in life, and it is arguable that she had no right to give without reserve. But she was acting upon the general commandment of God in the New Testament and upon the particular persuasions of her spiritual guardians, which were very strong.

She was allowed another respite when her brother-in-law, John, brought his wife Angelica to stay. Geckla became a great friend of the family but she was outside the secret. Even Mary, who had become a novice at the Sacred Heart Convent at Grand Coteau shortly after her conversion, in June, 1841, was not included in it by Pierce's request.

In April, 1842, Lord Shrewsbury wrote to say that he was at last able to offer Pierce a definite job as tutor to his nephew Talbot, and in May Pierce sailed from New Orleans. He had sold Gracemere and its effects with customary swiftness and acumen, arranged for Cornelia and the children to board in the convent, and taken Mercer, who was to be educated at Lord Shrewsbury's expense by the Jesuits at Stonyhurst, with him. He arrived in England in the beginning of July after a typically long and uncomfortable journey, including icebergs, "two awful-looking ones" which put them "in constant fear for several days and nights."

He installed Mercer at Stonyhurst and, owing to some delay in taking over Talbot, became travelling companion at two hundred pounds a year and all expenses paid to young Mr. Berkeley of Spetchley, heir to a large fortune. From England Grand Coteau appeared with a different emphasis. "Dear Grand Coteau! All the magnificence and greatness I am in the midst of is a poor, a very poor, exchange for solitude and holy quiet." His letters to his family are extraordinarily concerned with his own effect upon others and with his good fortune. He is also missing Cornelia and the children. One can only presume that his letters to his wife, which no longer exist, were along the same lines and wonder why she did not sense the hollowness of his sentiments and suggest a compromise. Perhaps she did—and he would not listen.

At the end of the year he set out with Henry Berkeley on his European tour for which, as he modestly admits, he was chosen because "of the access which I was able to give my young friend to High Society."

From Grand Coteau Cornelia's letters never hinted at the truth. They were mostly to her family and the John Connellys and were about such soothing subjects as autumn pruning and the children. Frank, or Bun as he was more often called, had fat, pink cheeks and untidy curly hair, and was just beginning to talk—an "enviable object," as his mother proudly claimed. Ady was learning the piano, and from England Pierce wrote to say that Mercer was becoming a fanatical cricketer. He was ten years old and his father regretted that he had not had time to visit him during his first two months at school.

For fourteen months Cornelia waited. She found it hard. "Mortification," she writes, "is absolutely necessary to acquire a perfect conformity to the will of God, since it is our own will and the disorder of our appetites which are the obstacles to this conformity, the former the means, the latter the end." But few other words remain of the loneliness and bewilderment of spirit she must have suffered while Pierce made his slow, enjoyable way across Europe. Those that do all suggest that she missed him dreadfully, both with her mind and her body, and that her energies were all devoted to combating this dependence upon him in preparation for their greater separation. She was a woman to whom her children were a source of pleasure and happiness, but it was upon her husband that her life centered and from whom her inspiration came. Yet nothing of this tearing apart of her heart showed in her manner or her face. She appeared, as always, calm and only occasionally allowed herself the release of writing in her diary, with, on one occasion, some humor "profit by all temptations!!!" and, on another, with some weariness, "O God help me to live, not I but Jesus in me, in His spirit of sacrifice and suffering, with only God in view, the reparation of His glory, the salvation of souls. For this end even suffering becomes sweet."

But the period of waiting came at last to its end. Pierce reached Rome and laid his petition before the ecclesiastical authorities. Nothing could be done unless his wife were pres-

ent. She was sent for at once and, four days after she received
the summons, she left Grand Coteau for New Orleans to
await further instructions. She was not, apparently, to go
straight to Rome. She was to travel to England first and to
stay with the Shrewsburys. Pierce himself would come to New
Orleans to escort her there. He did not like the thought of her
travelling alone with two small children, and it was, in any
case, a good opportunity to introduce young Berkeley to America. The introduction delayed them and they did not sail until
the middle of July. To make matters worse the trunk containing most of their clothes and $3,500 worth of jewelry was lost
going aboard. With typical resignation, but equally typical determination to retrieve it if possible, Cornelia wrote: "Perhaps
God wills us to be detached and poor, at all events it was a
mistake. So if it is lost let it go, only that we do all that we
ought to do to get it again."

On July 16, 1843, they sailed aboard the packet *West
Wind*, weighing in the neighborhood of 800 tons and belonging to the Philadelphian Line. The passage cost $100 and in-
cluded, as a subject for much pride, a piano in one of the
saloons. Like its competitors, the *West Wind* went in thoroughly for interior decoration and worthily represented the
American Merchant Marine, which managed to retain the
transatlantic service almost entirely in its hands during the
nineteenth century. But in spite of its pride in the fact that
"the Yankee packet was Lord of the Western Ocean," life in
the passenger class was comfortable largely by contrast with
those travelling steerage. There was not enough space to make
it anything else.

The life of the Philadelphian Line was not long. Begun in
1807, it only just survived the middle of the century. But during that period it ranked with the best, and Cornelia's first
visit to England, in spite of anxiety and confinement, was
made in the most comfortable circumstances possible to her
age.

She found England attractive and Alton as thrilling as
Pierce said. "When I came," she wrote back to America, "it
burst upon me as something I had no idea of. . . . I suppose
from six to twenty families come to see it in a day and are

shown through while the family are here, but the drawing room is so large that while we may all be at one end of it, strangers will pass through the other without seeing who we are."

It was a house befitting the premier Earl. But this gorgeous peer in his palace of huge magnificence and architectural solecism, built when the passion for Gothic burned at its height and at its most impure, was, in spite of it, a man of moderation and sound common sense.

He could understand and respect the chivalrous, improbable impulses that burned in so many of his friends' breasts but he did not indulge in them. He lived, beneath the façade, a simple life. He enjoyed his huge rooms and tiny, inconvenient windows with no sensation of losing himself in "*O Altitudo*," but with the sense of satisfaction that it was the right sort of house to have built; that its ambitious pinnacles and imposing buttresses reflected in spirit the physical glory of his state, which was kingly. He did not speculate upon their presumption or their architectural pretension—or upon the solidity of their foundations. He had more servants and more rooms than any of his Catholic contemporaries and most of his Protestant ones. He could radiate his dignity so effectively that it even protected and imbued his somewhat silly wife when she was with him. He was the sort of kind dutiful man who, in a slightly different sphere, would have hunted happily to hounds, represented his borough in another place, and bred a good type of gun dog. As it was, he employed the fashionable architect and enjoyed the fashionable pursuits of his day, which involved him in travelling, the pursuit of art, and the intellectual labor of representing the Catholic Church in England at nearly the most argumentative and bellicose stage of its career.

He was an earnest and excellent host, and the Connellys' stay at Alton Towers became more and more prolonged. Pierce seemed in no hurry. They would set out for Rome at their leisure. The young Berkeley's itinerary was of first consideration—and upon his wishes their financial status mainly depended. Cornelia was fond of her hosts and fascinated by the English countryside, but she could not have been at ease.

She had voluntarily abandoned the world, expecting only to see Pierce again when he was a priest or, as Pierce puts it, "when we were both in our long gowns," but here she was in the midst of parties, adulation, and witticisms and, more trying still, in the circumstances, with the near proximity of Pierce, delighted to have her back, delighted by her effect upon his precious society, excited, energetic, and exigent. The cloister seemed very remote, but he refused to abandon it. It could not happen just yet and meanwhile the world was near at hand and compromise an art he had been busy learning during the past few months.

Cornelia was having grave doubts about his intentions. Years later she told one of her nuns that had they acted then upon her judgment the resulting catastrophes would never have occurred. But though she must often have suggested to him that this was the time for turning back, before their lives were dislocated any further, he was determined to persevere. Obedience was natural to her and to her age and, in addition, she had for the past two years been disciplining herself to accept authority. Nothing of her trepidation showed. She smiled and talked in her soft voice with its slow American accent and fussed over the children who, immediately susceptible to the English climate, caught perpetual colds. She charmed and amused the people she dined with and enchanted even the servants at Alton, one of whom, the head housemaid, was to become one of her first nuns.

After delays and postponement, their course was firmly set —but by the longest possible route. To Paris, from Paris to Orléans by diligence, then Lyons, down the Rhône to Avignon and Marseille, across the sea to Genoa, and finally, after a protracted journey down Italy, to Rome. Frank was two and Ady only eight. They could not have been easy companions in the swaying, bumpy coaches, the surly, untidy inns, and the exhaustion of never knowing where the next night was to be spent. And all the time they were under the strain of finding suitable monuments and ruins for Berkeley to be entertained by, at the instigation of his tireless and tiring tutor.

But at last they were in Rome, the Pope was willing to see

them, and their cause was under consideration. They must both have felt the same release of mind and will as they had done five years before at finding yet another chapter of their lives starting with their arrival in Rome.

Chapter 4

TRINITÀ DEI MONTI

IT WAS on December 7, 1843, that Cornelia reached Rome for the second time. But if she had hoped for certainty or peace she was doomed to disappointment.

Pierce had already seen to it that notification of their arrival went ahead, and Prince Borghese invited them to dine the night they arrived. He was now a widower, for Gwendoline had died of cholera with her three small sons in 1840, and he was not yet married to his cousin, Teresa de la Rochefoucauld, who became his second wife in 1848. Pierce was too gratified to refuse and delighted by the way they were "magnified in the eyes of the people by the grand carriage and servants the Prince sent for us." Ady was delighted with Gwendoline's only surviving child, Agnes, who was nearly the same age, and spent two weeks playing with her before she was installed in the Sacred Heart Convent, Trinità dei Monti, which stands high up in Rome, guarded by the Borghese gardens behind and gazing down the Spanish Steps upon Bernini's barge in the Piazza di Spagna below. Cornelia already knew the Trinità. She had gone there on her last visit, and it was, besides, a sister convent to Grand Coteau and had probably had news of her coming from there.

The Connellys settled in an apartment in the Via Ripetta and entered upon that stage of waiting at ease which must attend the decisions of all potentates. The Pope was friendly to Pierce. Personality was among the things he counted permissible. He was as amused as Pierce when Frank, aged three and by now a "stout, red-cheeked, red-legged little English-looking boy," made them laugh in audience when, told to kneel down and kiss the Pope's slippered foot, "he jumped instead upon Ady's back to kiss it over her shoulder, and finished by giving the foot a crack with his handkerchief."

But the Pope's attention was not enough. The machinery of Rome moves slowly. There are the formulas and practices of two thousand years to navigate, arduous and agonizing formulas to those who suffer them.

For the moment the Roman authorities ignored the Connellys and they were thrown back upon their own resources. What should they do? They must provide for their children. They could not wait forever. Once again Cornelia was reined in from her purpose as she had been at Alton. The effort of self-discipline she had made during the fourteen months at Grand Coteau, and which would have carried her over any obstacles, was slackened for the second time in six months. There is nothing so undermining, so deteriorating to the will, as inaction, but, as always, Cornelia fell back on prayer. Her notes, more detailed and fuller than usual, advised her as sternly as before to "mortify nature one day at a time. Do and suffer one day at a time," and struggled, as before, with the problems of her decision. It is significant that they no longer mentioned Pierce's will. The problem of Cornelia's vocation had become a personal one and she faced it entirely on a spiritual plane—no domestic considerations intruded. "It is for the glory of God that we should be saints. God wills what is for His glory. Therefore God wills us to be saints. God wills me to be a saint. I will to be a saint. *Therefore I shall be a saint.* Live for Eternity. Eternity, Eternity, Eternity."

While Cornelia struggled with herself Pierce was occupied with worrying about his responsibilities and how he should provide for his family should Rome give an unfavorable verdict in his case. He made careful alternative plans, for several years ahead as well as for the immediate future, as a letter to his brother John shows. After describing them at some length he adds: "Our plans, however, are not certain as you see. Both of us will probably spend one or two more winters in Rome, but it is not, of course, so certain where Nelie will spend her summers. She may accept the Borghese invitation and pass this summer at Frascati with them. I suppose it is time enough to think of the next a year hence."

On March 5 Cornelia went into retreat at the Trinità and confirmed her decision:

"(1) If O my God Thou are pleased to place me in a religious life, I offer myself to Thee to suffer in my heart with Thee and for Thee not to do my will but Thine in the will of my superiors. (2) I offer myself to Thee to suffer the loss of any esteem whatever and to be despised without any exception. (3) I offer myself to Thee to suffer in my body by all my senses, by cold, by hunger, by thirst and in any manner whatever (and without reserves) that may the most contribute to the glory and the good of souls."

The Roman Consultors, to whom the petition for separation had already been presented, advised them that it was time to put their request for Pierce's ordination in audience with the Pope. Accordingly, on March 15, they knelt before him and handed the formal wording of their petition to "His Holiness, Our Sovereign Lord, Pope Gregory XVI." The petition pleaded their motives and the fact that Cornelia was already accepted as a provisional postulant by the Sacred Heart Convent at Trinità dei Monti while Pierce was provisionally accepted by the Society of Jesus. It went on to say: "A provision has also been made in the most suitable manner for the education and the future welfare of the three children granted to them by Divine Providence. The son, of eleven years of age, is placed at the college of Stonyhurst in England, which is under the management of the Jesuit Fathers, and the Earl of Shrewsbury has expressly engaged to take special care of him. The daughter, aged nine years, is being educated in the aforesaid convent of the Sacred Heart, here in Rome, while her mother is to take the veil.

"There is also a son, three years of age, who will be placed in due time where he may be taken care of and be brought up with every attention and may also receive, while his tender years require it, the assistance of his mother herself. The Prince Borghese has been pleased to take a generous interest in the future welfare of this last-mentioned child, and besides this, the petitioner will assign a capital out of his own private estate for the benefit of each of the said children."

The Pope, who was also their friend, accepted their petition but warned them that many months would elapse before they would hear a final decision.

But Bishop Flaget was in Rome that winter. He was in a position to persuade. Cardinal Patrizi, Cardinal Vicar of Rome, Cardinal Fransoni, Prefect of the Sacred Congregation of Propaganda Fide, and Father Grassi, S.J., Assistant General for Italy, were also impressed by the Americans. Unexpectedly the formalities were abandoned. They were not to wait months for their decision; they were to enter their respective orders at once.

On March 17, 1844, Pierce wrote to his brother John and, for the first time, broke the news of his intentions. "It seems only right that you and dear Geckla should know before anybody what will not now be long unknown to everybody," he began, and, later, went on to: "His Holiness sent for the Cardinal Vicar the day before yesterday, and told him he dispensed with all letters dimissory from America, and that His Eminence might give me minor orders immediately. This will perhaps be done before the end of Lent, and Nelie at the same time will enter the Convent of the Sacred Heart, where little Ady is, not as a novice but only as a postulant, remaining at liberty as long as Frank has need of her. . . . Cornelia will always pass her nights with him, and he has the most beautiful garden you can imagine to play in, large and high with a sweet view of all Rome." The letter ended with a jocular invitation to involuntary charity which must have been as grating to John Connelly then as it is to the reader now: "If you do not get all the amount of the debt from Grand Coteau you must consider what is wanting as given to a poor religious." But it also contained one paragraph which is surely sincere—as if, beneath all the pageantry and bustling ceremony, he had felt the thudding of his heart and known what it was to be alone with God. He was frightened and it made him honest. It is sad that he mistook his fear for a temporary and very natural anxiety. "It is a little uncertain if I shall finish my studies and go into my noviceship, here or in England, and the day of my taking the minor orders is not yet named. Indeed, it is all not a little uncertain, for who can tell how long he will be faithful? And nothing but God's grace will save one's courage from failing even at the last moment."

John's reactions, like those of Cornelia's sister, Mary, were less dismayed than the rest. Lord Shrewsbury, when he had been told before the Connellys left Alton, had replied: "What on earth are you doing? Breaking the human and Divine law by giving up your wife and children when no such sacrifice is asked of you. You must be mad." It was a tribute to Pierce's powers of persuasion that Shrewsbury quickly changed his attitude and remained Pierce's closest supporter in the events that lay ahead.

These quickly gathered impetus. By April they were in full spate. In Holy Week Pierce put on his "long gown" and received the tonsure. The deed of separation became public knowledge. On April 9 Pierce took Cornelia to the Trinità, where she formally entered as a postulant—the preliminary stage to becoming first a novice and then a nun.

On May 1, exactly a month after the separation was legally signed, Pierce received minor orders, the first step towards ordination, in the church of the convent, while Cornelia sang in the choir and Adeline, a little girl of nine, cried in a mixture of excitement, bewilderment, and misery.

Normally it takes six or seven years to become ordained a priest—and longer for a Jesuit. But though the Church specifies the length of time that should elapse between receiving minor orders, a subdiaconate, diaconate, and finally priesthood, it lies in the power of a bishop to alter this in certain exceptional cases. For a time, at least, uncertainty was laid aside. The Connellys' separation was officially signed and sealed and laid away in the Roman archives. There was nothing left but the slow, orthodox approach to a religious vocation; several years, first as a postulant and then as a novice, for Cornelia and for Pierce, since he had already taken orders in the Episcopal Church, however long his superiors thought he would need to acquire a proper understanding of his functions.

But the peace of mind that Cornelia hoped would accompany a relaxation from effort and opposition did not materialize, although the arrangements for her and the children's well-being were, considering the circumstances, good. "I am here," she wrote to her brother George, "as a postulant, though eating and sleeping in the house where the retreats are given, which is a large, comfortable house, cool and quiet. Powell, the English nurse I brought from England, takes care of Frank —she is a treasure of patience."

It was clear that Cornelia looked upon her stay at the Trinità as a preliminary to returning to America. "Before long," she wrote to George, "no doubt there will be a convent of our order established in that part of the country [where George lived] and perhaps I may be sent there, and then Martha [his future wife] will come and make a retreat with us and, should you be blessed with children, I will have the education of them."

But, in spite of having her children near, the year that followed was not a happy one. In every other way Cornelia was leading the ordinary routine life of a Sacred Heart nun. She found her bed hard, the room very cold, and the quiet frightening. She suffered from a feeling of claustrophobia that was both mental and physical. The dreadful finality suggested by the huge convent gates was echoed in a desolation of the spirit that brought with it no spiritual compensations. She was, perhaps, entering upon that familiar path of aridity and depression, "the dark night of the soul." But unlike so many of the saints, she was not suffering it in a vacuum. There was no protective layer of disassociation between her and the world. There were the children to be thought about, worried over, and, in Mercer's case, written to, and Pierce's difficulties to regard and comfort. She criticized herself for misplaced gravity and tried to smile as often as she could. She fought with herself in prayer and meditation, finding no comfort without and none within. She longed for death, doubted her right to it, convinced herself that her state of mind was a symptom of approaching death, and prepared herself to die. Everything lacked meaning. Her heart was empty, her mind listless. "Incapable of listening or understanding or thinking, I offered that which the others understood and forced my will to rejoice in the greatness of God and in my own dejection and misery." But it was no good. "My soul sleeps," she cried out in fear. Only her will remained secure against her malaise and such stray temptations as her longing for Pierce and thoughts about the children. There were moments of respite. She was suddenly happy because her director "thinks Frank ought to stay with me till he is eight years old. I think so, too, but I am so much afraid of having any reserves with God." But her body betrayed her. She was seldom well. What sign was there to show that she had made the right decision? Wearily she wrote: "Unless the Lord had been my helper, my soul had almost dwelt in Hell."

But nothing of this appeared. Pierce visited her every ten days and listened to Ady playing the piano or Frank reciting. He brought him "a little guitar" to encourage him and the same evening "sent us a treat of ices for all the house." It was St. Peter's Day and at ten o'clock, when the ice creams were eaten and the community in bed, the Girandola, the most famous fireworks in the world, burst over Rome.

In spite of his new religious status Pierce was still in trouble with his family for his snobbishness. He wrote in protest: "I wrote what I did because I thought it would interest you and not, I hope, because my heart was more in such things than in religion. And then, too, it was natural that I should tell you whatever promised to be of advantage to our dear little ones."

Cornelia herself was not immune to Pierce's affectation. In the midst of this period of trial and desolation she could write to her brother George congratulating him upon his engagement and adding, with some pique: "We have here a most sweet superior. She is by birth a Marchioness. The house is for the nobility and all the children are noble. There is another house of this order here which is for the second class of people. *But all that does not interest you.*"

Such comments were very superficial. In fact, some part of her unhappiness may have been due to the state of the convent itself. The Sacred Heart Order had not been founded long. Its foundress, Mother Barat, was still living as head of her house in Paris. Like most convents and many institutions during their early days, it was going through a restless and trying time. In 1839 the Holy See had formulated certain decrees to try and draw it more into line with the constitution of the Jesuits. The results had been disastrous. Each order has its own stamp and spirit. The Church provides in canon law a basic rule to which all new orders must conform. But the ruling is a skeleton only, liable to many permitted deviations of phrasing and practice. And in such deviations the spirit lies. To tamper with it is often to destroy it. The nuns, at first dismayed by the change, became slowly perplexed and then angry. Four years later Rome annulled the decrees and saved the Society. But this was only the year before Cornelia entered the Trinità and the vibrations of discontent were still spreading from the forgotten cause.

Barbara Charlton, an eccentric and outspoken old lady when she wrote her memoirs, remembered Mother Barat's house in Paris vividly, if not with much affection. Writing of it as it was in 1828 she says: "The Sacré Cœur that I went to was certainly a refinement on other convents of that day—although the English girls at it suffered somewhat from neglect. It was housed in the princely domain of the Hotel Biron. The *règlement* was perfect; no regiment of the line could have had a better discipline or been more smartly drilled. The rules were very strict, the principal object being to dry up all the springs of affection in the human heart and imbue the nuns with an icy, stand-off manner towards their pupils. It cannot be denied that the religious instruction was simply perfect. . . . The year 1829 was almost a duplicate of my previous year there; the same beautiful church ceremonies on Feast days, the same exquisitely organized Processions in the grounds that feasted the eye if they did not touch the heart."

Barbara Charlton is not an entirely reliable guide. Brusque, amusing, and determined, with a shrewd eye for motive and a loathing for pretense, her observations, though always based on fact, reveal a flare for the dramatic which is not always trustworthy. But in this case Cornelia's reactions bear her out. She had decided, after more than a year, that she could not become a Sacred Heart nun—a decision that was shared by her superiors, one of whom wrote, somewhat cryptically, to Mother Barat that Cornelia was more fitted to founding her own order than to remaining in theirs.

On November 12, 1845, Cornelia wrote to her sister Adeline: ". . . and now dear Ady to explain why I have not answered your letter immediately, the truth is it would then have passed through the hands of the Superioress here and would probably not have been such as would have pleased her, for I considered myself obliged to announce to her, nine months ago, that I doubted very much that I should ever enter the order of the Sacred Heart tho' I had no doubts about my vocation to a religious life . . . the nuns here are very good and kind and there is nothing whatever with respect to ourselves that I would wish different from what it is [but] I bless our dear Lord again and again that I have been prevented so wonderfully from taking any promise or obligation upon me with respect to this French order, for it is not the one for our country. Our own dear country women must be led to a perfect life by meekness and sweetness and not by fear. I shall ask your dear brother Pierce to tell you a great secret which you must keep as your heart or you will never be trusted again. . . ."

It is tempting to wonder what the secret was. Clearly nothing to do with Wiseman's ultimate plan for her since she is still thinking in terms of America and, from the tone, nothing to do with Pierce's change of heart. For at the same time as Cornelia firmly faced her incongruity in an order so alien in temperament, and told her superior her doubts, Pierce decided that he was not called to be a Jesuit and wished to be a secular priest.

By the end of the year, 1845, the tension was beginning to relax. Mother Barat had come to stay at the Trinità. With an intuition and kindliness at variance with Barbara Charlton's verdict, she insisted that Cornelia should live in the convent, although she no longer wished to enter it, until she could decide where her proper vocation lay.

She stayed there a year.

Meanwhile, on July 6, Pierce, who had preferred the more congenial atmosphere of the Collegio dei Nobili to that of the Jesuits, was ordained priest. The usual procedure had been considerably shortened, for it was just over a year since he had received minor orders. A few days after, on June 22, he received the Order of Subdeacon, and that of Deacon on June 29.

On July 7 he said his first Mass in the convent chapel—its great doors flung open to embrace a large and unusual congregation—among them the Shrewsburys and a number of people eager to record their comments. Several of these were in flat contradiction. Lady Mary Arundell, a cousin of Maria Edgeworth's, wrote to her sister-in-law, Mrs. Doughty, to describe the scene and ended: "I have since heard that when the parting was over, Mr. C. having torn himself away, Mrs. C. fell on the ground and remained there some time, and on rising there was literally *a pool of tears* on the floor—but both are going on well. This is true heroism. Such things redeem this horrid nineteenth century in one's opinion. The events were written by my dear Colyer from Rome, of course he had some hand in it, to a very interesting agreeable Puseyite convert, Miss Bowles, whose conversion made some noise at Rome last winter." Her letter casts an interesting sidelight on Emily Bowles, who was to play a large part in Cornelia's life and who, with an irony that only retrospect can reveal, was still probably unknown to her. But it is belied by another letter, this time to America, from a young man writing to his Cousin Deborah: "This morning at about ten o'clock Mr. Pierce Connelly sent word to the college for some of the American students to go and assist at this his first Mass, which he celebrated in the church of the convent where his former wife lives. We arrived, when Mass had begun, and there were a good many persons there who wished to receive communion from him. Among them his little daughter . . . she wore a wreath of flowers on her head, and first, before giving the communion, Mr. Connelly turned from the altar and addressed her publicly for about fifteen minutes, exhorting her to remember this day, and celebrate the anniversary of it, not only here but in Heaven. It was a very affecting scene—one of the most affecting scenes I ever beheld.

"After Mass we went into the sacristy to see him and congratulate him, but he was entirely overcome and could scarcely speak with us, and invited us in another room to congratulate Mrs. Connelly. I have seen so much in the American papers about Mrs. Connelly pining away upon Monte Pincio that I was almost surprised to see her so joyful. Indeed I never saw any person more so. I am sure it is the happiest day of her life."

Indeed it must have been a case both for relief and for celebration, although *Dolman's Magazine*, an English Catholic review, cautiously and acidly remarked: "It is surely to be lamented that young persons should be permitted to bind themselves to callings incompatible with their matrimonial engagements during what may prove to be only a fit of exalted enthusiasm."

Ecstatically, Pierce wrote to America: "I wanted to write to you when I put on the cassock but I felt afraid to write about it. It seemed too great to count upon, and till the blessed day I said my first Mass I never could feel sure of it." Here was a little of the awe that attends so many ordinations and which Newman expressed so accurately in a letter to his mother after he was ordained deacon in June, 1824: "It is over. At first after the hands were laid on me my heart shuddered within me. The words 'for ever' are so terrible." "For ever," he adds, "words never to be recalled. I have the responsibility of souls on me to the day of my death."

For Cornelia the months that followed were as hard as those that had gone before: anxiety about the future, sudden inspirations and corresponding depressions, strange spiritual attractions drained of their vitality by equally strong repulsions. And then, quite suddenly, the command of the Pope that she was to join no existing order but to help found a new one in England.

Such an idea stepped from the bounds of orthodoxy into extravagance. It was a breathtaking, fabulous suggestion that a woman who had borne five children, had only recently left her husband, and was not even a professed novice should calmly leave Rome for a country she had only once visited for a few weeks in order to start a new teaching order. But so deeply had the Connellys' piety impressed Rome that such disadvantages slipped by unnoticed.

The idea, of course, was not as sudden to the main protagonists as it seems. Although we have no evidence for them, discussions must have taken place endlessly between Pierce and Cornelia about their plans—their failures, their hopes, and their ambitions. These, in turn, Cornelia would have confided to her spiritual directors. At some stage, and through one of their friends or advisers, the suggestion of helping on the work of education in England must have arisen—probably through Lord Shrewsbury, who was constantly in Rome and constantly in touch with Wiseman, whose main interest, since he had become Vicar Apostolic of the Midland district, it was. In the enthusiastic, plausible hands of Pierce Connelly it would not take long for such a suggestion to gain strength and conviction. At this stage Cornelia's directors, who were both sympathetic and admiring and who appear to have been imbued with the same crusading desire for the conversion of England which stirred so many Catholic breasts in the nineteenth century, must have added their encouragement.

By slow degrees, and perhaps through various channels, the suggestion reached the Pope—perhaps even through Pierce himself, who was acting at the time, in a part-time capacity, as an official attendant at papal levees whose duty it was to introduce all American visitors. But whatever its beginnings —and a year later Pierce wrote to his brother, "You ought to know it was no doing of Cornelia's coming to England, she had only thought of America, and it was in obedience to her directors"—it was certain to gain more august support quite soon. For, from their first appearance in Rome, the hierarchy seem to have been ranged behind the Connellys.

The idea that Cornelia should go to England to help Wiseman in one aspect of his fight for England—in the field of education—was put to her by the Pope. Tradition alone supplies the fact. It does not, unfortunately, annotate it. We do not know how he worded it. He was, we do know, extremely vague. His request that she draw up proposals for a teaching order with the help of her spiritual directors was the sort of light, expressive suggestion that conversation makes easy and formality forbids.

Cornelia is not the only founder to have started an order on the command of authority and not from inspiration, but

she must be unique in having undertaken it with so little preparation and upon such vague terms.

The actual composition of the rule was, however, not at all
vague. The founding of an order is subject to strict and legal
formalities, which the Church scrupulously enforces. There
are certain practices—spiritual retreats, mental prayer, the
vows of poverty, chastity, and obedience, etc.—which are common to all religious orders. There are stern regulations guarding the terms of endowment and property which aim at
safeguarding the society from the possible fickleness and sus-
ceptibility of the individual and the individual from the possible greediness and inexorability of the society. There are
differences within the general rule—the enclosed orders differ
from the unenclosed, the contemplative from the active. But
it is only the careful interpretation of this general rule, the
choice or omission of certain aspects of it, the phrasing and nature of the adaptation, which seems so slight on paper and
means so much in fact, that mark the temperament and intention of the individual rule.

Cornelia, with little knowledge of ecclesiastical convention,
had to have a basis on which to work her ideas. She chose the
rule of her beloved St. Ignatius, founder of the Jesuits. But
she was a woman who loved lightheartedness and joy and,
even in her unhappiness, sought to preserve them. It was natural to her to associate such things with the innocence of childhood and to envisage God in terms of them. It was in this
likeness that she fashioned Him. And as she worked upon her
rule in front of a picture of Jesus as a child in His mother's
arms, the association of ideas was lent authority by a sensation
she had that the child smiled upon her work, and by a dream
in which a voice seemed to repeat the words, "Society of the
Holy Child Jesus." It was a name that appealed to her imagination and her affection for the Society of Jesus. She decided
to give it to the order she had been asked, one day, to found.

Hers was to be an active order. For it she rejected total
poverty and enclosure, extra fasts and bodily austerities. Her
nuns were to be divided into two ranks, choir sisters who were
to be educated women who would teach and bear responsibility, and house sisters who would do the household work. She

took special care to make the latter feel included in every aspect of convent life, for "the choir sisters and the house sisters, although engaged in different employments, are yet under the same vows, and all form one and the same family, bound together by the mutual ties of esteem and love."

All the nuns were to be postulants for six months and novices for two years, after which they professed temporary vows for five years. It was to take them seven and a half years before they could be fully professed and make their perpetual vows. Even so, these perpetual vows were not solemn, in the sense that a priest's vows are, and could be dispensed by ecclesiastical authority.

The rules of admission which applied to prospective postulants were many. They must be known to and voted for by the community. They must produce a certificate of Baptism and Confirmation, have a spotless reputation and "a well-ordered mind and an exterior exempt from any grave deformity." They must possess "good judgment, be of an open, docile, sociable, and cheerful disposition," and have "a temper of mind solid and strong enough to undertake and sustain the sacrifices required by the religious life; to have no indication of epilepsy or any contagious disorder." They were "not to be remarkably eccentric nor to betray any symptoms of insanity." Nor were they "to be in debt," nor "to be a widow having the support of children." They were "not to have parents dependent on their pecuniary support" and they must provide "a dowry or other means of support" (to protect them in case they should leave the order as well as to support them within it). This dowry was to be in the form of a capital sum ("invested in safe and profitable securities") of £1,000, or in an insured annuity of £50. This could be, and often was, reduced by General Council to £400 capital or £20 annuity, and sometimes exempted altogether.

The government of the order, although it was based upon the same careful definition which governed nuns' dowries and convent endowments, allowed more scope for individual interpretation.

It was Cornelia's intention that "the houses of this institute" should be "under the immediate jurisdiction of the Ordinary [Bishop] of the Diocese who shall exercise over the houses and sisters all the authority granted him by the Sacred Canons and the Apostolic Constitutions." But "The general government shall be exercised by the Mother General," whose powers, both spiritual and temporal, were great. Realizing how absolute her power might become, Cornelia sought to restrain it by democratic means. She was careful to define every occasion on which a Superior must seek the Bishop's advice, and to leave room for many more occasions which were outside immediate possibility. She also established the office of General Monitress, whose duty it was to "admonish the Superior General frankly, and with great humility, of any faults she finds in her which might have a prejudicial effect on the Institute. It is her duty also to convey to the Superior General any well-grounded complaint she may have received from any of the sisters, but without mentioning the sister's name." There was to be a local Monitress in every convent to provide the same countercheck upon the local Superior. The clauses defining the election of a Monitress were as carefully worded as those concerning a Reverend Mother. "The Monitress to a Superior General was to be elected from among the general assistants by secret vote at the General Chapter." General Chapter was an assembly, composed of two representatives from each house, which was intended to meet every three years to elect the Superior General and her four Assistants, who were in turn to elect the other leading officers of the Society. A nun could be elected to the same office for several successive terms, or changed to another, but the moment she ceased to hold office she automatically returned to the status of an ordinary nun. She carried no insignia of the rank she had once held beyond the order in which her name was called in Chapter.

Cornelia's rule laid special emphasis on the fact that "no sister shall at the same time hold incompatible offices unless for grave reasons sanctioned by the General Council, and sanctioned by the Ordinary." As examples of incompatibility she quoted "the office of Superioress General with any other" (except that of the mother house) and "the office of Auditor with that of Superior of any kind, or with the offices of *Eco-*

nome or Treasurer." It must be remembered that her rule did not take account of the difficulties of foundation—at first, of course, a Superior General must be everything—but was written for the running of an established order. With this in view she entered into details of expansion with great care.

Her rule covered many printed pages and was divided into chapters considered under the headings "The Institute," "Constitutions," "Administration," and "Directory," the last including special instructions suitable to each office. It was full of good sense and kindness, a finely wrought map of religious endeavor which must always be encouraged, but protected, at the same time, from excess and lack of foresight. Cornelia defined "the spirit of the Institute" as one which "embraces in a very special manner the virtue of zeal, because its chief end is our sanctification and the salvation of souls." But this virtue must be sensibly conceived; it must be "a well-regulated zeal, a humble and disinterested zeal, a courageous zeal, a gentle and insinuating zeal, a patient and persevering zeal, a discreet zeal."

Her emphasis was always upon moderation and love. She could see no need for holiness to associate itself with drabness, or zeal with lack of taste. Even on small points the insistence remained. The Infirmary "must be kept very clean, the beds well made and the rooms dressed with pictures and flowers. The remedies should always be presented with cheerfulness and sweetness." There was to be no gloom in dedication.

The months she spent in drafting a rule put Cornelia in the embarrassing and anomalous position of founding one order while literally under the roof of another. It could not have been easy for her superiors to stomach. There was some justification for seeing that the way was not made too easy for her. She was certainly not lacking in tests of endurance of the kind that community life makes so easy to administer and which are so hard to bear—the small slights, the casual overlooking of effort, the careful reminder of mistakes, the skillful appropriation of extra, and unappealing, sorts of work.

And then came the summons and her release. She must go to Paris, to the convent of the Assumption in the Avenue de

Chaillot, and wait for further orders. She had not taken any vows beyond her original vow of chastity. She was free to depart from the Sacred Heart and to place herself wherever her spiritual directors thought fit. With her faithful English nurse, Powell, whom Lady Shrewsbury had found for her two years before, Ady sad to leave Rome, and Bun beside himself at the thought of seeing Mercer again, she left for Paris on April 18, 1846.

It was not at all like her previous journey to England. She travelled without Pierce and she travelled steerage, where space was cramped and unhealthy, and the overcrowding and lack of sanitation must have made her seasickness seem far worse.

Pierce, writing to his brother John on April 28, is either deliberately vague or else the exact nature of Cornelia's voyage is still unknown. "Father Grassi, Nelie's director, had very nearly sent her to America, but Lord Shrewsbury so strongly argued in favor of England that she is now on her way there, where she will probably enter into religion, but it will be with the hope of connecting England and America together in a new congregation under St. Francis of Sales."

Pierce's enthusiasm for the Jesuits had been on the wane since his ordination. He had tried to persuade Cornelia to let her rule rest upon the precepts of St. Francis rather than upon St. Ignatius. But Cornelia was undeterred, though their discussions were long. Did he see himself as St. John of the Cross to her St. Theresa? However rarefied their relationship had become, he did not attempt to hide his delight that he was going to be in England near her, which an offer of Lord Shrewsbury's made possible.

He was becoming weary of Rome, in spite of such excitements as the Russian Czar's visit to try to persuade the Pope out of sympathy with the Poles—a visitor whom Pierce, writing on December 6, 1845, regarded as "the modern Nero. . . . I trust and believe there will be no public demonstrations of honor . . . and that the Pope will neither receive him alone, nor allow him to leave his presence without speaking to him some few and holy words of expostulation and reproof." He had a certain amount of reason to concern himself with the Pope's movements in his capacity of sponsor to American visitors at the papal levees. But the thrill was wearing a little thin without sympathetic companionship, and in May, 1846, he eagerly accepted the post of tutor to Talbot at Alton. A month after Cornelia he sailed for England, full of enjoyment, "although you will think I am learning to be poor when I tell you that the hat I now wear is the only one I have worn, winter and summer, for more than two years."

In August the Pope died. His successor was elected, Pius IX, a man of very different caliber, who filled Metternich with dismay, and Europe with delight, at his election. Giovanni Maria Mastai-Ferretti became Pope at the age of fifty-four on a wave of popular feeling. Liberal, reforming, idealistic, he at first handled his dangerous inheritance with a mixture of sensitivity and acumen. The disillusioned reserve and cynical caution of his later years was entirely unheralded for the present. He had not yet learned the danger of distributing power too quickly. He had not yet fled from Rome. He was *Pio Nono*, the people's choice, widely acclaimed, the champion of liberty and supporter of the oppressed. Cornelia took the news calmly, and with an affection for miraculous happenings which was typical of her. She loved the fairy-tale side of the Church and was delighted that "there was a dove flying around the Chamber of the Conclave of Cardinals during the whole time of the election, which they endeavored in vain to drive out." Of Pierce's reaction we have no hint. Yet, for him, the repercussions were to be great.

Part of her delay over her movements may have been due to this. But in August Wiseman wrote to ask her to come to England, to his district, the Midlands, and begin her work there. She arrived in England on August 15, the very day that saw the Royal Assent given to the Religious Opinions Bill, which removed the last serious disabilities for Catholics. Mercer, "crazy with joy at the thought of his vacation," joined her at once, and with her three children she went immediately to Spetchley Park, young Henry Berkeley's home. It was there that Wiseman saw her and for the first time made clear the nature of the order he wished her to found. He would like her to start straightaway. She was to go to Birmingham, to the

convent of the Sisters of Mercy, to await orders there. Before
she went he would explain to her a little of what he meant to
do, of what England was really like, and of what he required
of her. The project was formidable, the explanation fascinating.

Part Two

Chapter 5

ENGLAND

ENGLAND IN 1846 was a confusion of crosscurrents. Political blimpery moved slowly but inevitably backwards before the vigorous onslaughts of Lord Shaftesbury and the Chartists. Religious activity, rapidly revived in the Church of England, and reflected by the reformed Parliament of 1833, was finding a dangerous rival in the new Catholicism represented by Wiseman and the Italians, Fathers Gentili and Domenico Barberi. The war of the Tractarians had reached its climax with *Tract* 90 but had not finished when Newman went over to Rome and was lodged in Birmingham. The Gothic renaissance burned as furiously in the realm of poetry as in the realm of architecture. Pudding molds were still made in Gothic shapes for fashionable hostesses. (Some years later Barbara Charlton was to amuse Wiseman at dinner by presenting him with his pudding set in the shape of a Cardinal's hat.) It was the year Pugin went mad, only five years after the dedication of his St. Chad's in Birmingham, with its introduction of Gothic vestments and a rood screen, forbidden since the Reformation. The scandal had been great—in spite of a Mass by Haydn as a concession to public taste. But already in places the fervor was wearing thin. There was a defiant group of Italophiles who were to win through to final victory with the Brompton Oratory. Newman, Faber, Barberi, and Gentili were drawn up against the serried ranks behind Shrewsbury, Pugin, and Ambrose Lisle Phillipps in favor of Gregorian chants and Gothic array. They wore the knee breeches and shoe buckles of the Italian clergy indoors and, in spite of the law, flaunted themselves defiantly, if hurriedly, on the short journey along the sidewalk which separated their church from the presbytery. Some even went to such fantastic lengths as to spit in church—a practice which, they said, denoted the feeling of being at home there.

It was an age of boisterous pamphleteering. Nobody pulled his punches. In the world of Catholicism *The Tablet* angrily led the way, under the editorship of Frederick Lucas, a raucous supporter of O'Connell and loudly scornful of the Tractarians. On both grounds Lord Shrewsbury disliked it intensely. "It is a sad reflection on us," he wrote to Ambrose Phillipps in October of 1841, "that we can never have either a respectable magazine or newspaper—I wish *The Tablet* were done for, for it puts us in a very odious light and keeps up a deal of bickering." The complaint was a mild one. It was echoed on every side in less commendable language in an age of thrilled partisanship. The tidal wave of exacting belief that had swept away the monarchies of Europe in an effort to interpret the rights of man had merely washed the shores of England with the intellectual residue of a force already spent. But rhetoric was a good substitute for revolution. The English revolutionaries were hot in debate if not in action. Enthusiastic, robust, inventive, the England that Cornelia came to was able to sustain any number of cracks without breaking. Her own corner was particularly vulnerable—it was sharply divided into the old Catholics and the new.

The old consisted of the few who, for three hundred years, had given their lives, their wealth, and most of their property for their Faith and who, as Parliamentary reforms gradually released them from danger, found themselves leading, by force of habit if no longer by force of circumstance, the brave, restricted, dogged lives of a minority. Before 1791 they were forbidden to enter the legal profession, and it was not until 1829 that they were given the right of serving in Parliament or of accepting most positions of rank and all commissions in the Army or Navy. They had grown so used to persecution that they still remained morally entrenched against it. For years their sons had been sent abroad to be educated and had returned, for the most part, to marry into a strict cousinage and to settle down to become conscientious country squires, as far as possible out of the way and mind of the Government. They disliked innovation; they had grown to resent and mistrust frivolity as a luxury they could not afford. To outsiders they presented a united if uninteresting front. Among themselves they appeared a proud, unyielding, and powerful sect.

To them the new Catholics seemed hopelessly affected, dangerously clerical, and horribly foreign. For the new Catholics consisted, on the one hand, of men like Wiseman, whose proud boast it was that he had "grown up under the very shadow of the Apostolic Chair," with his passion for protocol and ceremony, with his ultramontanism, his respect for ritual, his faith in scholarship, and his fondness for seeing the two sides to an argument. There was, on the other hand, the huge influx of converts following the Oxford movement: men like Newman and Ward who had moved from discussion to conversion by the processes of reason and had not been afraid to follow where their conclusions led; who brought to their new faith the vigor of the old, a new contemporary enthusiasm for externals, and recruits from what David Mathew describes as "the whole section of English life which the [old] Catholic community did not penetrate, the clerical and academic worlds, the new industrialism, the groups from which the Civil Service were recruited, the great mercantile groupings of the City of London."

In a nutshell, the old Catholics, in whose hands authority and power had lain for so long, were laymen. They lived upon the inherited memory of the years when priests had meant the threat of fines or death to those that harbored them and where, in their straightened, hidden chapels, there was little room for ceremony and no desire to prolong, by it, the dangers of detection. Those that came by night to bring them Mass had come as swiftly as messengers and stayed no longer. During this period, and long after it, the continuity and life of the Church had been upheld mostly by the landlords and their kin. The new Catholics, by contrast, were churchmen, burning with missionary zeal and a sense of religious destiny, fired with enthusiasm and the fervor of first belief.

Of course the groups met and, at places, crossed. The sons educated abroad provided the greatest opportunity for compromise: among them Wiseman, by birth an Anglo-Irish Catholic and ardent loyalist, by training a churchman of a foreign florid school. He lost no opportunity in trying to push home his advantage and achieve some measure of reconciliation. It was unfortunate that he got little support at first from the old because, by inclination and behavior, he had committed the sin of joining the new.

But there was always one sure way to the fountainhead—through education, particularly for women. There had been plenty of willing and excellent helpers for the poor and destitute during the last twenty years, but there were few able to educate young women, especially the daughters of the upper and middle classes, the daughters of the old Catholic landowners on the one hand and the daughters of lawyers and university dons on the other. There was, it is true, the Bar Convent at York which had been there for a hundred and fifty years. But it was strictly enclosed, thought baths modern and wicked, and had little contact with the lives its pupils were afterwards expected to lead.

It was not only Catholic girls whose situation was so lamentable. The whole picture was a somber one. For years no one had considered girls worth educating. So long as they were pretty and learned to master the drawing-room accomplishments of their age, to dance and sing a little, to do japanning, filigree work, and water colors, and so long as they were kept in demure seclusion until the days of their gaucherie and coltishness were over and they could be presented attractively enough to acquire a good rich husband as speedily as possible, that was all that mattered. For the most part, and certainly before the twenties, they did not go to school. They had governesses. And the governesses of the late eighteenth and nineteenth centuries were a miserable lot, some of them barely educated themselves. Impoverished gentlewomen, often the daughters of clergymen, they took the only honorable alternative to matrimony provided for them before Miss Nightingale's other solution. It was the nearest they could get to a profession while at the same time maintaining an air of respectability—a ghastly between existence, despised and teased by the servants, suffered and treated casually, and often cruelly, by the family. Lonely and unpopular, they struggled, if they were conscientious, against their own lack of training, their employers' lack of belief in the importance of their job, and their pupils' disinclination. If they were not conscientious they need not even have the talents their credentials boasted. Mrs. George Martineau, relaying gossip to Harriet, throws it out as an aside that "there is unusually for the Knoll some servant trouble. Caroline's new help is a girl who spends most of her time sitting on the kitchen table picking her teeth with a pin. She can neither read nor write, but she leaves them to become a schoolmistress."

They were not all as bad as this. Some of them like the Brontës and Maria Edgeworth, showed fire and spirit amidst great difficulties. But for the most part they were a growing and unqualified class. Their predicament was terrible until Queen's College was founded to give them a proper training and to safeguard them in their retirement. During the forties more than a hundred governesses advertised daily in the *Times* for situations paying an average salary of £35 a year. By 1850 there were 21,000 registered governesses in England. It was already becoming more fashionable to go to schools. Many of these schools were opened by retired governesses like Miss Ann Sharp, governess to Jane Austen's nephew and nieces, and housed in prim villas in a village with a board reading "Young Ladies educated and boarded," the sort of school where Emily Brontë worked from 1836 to 1839—Miss Patchett's Academy for Young Ladies at Law Hill, near Halifax, where she worked from 6 a.m. to 11 p.m. and where the invigorating harsh routine has already been committed to fiction.

That was the hard side of the picture. But even the happier side was difficult to bear for the intelligent or ambitious child. Miss Beale, remembering her own school days, wrote: "It was a school considered much above the average . . . yet what miserable teaching we had in many subjects; history was learned by committing to memory little manuals. Rules of arithmetic were taught but the principles were never explained. Instead of reading and learning the masterpieces we repeated week by week the lamentations of King Hezekiah, the pretty but somewhat weak 'Mother's Picture' of Cowper

and worse doggerel verse on the solar system." It was unstimu-
lating and uninvigorating monotony.

In 1846 the situation was not much improved. Queen's
College was not started until March, 1848. A few foreign
Catholic orders had sent some branches to England at the
request of their Bishops in the last ten years, the Sacred Heart
and Notre Dame among them. But they were not English,
their sentiments and their system were foreign, and there was
no order to correspond exactly to Wiseman's wishes.

Mrs. Connelly, he must have thought, was not only a
charming and beautiful woman, acceptable to the society
which he had in view, but she knew and understood children
and had had considerable practice in dealing with untoward
circumstances with unruffled humor and tact. She had, moreover, herself received a first-class education, was armed with
ideals and enthusiasms and with none of the prejudices and
traditions of the English past. She was just the person he
needed to face the childish brawling mob which the English
Catholics had become. She must undertake the task at once.

Typically, and as he was to do in another context and with
more serious consequences, two years later with his pastoral
From Out the Flaminian Gate, he overlooked all political obstacles and irritants. Cornelia was a stranger, almost without
friends, without money, and without a single companion. She
was also in the somewhat ludicrous position of becoming a
Reverend Mother before she had been a novice, or certainly
at the same time as she became one, she had the care of two
young children, and her circumstances were, to say the least of
it, strange. Here she was in a country "noted as much for its
Protestantism as for its devotion to family ties," open to every
sort of criticism on every sort of score and given the job of
allaying suspicion and of educating complacent English children whose fond parents, whether Catholic or Protestant,
were proud of their conventions and their prejudices.

Her immediate future, however, was clear. She was to go
to Birmingham to the convent of the Sisters of Mercy at
Handsworth with her children. After she arrived she was at
once joined by Mercer, excited and delighted to be with her

again. They took up their affection and intimacy again as if they had never been separated.

When Mercer went back to school Cornelia had not long to wait for disciples—devout young women who were eager to teach and who found, in the idea of this new order, an opportunity that they had not thought existed; and other candidates from a more orthodox sphere, young ladies recommended to Cornelia by priests or Bishops who had heard well of her, acquaintances who had known her and wished to follow her example. Sister Austin, a lay sister and former housemaid at Alton, belonged to the second contingent; Emily Bowles, to the first.

Emily Bowles, one of the witnesses to Pierce's first Mass in Rome, was a very different proposition indeed. She was the daughter of Newman's great Oxford friend, E. C. Bowles, who, like him, had taken orders in the Anglican Faith and, like him, resigned them. They had in fact been baptized into the Catholic Faith together on the same day. Emily may have known the Connellys in Rome, but she was probably told the details of Cornelia's new project by Newman himself, who was in Birmingham, at the new rectory of St. Chad's which housed the Oratorians, and who was seeing a great deal of Wiseman at the time. She embraced the idea with impetuosity.

Emily Bowles was a bluestocking. Talented and exuberant, her fervors and energy constantly overflowed her intentions and ruined her effect. She certainly did not suffer from that brittle surface polish which dismayed Newman so much. "He always seemed to me," wrote Lord Blachford, "to have a kind of repugnance to the highly finished manners of the man of the world. Nothing covers what is behind it so completely as moral and physical polish. It reveals nothing but what it reflects."

After Emily's arrival, Sister Aloysia Walker, a lay sister and the first nun to join Cornelia, commented evasively on Cornelia's patience "under so many trying and annoying circumstances." But at first all went well. The three women, Cornelia, Emily, and Sister Aloysia, were as awed by their adventure into education as by their initiation into religion. All three were pioneers and, as Cornelia told them after Wiseman had conferred their novices' habits upon them: "As we are all novices now we shall learn perfection together." Cornelia lacked the advantage of time and experience, "but," as one of her early nuns wrote, "she was far advanced in perfection and understood practically the science of the saints."

In October, 1846, Wiseman announced that he had found the right place for Cornelia to begin. It was one of Pugin's outbursts, the building that flanked his church and presbytery of St. Mary's in Derby. It belonged, in part, to Mr. Syng, the parish priest, but Wiseman had undertaken to be responsible for the debts incurred in acquiring it. Derby had already a population of forty thousand, and three or four thousand of its younger men were employed in silk or lace factories, or in the Crown Derby works. It was a heavy industrial town boasting a few town houses belonging to the local aristocracy, of which Pugin's building was originally one. It had been built, at great expense, for Mrs. Beaumont, Lord Lonsdale's daughter. Would she and Emily come and see it—it seemed perfect?

Wiseman enjoyed initiation. He did not always enjoy the detailed labor of putting a plan into action. When Cornelia saw it she remarked with justifiable irony: "This is not Bethlehem." Nor was it. Bleak and rambling, it rose grandiosely out of the solid Midland stone which gave it birth. It was cold, vast, and impractical and it was intended to house and be run by three impoverished women. "Dr. Wiseman," wrote Pierce to America, "has, much against her will and even her judgment, made her take possession of a large and beautiful convent. She wanted to begin in a more humble and quiet way."

But there was no alternative to obedience, and for the first time as a nun her calmness of spirit was to be practically tested.

She was faced with no prospects, no money, and a great barrack of a house to keep clean and respectable. "The convent was quite empty," wrote Sister Aloysia, remembering their arrival, "except the parlor, and there were some bedsteads with beds and pillows in the dormitory. There was a leg of mutton in the kitchen, and some potatoes and carrots on the fire, but no knives or forks or plates, or anything else in the place. The priest's sister, who was also his housekeeper, lent us a few things so that we soon got some dinner. The first thing after dinner was to begin and arrange a room for the chapel, as the proper chapel was not yet finished . . . then began the airing of rooms, making the beds and attending to tradespeople who had been recommended to call for orders. Reverend Mother's great anxiety was to have every place dry and well aired." They must all play many parts. "I was put into the kitchen to be cook, refectorian, portress to the back door, night visitor, caller, and bell-ringer. For though the convent was empty we began order and regularity as if the house were full," wrote Sister Aloysia. Cornelia herself did most of the cooking; the others had not cooked before. She also did a lot of the cleaning and sewed the dresses she had designed for the nuns to wear as well as receiving endless visitors, from Bishops to tradesmen. Within a few days, and though Emily Bowles had not fully recovered from the sickness brought on by her journey to Derby, they took over the care of the parish school, which, again according to Sister Aloysia, "was being taken care of by an old-fashioned person who seemed to me to be always carrying a cane in her hand." It contained two hundred working-class children who were destined, later in life, for the stark, grimy factories of Derby. The conditions in these appalled Cornelia. It was her first introduction to English poverty, and the year of the potato famine in Ireland which had resulted in thousands of poor Irish laborers' coming over to seek a livelihood. They swelled the already large numbers of those seeking work in the factories and made the conditions worse. Food meant more to them than religion, and they willingly exchanged their Faith for a loaf of bread—held out as bait by certain Protestant proselytizing societies. Cornelia at once offered to provide day and night classes, not only to help teach them their religion but, first of all, to teach them to read. Since Sunday was the only day they had free, she started Sunday schools, so that the elder sisters of the children she taught all week could learn the same lessons.

She had very little in the way of funds. What private income she still received from the family estate had all gone in furnishing the convent, and she was not in a position to receive dowries from her nuns, who were not yet professed. The enterprise was endowed but the endowment did not meet the requirements. Later on, Cornelia was always to insist that the important rule for an educational order was that it should pay its way. But at the moment it was impossible to remain solvent by combining a private boarding school with a parish one, which later was her usual custom. Lord Shrewsbury was, as always, a great support. He sent her money for her factory girls and for her poor school, and when she wrote to thank him she added: "But you may be sure that we shall do with you as we do with our dear Lord—the more He gives the more we go on asking!"

All the money she was sent, or given, was reserved entirely for the children. The nuns themselves lived simply and poorly. There was often very little to eat beyond stewed bones, and on one occasion "when the boots she had been wearing from the beginning began to wear out a Sister covered them with one big patch, or rather a piece of cloth, put all over to hide the rags."

Cornelia herself gladly embraced these signs of poverty. "I have seen her kiss her old patched clothes with great reverence," wrote Sister Aloysia. She was soon joined by three other postulants, among them Sister Austin, who was overcome at having to awaken Cornelia in such different circumstances from the last time she had seen her at Alton: "At half past five in the cold, she would be so ill and weary, but she was always out of bed and on her knees in a moment."

The physical tribulations were comparatively easy to bear. Even when "a rat trap that was shown to her snapped on her finger with its great iron teeth she said nothing . . . we never heard till afterwards how much it hurt. She would have considered it immortified to speak of it."

But there were other problems besides the physical. Among the first batch of candidates who offered themselves as postulants, including a young girl, Veronica, of sixteen who wished to become a lay sister, there were several unsuitable and several who found themselves unsuited to the life of a convent. Their going worried Sister Aloysia, who saw in it a personal disloyalty to her beloved Cornelia. But Cornelia herself was unmoved. "If they are not called by God," she used to say, "they will do no good, so they must go."

Those that remained often provided greater cause for anxiety. By the spring of 1848 Cornelia had garnered a community of eight, the last addition being Maria Buckle, the daughter of some old friends in Rome, who came to the Derby convent to make a retreat and found herself suddenly overcome with a desire to enter it. This she did not long after—at the same time as a cousin of hers, Mary Ignatia Bridges. They were both to outlive Cornelia as nuns.

Sister Maria Joseph, as Maria Buckle became, was, like Emily Bowles, a convert—opinionated, critical, and clever. But whereas Emily suffered from impatience, a strong will, and a tendency to argue every inch of the way, Maria Buckle found herself continually undermined by her own sensitivity. Her generosity and high ideals found difficulty in surviving the self-analysis she subjected them to and the scruples that constantly worried her—the dreary, frightening ghosts of her subconscious. Later, she insisted that it was Cornelia's exact mixture of severity and kindness which saved her. In an age in which people felt no reluctance to demand the same sacrifice from others that they would willingly make themselves, Cornelia drove her nuns hard. But she also insisted that at any hour of the day or night, and the convent night is not a long one, Maria should come to her for comfort. She often did so.

Like Emily, Maria poured her longings into prose and verse. Unlike Emily, whom Cornelia had almost at once set to writing and publishing a school history book, she was forbidden the luxury of self-expression. Cornelia had decided that she could not afford to let blood as Emily, with her inordinate will and energy, could. But Emily, though she found religious discipline hard, gave too much evidence of sincerity and effort to be sent away. And besides her talents, and the tactlessness with which she so often employed them, there existed a fount of good will and natural charm which Cornelia found hard to resist. Struggling through the labyrinthine ways of personality and psychology, Cornelia learned to temper precept by practice and to carve theory out of experience.

It was her firm belief that goodness could not be cut to one pattern: "We die not to our good nature but to our bad." Every soul has its individual character and purpose. She shrank from what she calls "the tyranny of interfering between the soul and its creator." "Be yourselves," she would say to her nuns, "only make those selves what God wants them to be."

In 1847 Cornelia, on Wiseman's advice, opened a small boarding school for young ladies, in the Patchett tradition but with very different methods of teaching. The prospectus advertised, at a fee of twenty-five pounds per annum, "English and French, Writing, Arithmetic, Geography, History, Grammar, Singing and the principles of Church Music. Drawing, Plain Needlework and every kind of embroidery, tracing, point-lace, stitch, etc." But the English ability to sense a scandal in any innovation showed itself at once. She proposed to teach her young girls French. Even Wiseman's confidence faltered. "I have some doubts over the prospectus as to the teaching of French. The present French literature is so wicked that the temptation to read it is better removed, though much indeed is translated."

Cornelia did not give in. She kept the French and added Latin to the curriculum. Soon, for the school year was a long one in the days when children only returned home for six weeks in the summer, they were reading and enjoying *Athalie* and *Esther*.

The convent was beginning to prosper. But ever since Cornelia had come to Derby and begun to learn the principles of authority and administration, she had had a growing private difficulty to contend with. It arose, as expectation might suggest, from the curious unrest of her husband.

From the moment that Pierce left Rome, in May, 1846, a month after Cornelia, he appears to have been miserable and unsettled. Life at Alton as Talbot's tutor, pleasant and comfortable though it might be, was no longer so exciting without Cornelia. He had been happily married for too long not to miss it now. He wanted Cornelia to share his enjoyment, to tease and flatter him about his success, to laugh at his jokes in private while she upheld his dignity in public. He wanted to hear and talk about the children, to be comforted in his loneliness. In fact, he wanted his wife.

When Mercer returned to Stonyhurst after his summer holidays spent mostly with Cornelia, Pierce's dissatisfaction started to grow in earnest. He had not seen Cornelia since he left Rome and he was still discouraged from doing so, both by his ecclesiastical superiors and by letters from Cornelia, which showed the tenor of Wiseman's opinion against such a meeting.

The English Bishops were unanimously against it. English conventions were not those of Rome. Their imaginations were not so easily reconciled to the picture of a married couple having deliberately chosen a life of celibacy and yet meeting continually for conversation and visits to the children. "What a consolation to have her in the same country," wrote Pierce to his brother, "though I have not yet been once to see her. It is so difficult in a Protestant country that I thought it best. In Rome, of course, every week or ten days I saw her."

Over this matter of Pierce's and Cornelia's relationship Emily Bowles sided unconditionally with the Bishops. She was terrified of prejudicing the reputation of their precious new order and begged Cornelia neither to meet nor even write to Pierce until she was at least professed. In spite of being opposed to Emily's opinion, Cornelia saw and accepted the sense behind some of her arguments. A rigid etiquette was therefore imposed upon the manner in which the Connellys handed over the children to each other before, or after, an exchange visit, although Cornelia continued to write to Pierce and to receive letters from him.

One of the immediate decisions that faced them both was over Adeline's and Frank's schooling. Cornelia's plans were so unsettled when she came to England, first at the convent at Birmingham and then at Derby, that she could not make up her mind whether it would be best to keep the children with her or, for a time at least, to send them away. Pierce was as undecided as she, and it was mainly for this reason that they wished to meet.

In a strange and revealing letter from the heart, one of the few letters which has come to light from Cornelia to Pierce, and which only does so because Pierce later published it in one of his pamphlets, she wrote: "I have waited until now, hoping, if you came in an early train, you might drive up to the door to see and kiss little Frankie without getting out, and I have hesitated whether I should go to the train or not; but Emily is so very fearful of a word being said—so much about all the remarks that were made about your coming to England the same time that you knew I was to come, etc., I think I have made up my mind to leave the decision about Frank to you, the father. Emily is much *too* anxious *not* to have him but I think myself, if he could be with a motherly schoolmistress and little boys it will be better. Her proposition [for me] not to see you until I am professed is absurd. But you see things are to go on at a nice pace in England. I am disgusted with the clergy and the grossness of the people that seem too coarse to understand spiritual things. I was so much disappointed in not hearing from you this morning! And I relieve myself during the time Powell is waiting for you at the train by just taking my paper to write what comes into my head."

It is clear that Cornelia was as much disappointed by their separation as Pierce, although later she wrote in pencil against a copy of this published letter: "If I wrote this letter it was a confidential expression of momentary feeling, certainly not founded on facts." But her feelings were for the moment roused. For the sake of peace and privacy she agreed, according to Pierce's testimony, that he should send his letters to her in unfamiliar envelopes which she had addressed to herself "in a feigned hand."

At the same time she decided, with Pierce, to send the two younger children to school—Adeline to the Convent of the Holy Sepulchre, New Hall, Chelmsford, and Frank to a school for small boys kept by a Mrs. Nicholson at Hampstead—both far away.

For the time the children were happy and Cornelia managed to write quite cheerfully to Mercer, back at Stonyhurst, about "the nice school at Hampstead where I put our darling little Frank. Such nice little boys of his age [four] and some still younger, and he is so happy. Mrs. Nicholson says he has only cried once since I left him." But she soon became, on the evidence of Sister Aloysia, lonely without him. He was a very small boy and she had never been without him. To make matters worse Adeline had begun to miss her badly. "It is so hard to be without Mama," she wrote, and "copied for my dearest, darling Mama by Adeline Connelly," she scribbled passionately on her edition of "The Boy Stood on the Burning Deck."

Towards the end of 1846 a change in Pierce's predicament postponed his unease. He was succeeded as tutor to Talbot by Mr. Paley, a grandson of the famous theologian Dr. Paley, and became instead assistant chaplain to Dr. Winter, Lord Shrewsbury's house chaplain. But his finances were still a cause for worry. He was getting only one hundred pounds a year from Lord Shrewsbury and, though he had a fair income from his American estate, this had to be preserved in trust for his children, while Adeline's school bill alone cost him forty pounds a year. "Things are very quiet and slow just now," he writes, with that familiar wistfulness which always heralds some unexpected and tumultuous course of action.

It did not take long to develop. On March 4, 1847, nine months after his arrival in England, Pierce decided he could wait upon discretion no longer. Taking Dr. Winter, who was both his confidant and his friend, he went on a surprise visit to Derby to see his wife.

The convent was in an uproar. It was outrageous and improper. Emily took it upon herself to write reproachfully, and without the customary permission to do so, soon after he left. "Why did you come here? That little gratification has done us very great harm, and will do us much more. I wrote to Wiseman that you had been and he beautifully says this morning 'I am sorry, very sorry, for Mr. Connelly's visit. I know that Dr. Walsh will be exceedingly grieved by it. We are debtors to the unwise as well as to the wise, and a young house must escape even ill-natured censure as much as possible. It ought not to have been done without leave at least!' Oh, my dear, dear brother do be wise in time. I beseech you to listen to advice when it comes from legitimate authority though from Vicars Apostolic. No blessing will ever come from despising it. Give up even what you think your due, if the will of God so declares itself in the circumstances."

It was unfortunate that Emily should have written, and even more unfortunate that this was the letter she chose to write. To have the criticism of a third person, and that person Wiseman, to whom Pierce was particularly sensitive, passed on at second hand and worded as final is incensing. And Pierce was incensed.

When Cornelia heard that Emily had written she, too, was most upset, for she knew what its effect upon Pierce was likely to be. But though she wrote to try and calm him she acted upon advice and made no move to see him. It was, though she did not know it, the beginning of their real separation. From now on their understanding was no longer complete. As Pierce's protests grew louder and stronger Cornelia became more reserved. Much later she told Wiseman: "I allowed him to write all these things without answering anything that I thought would irritate him to have contradicted." She hoped, as perhaps experience had previously shown her, that sympathy would soothe away the memory. But this it failed to do.

Alone, without Cornelia to sustain and comfort him, Pierce began to brood about his children. Somewhat belatedly, their circumstances struck him as being rather sad. For the first time, and with some justice, he saw what the future would be like for them in the half-world of foster schools and institutions to which they were condemned. But, typically, it did not occur to him that their situation owed anything to him. He began writing to Cornelia, as references from other letters show, implying that Wiseman was trying to prevent their acting together over the children. His anxiety over them was perfectly genuine, but he refused to lay the responsibility at his own door. In spite of the fact that Wiseman had nothing to do with his relationship with the children, his resentment against him grew.

While Pierce worried, complained, and confided his complaints to Shrewsbury and Dr. Winter, we have no knowledge at all of what Cornelia thought, except for Sister Aloysia's testimony on Adeline and Frank leaving for school. "Never shall I forget the struggle of that separation. It was, I think, one of the greatest sacrifices she had to make." Did Cornelia have any premonition that she would never see Frank, as a child, again? If she did, she had already begun to follow the advice she gave Maria Buckle a little while later over a serious private unhappiness: "Courage, confidence—and silence."

While her own three children were away at school she gave all her energies to those under her care—especially the naughty ones. She understood, protected, and tolerated them. A little later two girls of two and four, the Ladies Agnes and Agatha Tollemache, came to school. Frightened, like so many children, by the somber black dresses of the nuns, they stood sullenly by the door—defiant, solemn, and miserable. They responded to no one. But when Cornelia came, smiled, and sat them on her knee they at once capitulated. Yet her understanding of other people's children was bought at tremendous cost—as the life of her eldest son shows—the failure to understand her own.

We do not know much about Mercer. He is a shadowy figure, their eldest child. And yet the life of his parents, always unorthodox, usually unhappy, and sometimes farcial, was, for him, the greatest tragedy.

When Pierce brought him to England for the first time at the age of nine he was, to all appearances, an ordinary little boy, hugely excited at sailing the Atlantic alone with his father, at going to a new country and a new school, of having a pony to ride at Alton. But his excitement was controlled, his manner quiet. For he was by upbringing gentle and by inclination dreamy, harboring his enjoyment to savor it later in that imaginative region where time can set no hateful limitation and where the pains of reality can be softened and denied by "the pale cast of thought."

He stands, in the little colored miniature his father always kept of him, with one hand on a chair, a pretty boy with warm brown eyes and wavy brown hair. The eyes set widely apart are a little belied by the meager feminine mouth. It is a long face, the expression sweet and anxious. There is an air of timidity about him standing so conventionally to order in his pale blue trousers and his tight black coat with its smart brass buttons.

He was brought up in an atmosphere of intense religious fervor, of permanent exhilaration, and he did not remain untouched by it. At the age of twelve he wrote to his mother, as Cornelia relayed to her brother in July, 1844, to say that "he had lately felt a burning love within and speaks with so much feeling that it is delightful to think of." His natural sensitivity had been carefully nursed, and he must have been as responsive to the nuances and shades of spiritual progress, of the minute importance of venial sin and the purification of motive, as a professional and adult Christian.

From the age of nine onwards he was separated from both his parents for long periods. He was sent to an English public school in the days when discipline was notoriously harsh and the boys like unpent animals. "The English boys," Cornelia wrote many years later, "are rough fighting boys and glory in combativeness in college—and they get flogged too for naughtiness, but at home with their mothers and sisters they are gentle as lambs. I always regretted having sent dear Mercer to an English College and would never have consented to sending Frank."

We do not know what Mercer thought of Stonyhurst. The school records give nothing away. His name figures only in the class lists. In spite of his love for cricket, he was in no teams and he won no prizes. He made no friends but he did not sound unhappy. He had quickly become "a proper little English boy with rosy red cheeks," and two years later, when his parents were in Rome, he had already mastered the difficult art of writing crossed letters neatly.

He was not neglected. Cornelia sent him food and money and accepted, with some amusement, the daydreams which filled his letters to her. She was not greatly worried about him. His progress if uninspiring was not bad, his daydreams were not yet threatening his ability to cope with reality.

When she arrived in England in the autumn of 1846, she was too delighted at seeing him again after a gap of three years, and at finding him so thrilled and affectionate, to be much worried by his slight evasions and vague explanations. He had always been vague. His inability to spell, his sudden bursts of temper, and his scatterbrained schemes were old enemies

to score off. She wrote to him from Birmingham when he went
back to Stonyhurst:

MY DEAR MERTY,

I am very glad you have found time at last to write for
I began to think you must certainly be building your airy
castles since I had been so long without any demonstration
of your reality . . . you have written so much that pleased
me, but you have not said anything about your faults that
you promised to mention to me you know. Can it be possible that you have not been in a passion since you last
wrote? How delightful that would be! Be sure to tell me
when you write again if that is so.

I think I must make a little note of the words you spell
wrongly so that you may correct yourself a little more than
you do, for you have been spelling the same words wrongly
for the last year, such as:

> Ofended for offended
> Writte for write
> Enought for enough
> Remaine for remain. . . .

You may be quite sure of getting a 'Xmas Box if I can
find a way to send it, which I shall enquire about. I thought
you were allowed 10s. pocket money. Would you want 10s.
more do you mean? And would it be necessary for you to
make merry to your heart's content?

God bless you my dear boy and help you to put away
flash and vanity with courage and generosity. I press you to
my heart. . . .

This is no more than natural anxiety expressed in the customary idiom of the day. All parents exhorted their children
constantly, encouraging them in the name of God. Cornelia's
letters to Mercer were on a high and moral note, but not un-
duly so for her age, and to a child who had, from his early
childhood, been used to lofty sentiments and high ideals. But
it had no effect.

From the moment that Mercer saw his mother again after
her return from Italy and the Trinità dei Monti he seems to

have deteriorated. It is as if the remote world of make-believe
had been punctured beyond repair. He had loved and venerated Cornelia, written to and confided in her. Her life and
sacrifice had been envisaged between them in pious general
terms. But now he was suddenly brought face to face with
reality—with Cornelia in a black unfamiliar habit, living in
an institution as its head, called no longer Mrs. Connelly but
Sister Cornelia, obeying and imposing a strict routine, a creature of God's—no longer his mother. The deep-seated conven-
tionality of the schoolboy was violated. It was nothing superficial and it could not be remedied.

He began to get bad reports. He not only refused to make
friends but he flew into sudden blinding rages and then took
refuge in sulks and wild improbable imaginings—some of
which he still confided to Cornelia. They were dreams of compensation. In them he was a general, a commander, a hero.
But in reality he was a boy who could not come to terms with
life, who had tried to get extra money out of his mother and
smuggle it past his masters. She wrote to him in great distress:

My Dear Merty,

I have your second letter and was very glad to know that
you had not been in a passion but once, but I feel sorry for
that once. Try, my dear boy, to laugh at yourself as if it
were another person. You would very likely have laughed if
the same thing had happened to another, so why not laugh
at yourself. . . . There is one thing in your letter that I do
not like. Merty, Merty be open and despise duplicity as belonging to the father of lies. Now my dear boy go to Mr. W.
and explain with openness why you wished me to put the
money in the cocoa. If you wished to hide it why ask for it?
Explain this to me with courage and generosity, and if there
is anything to make you feel ashamed about it, do the
penance that will cure you of ever doing the smallest action
that will savor of deception. O Merty, Merty, nothing so
wounds my heart as to suppose you capable of any duplicity!
But, if it is so, make up for it with courage and humble
yourself to the Father Rector, and ask him to help you to
purify your intentions and desires. There was no fault in

asking for the ten shillings, and I should be so glad to send them to you, but never to conceal them or put them in the cocoa like a rogue! O Merty, God sees into the cocoa and into our hearts. . . .

Mercer was nearly fifteen when he got this letter. He could hardly be expected to react to it with much grace. It was a letter to a child, demanding the same desires and purity of motive as the sender. In its successor Cornelia wrote: "Indeed I can tell you that some of our little girls would put you to shame. Not that they are any more clever than you are, on the contrary, but they are docile and ready to learn how to reason and how to act." She seems to have been totally unaware of Mercer's predicament, of the tremendous disadvantage he suffered from, his father a priest and his mother a nun. He could imagine, if he had not experienced, the remarks of his companions that made him an excuse for sniggering and nicknames that were not founded in affection. Her letters emphasize the convent life rather than avoid it, accentuating the dreadful parody of a home which was all he had. No wonder he found it hard to make friends, only too easy to fly into passionate rages. It is not at all strange that the boy he most avoided, in spite of frequent encouragement from Cornelia, was young Henry Berkeley, Lord Shrewsbury's protégé and Pierce's former pupil. For Henry knew everything of his history and was in a position to exaggerate it cruelly with the lift of an eyebrow or a well-placed sneer. But Mercer could not tell his mother this. He was not articulate, he could not explain what was wrong to himself, and it was not the age for sharing introspection. But he loved her still in spite of his resentment. He wrote to say that things were getting better.

Superficially only, for his reports got worse and his dreams of war continued. "Time enough to think about the wars," Cornelia intervened casually in a postscript and then, just after Christmas, "My dear Merty, I had hoped to hear that you had got your box of cakes and pies in time to make merry on Christmas Day. I sent it three days before on purpose to make sure of it for that day. If it has not reached you I suppose it is at the Brown Inn, Preston, where you said it was to be left.

. . . Perhaps you would like to know something about us at the convent, though I must take this for granted, as you do not express the wish in any of your letters." It is strange to find Cornelia so sensitive to other people's needs, so blind to her own son's. Perhaps it was that she cared too much what became of him and saw him too little. All she felt and feared had to be said at once. She could not ply him with tact and persuasion as she could if he had been near her and her life a normal one. His father, too, was beginning to behave oddly and an uneasy association between them may have influenced her attitude. To her his integrity and his soul meant far more than his physical well-being. It could not have been otherwise. Volumnia is not alone in ambition for her son, and of all ambition's forms the desire for eternal salvation is the most agonizing.

At the end of the year 1847, Mercer failed his examinations miserably. His father was too angry—and perhaps too much embarrassed by the thought that Lord Shrewsbury was paying for his education—to see him. Cornelia wrote:

MY DEAR MERTY,

I did the best I could to induce your dear Papa to go to the Academy, but it seems you have been disappointed. I am sorry my dear boy that you should take every little thing to heart as you do, and talk about borrowing a piece of paper as if anyone might not borrow paper and return it; and you know that you are allowed to buy all that is necessary for you and let it go into your account.

Oh Merty how you will grieve over the education you have wasted! Five years time and expense purely wasted! I do not ask you if you distinguished yourself, or if you had any prizes. Your letter gives me no hope. What is to become of you? Even our little girls who have been with us three months, coming to us quite ignorant, write at the end of that time better than you do.

You know that you will have to depend on your own efforts for an honorable livelihood, and that what we have will neither go to you nor to Frank but to Ady, and that is but just, as she could not do what a boy could do.

Ah Merty, will you give me some hope that you may be fitted for something? I fully impressed upon you that you would have to depend upon your own efforts after leaving College. If you would but try to study. If you would but do what you are doing, there might yet be time, and we might still hope! Oh if this were the case what efforts would we not be willing to make for you, and what sacrifice could we refuse you? Will you make us bless the day that you were born? For you have the power to make us either deplore it or bless it. Ah, Merty, your Papa will not try you beyond a certain point, and this may decide your destiny for this life.

If you have anything to tell him about the examination and prizes, that will be in any way favorable, I trust you will communicate it to him at once. May God have pity upon you and upon us! Oh if I could tell you what I suffer on your account you would pity me, my child and pray for

Ever your affectionate mother, C. C.

Cornelia never saw Mercer again.

He was caught up by events that swept him away from his mother, and over to America, and which had their origin in the strange and growing disquiet of his father.

Chapter 6

THE THIN EDGE

EVER SINCE he came to England, in May, 1846, Pierce had suffered from a sense of disappointment and aimlessness which had been alleviated for a time when he was made assistant chaplain to Dr. Winter instead of tutor to Talbot. His letters show that he was pleased with the job—in fact, they give it more weight than the church register implies, for this makes no mention of his name. Technically he held no office; it was an honorary post, created by Lord Shrewsbury, who was always helping aspiring young priests. They surrounded him, moving quickly and eagerly within his orbit like the small and flashing fish who move above and below, but always in pace with, the slow majestic course of the whale. Not many of them stayed as long as Pierce.

After a time, however, it became evident that there was too little for him to do. He began to take an increasing interest in Cornelia's convent, and, even before his startling appearance in Derby, he had written, in January, 1847, to a friend of his, with whom he had been a novice at the Collegio dei Nobili in Rome, to suggest that he come to England as a chaplain to the community at St. Mary's in Derby. They were by now in need of one, their numbers having grown steadily in the first few months. At the same time he wrote to Cornelia extolling the virtues of his Italian friend, Don Samuele Asperti, and explaining what he had done. At this stage Cornelia had no special reason to mistrust Pierce, and they were both in complete sympathy over the "gross-hearted" English. There was, besides, a shortage of Catholic priests in England still. She easily gained permission from harassed authority to send for Asperti.

Pierce had taken his first practical step towards interference. But Asperti took a long time to arrive—he did not reach England until October.

In the meanwhile, both before and after his visit in March, Pierce turned his mind to public affairs. It was the alternative Cornelia had hoped for him. Some time later, she told Wiseman, when she was describing the manner of his downfall and the restless curiosity that preceded it, that she "thought he would [soon] get some other crotchet that would have caught his inclination and thus his thoughts of authority over us would have gradually died away."

At first they did. There was plenty to occupy him. Seeing himself as an Éminence Grise, with Shrewsbury upon the throne, Pierce encouraged him to enter several new arenas and to write letters on subjects varying from "the inconvenience, delays, and detriments of Appeals to Rome" to Irish politics. Against one man, or rather his works, Pierce felt particularly strongly. The man was Father Faber, a convert like himself and one of extreme feeling. He was an Oratorian who belonged by sentiment to the Italophile branch of the new Catholicism, and was one of its leaders. Contributions of his had just been published in the first volume of *Lives of the Saints*, in which, by leaving out every fault and putting in every miracle, he had achieved an astounding result. Somehow his theme, the psychology of sanctity, had survived such historical distortion but it was sung on such a high note of frenzied emotionalism that it nauseated many more than it thrilled—among them Pierce. He persuaded Shrewsbury to lead a crusade against it and work for its suppression. His activity got him into trouble with *The Tablet*, which backed Faber to the hilt, and never forgave him. Shrewsbury remained delighted with Pierce's perspicacity and his direction. In him he felt he had found "a man of larger views and sounder principles" than himself. *The Tablet*, stung on several occasions by their combination, complained, at a later date, that the "noble Lord had found in this private chaplain an adroit flatterer of his weaknesses, one who ruled him to his own evil purpose by this skillful subservience; who made him preposterously worship himself as a great statesman, a great theologian, a great guide and teacher of the people, a great censor of all spiritual authorities, a great director of the Holy See, and in all these characters pulled the strings of the puppet and made it do the work with which Mr. Connelly was unable to meddle in his own proper person. All this was done on the strength of Lord Shrewsbury possessing broad acres, an ancient Earldom, moderate abilities, and a judgment very likely to be led astray." Lucas was enjoying himself. In Pierce he had found a good stick with which to beat one of his oldest opponents. But beneath his sneers and ill-temper there was a hard core of truth.

For as Pierce became more absorbed in public matters, and managed to keep Shrewsbury pleased and stimulated, his imagination began to run ahead. Confused by the attention he got as Shrewsbury's protégé, he began to see himself as the leading actor on the stage—and to dream and act accordingly. But his success was greater farther away from home. At Alton the servants were becoming doubtful of his intentions. They began to view him with suspicion. Thomas Ward, Lord Shrewsbury's agent, especially disliked him; his manners were too plausible and smooth. The Wards' small daughter, racing across Alton Park on her quick little pony, succumbed to Pierce's charm but she could not persuade her parents.

Gradually, a great ambition began to shape and take possession of his mind. He had always been enamored of the Roman hierarchy, and was accustomed to consorting with the Princes of the Church. Having gone so far in his forty-three years, might it not be possible that he would go still further, that he might, one day, be made a Cardinal? Once the possibility, remote as it was in fact, had occurred to him he lost no time, as usual, in trying to realize it.

A letter in *The Tablet* of May, 1849, signed "Peregrinus" (whose real authorship, although one suspects Lucas, it is impossible to trace since the appropriate *Tablet* files were partly destroyed by fire), refers tantalizingly to this period and describes the more startling of Pierce's activities. "Being in Bavaria I was much amused by a story that had just got abroad of an English priest who had written to the Bishop of Munich, urging him on in the performance of duty to excommunicate poor Louis Philippe, and on making further inquiries I found the writer of this epistle was Mr. Connelly. Of course, the Bishop humbly represented his want of jurisdiction and, indeed, the impropriety of the proceeding altogether, but it was with great difficulty the good prelate obtained exemption from the mandate which Mr. Connelly had laid upon him."

The letter goes on: "As for the project of obtaining the Cardinal's hat, although it was new to me, yet it hardly excited surprise, for some time ago it was said that His Holiness intended to send an envoy or nuncio to Ireland, and it was as commonly believed that Mr. Connelly aspired to the employment. It is well known, too, that a seat in the sacred college is often the reward of such a mission as Mr. Connelly wished to undertake."

Pierce's efforts against Louis Philippe were rendered unnecessary by the ending of the July Monarchy, which forced abdication upon the French King. He fled to England and, by a curious coincidence, the year 1849 was to find him living in St. Leonards, where Cornelia and her nuns had been moved, and frequently attending Mass at her convent.

In spite of his ambitions, Pierce was not sent to Ireland. The present Pope did not, like the last, know him personally and he was no longer in the position of court favorite. Moreover, Rome had more to think about than the personal ambition of her priests and prelates. For the papacy was riding upon a hysterical wave of popular feeling that might either carry it safely across the conflicting political currents that beset it, or dash it against the rocks of liberalism, at which it had itself connived, upon the other side.

At some stage in this period it must have become clear to Pierce that he was unlikely ever to obtain a Cardinal's hat. It was then that, in all earnestness, his thoughts turned to another attractive possibility—that of gaining immortality as a founder of a religious order.

When he had finally decided against the Jesuits, and had joined the Collegio dei Nobili in Rome, Pierce had wanted Cornelia to model her rule upon St. Francis de Sales' and not upon that of St. Ignatius. He now began to take up the point at length in his letters to her, and to agitate for a reconstitu-

tion of her rule, the first draft of which had already been sent
to the Congregation of Propaganda Fide.*

Cornelia wrote back evasively. As she said later to Wiseman: "You have no doubt been astonished at the tenor of Mr.
Connelly's letters to me. I allowed him to write all these
things without answering anything that I thought would irritate him to have contradicted." She was still hoping that
"some other crotchet" would capture his imagination and lead
it away to safety.

But Pierce was not to be palmed off with soothing words.
He wanted action. His first attempt to achieve it, his visit to
Derby, brought him up sharply against authority, and the person of Wiseman. For though no letter still exists, it is almost
certain that Wiseman wrote to Pierce, as well as to Cornelia,
to suggest that he should adopt a more regular procedure before trying to see her again. At any rate Pierce was soon writing to Cornelia, as her later references show, to complain of
how insulted he had been by Wiseman and to imply that the
Bishop wished to prevent their acting together over the
children.

As the grievance about his children grew, so did his conviction that Cornelia was being misunderstood and mishandled
—in spite of the fact that Cornelia's concurrence with Wiseman suggested quite the opposite.

Pierce's next agitation was on another score. He was beginning to resent diocesan authority—especially in the person of
Wiseman. Why should Cornelia's rule come directly under a
Bishop? Many of the French orders did not. He began writing
to Wiseman himself, to persuade him to allow Cornelia to
take her final vows. He hoped that, after her profession, she

* The department of the Vatican which deals with all matters concerning mission territory, which England was until 1908. The Sacred
Congregation for the Propagation of the Faith (Propaganda Fide) exercises jurisdiction over all mission territory in the world. According
to its strict definition, "Mission territory comprises all parts of the
world where the hierarchy has not yet been formally established or
where, although the hierarchy is already established, the Church is
still in its formative years." It is interesting that, although the
hierarchy was restored in England in 1850, it remained mission territory for another fifty-eight years.

would become more independent of the Bishop—a view dictated by expediency and not at all in accord with that of 1845, which he had expressed in a letter from Rome to a friend in America: "Yesterday my Mass was for the convent at Grand Coteau (Ah! if it were under its own Bishop instead of under a female head in Paris!)." Wiseman refused, explaining that the canon law required a full year of noviceship before profession. He might have added that Cornelia's vocation had already been exceptional and that it would be foolish to make it more so.

Up to date, Wiseman had been almost unaware of Pierce as a personality—still less as an ill-wisher. His diocese, the battle between the old Catholics and the new, his editorship of the *Dublin Review*, to which he was also a regular contributor, occupied him all day and most of the night. He was full of new plans and quick sympathies, encouraging, innovating, and —a cause of special disquiet to Pierce—converting.

It was five years before the restoration of the hierarchy. The old hierarchy had disappeared two hundred years before, the outward shell with its administrative and constitutional scaffolding, its dioceses and sees, absorbed into the Church of England. The position of the few Catholic Bishops was vaguely defined but, within its limitations, very powerful. They were sent as missionaries, Vicars Apostolic, owing their allegiance and authority directly to Rome but each supreme in his own sphere. They were answerable to no careful modifying body. There was no such thing as an ecclesiastical court of investigation. Their decisions were absolute and their dioceses far too large. But if they made mistakes they bore a great burden, and they were, on the whole, a conscientious and reliable body of men.

From 1688 until 1840 there had been four Vicariate Bishops. In 1840 four more were allowed. Seven years later, as Pierce was working himself up to his final irrevocable gesture, Wiseman took the lead when he was temporarily appointed Vicar Apostolic of the London district. But as the appointment did not become permanent for some time he continued to live in and direct his Midland district until Bishop Ullathorne was appointed to it in 1848. Meanwhile, in 1847, he went on an official visit to Rome.

By October of the same year Pierce had completely changed his tune. He was now demanding that Cornelia should not take her final vows at all, on the grounds that he would be responsible for any debts she or her congregation might contract. This idea, which took firm root, was soon to flower, overabundantly, into print and was founded on the belief that it was quite unnecessary for Cornelia to become a nun—that a vow of chastity was sufficient. The inevitability of her vocation had struck him, and with it the completeness of their separation, the depth of her loyalty to another authority. They were no longer playing a game of his invention which could be tidied away at the end of the day—though one of his counters, Don Samuele Asperti, was just coming into circulation.

Dr. Samuele had at last left Italy. He departed in August shortly after Wiseman's arrival in Rome, and one of his first tasks on reaching England was to visit Pierce, and Dr. Winter, at Alton in order to dissuade him from interfering further with Cornelia's vows, which were in fact made in December of that year. It was Asperti's most successful attempt at mediation. He remained "my dear, my very dearest," in Pierce's affection.

It is impossible to decide what were the contributory causes to Pierce's next move—ambition, indignation, passion. Be that as it may, suddenly and without warning, beyond the feeble pretense he had made in letters to Cornelia that the Church was conspiring to deprive him of them, he removed his three children from their English schools and fled with them to Italy.

Some time later, Pierce admitted that his chief reason for taking the children was to hold them as hostages and with them to tempt Cornelia back. But an editorial in *The Tablet* suggests other motives for his departure to Italy. "First, it is said that his main business was to use his influence in Rome to procure in the rules of his wife's order such a change as would allow him to have the management of it in his own hands, to stand to it in the nature of a patron and director, and to have the comfort of habitual amicable conversation with his wife. Second object to his journey was supposed to be the Diplomatic Relations Bill, which was then under discussion; and certain stories of letters misdirected and misdelivered in Rome were current a year ago [*The Tablet* is dated May, 1849] and seemed to implicate him in the Whig plot against the Church. We give less weight, however, to this second rumor than to the third. It is said that about, or a little before, that time a friendly unofficial letter had been addressed to Lord Shrewsbury from Rome, asking him to suggest some English priest for a Cardinal's hat. The dignity of Cardinal requiring a moderate income for support, and the allocation of Roman livings or benefices to foreigners being unpopular, it was prudent to look out for a priest whose private fortune would suffice for the burden. When this circumstance came to Mr. Connelly's ears, we are told that he straightaway overlooked the small circumstance of his not being an Englishman, or even a British subject, and forthwith proposed himself a candidate for the vacant hat. It occurred to him that he had the money; that his graceful and majestic figure peculiarly fitted him for the scarlet; and that the occupation of Cardinal would be very suited to his turn of mind. Lord Shrewsbury, much to his credit, is said to have discouraged this ambitious pursuit, but [he] pressed his suit for the Cardinalate with great vigor, and gave himself out in Rome, we are told, for Lord Shrewsbury's candidate." Whatever truth lay in the second and third points and in the current rumor that, far from getting votes towards his hat, Pierce had had to make a public recantation of heretical expressions he had used in his sermons, the first was certainly true.

Unknown to Cornelia and Wiseman, Pierce had composed, and sent to Propaganda, a revised rule which laid great stress upon a clause demanding exemption from episcopal visitation. Neatly written in his own hand on fourteen pages of folio, this strange document contradicted a great many of Cornelia's provisions and was based on an incredible assumption of detail. Nothing was said of the spirit to prevail in the order beyond that "it shall follow the Rule of St. Augustine . . . the annotations of St. Francis of Sales thereon being of the same authority as the Holy Rule itself. And the constitutions

which the same blessed St. Francis gave to the Venerable Order of the Visitation shall be for precepts and counsels to this
little Congregation where it be not otherwise ordered, or they
be not at variance with the double object of the congregation."
This new rule in its entirety Pierce wished to substitute for
the one already submitted by Cornelia in 1846.

Pierce spoke excellent Italian. In Italy his reputation for
piety had been preserved by his absence, he was a friend of
Cardinal Fransoni, and his plausibility was extreme in any
language and at any time. It was not surprising that in an age
of slow communication from abroad and high national excitement at home, Rome, or that part of it concerned, came to
accept him as the founder of the Society.

The first intimations reached England in the spring of 1848
in a letter from Pierce to Lord Shrewsbury stating that he was
trying to obtain necessary and sensible modifications of the
rule. A few days later Asperti got to hear of it, told Cornelia,
and was sent by her to visit Bishop Walsh and Bishop Wiseman. Reading between the lines, it is obvious that Wiseman
had been sent a copy of this modified rule, and under pressure
of work, and on the assumption that it was already known to
and derived from Cornelia, had failed to read it. "They asked
me," wrote Asperti to Propaganda, "whether Mother Connelly knew nothing of this rule, and on my replying that to us
[at Derby] it was absolutely new, they did not know what to
say or think."

Pierce's new rule was indeed alarming. "These constitutions," he had insisted in his covering note to Propaganda,
"were given in the year 1846 to the Cardinal Prefect. I had
prepared them for a small congregation which the good God
had long inspired me to found with the aid of a holy woman
who was most docile to me." Throughout he refers to the Society *que j'ai enfantée,* and makes the quite untrue claim
that the community had grown so rapidly that it had fourteen
novices and three hundred school children and that conversions were so numerous that "on one day forty young people,
who were Protestants of various ages from twelve to eighteen,
were baptized conditionally." It is not difficult to detect the
same thread of ambition, the same desire to chalk up success.

Wiseman was in fact only too relieved that among so many difficulties Asperti should arrive and appear willing to cope with one. "Dr. Asperti's visit was very opportune for affairs at Rome," he wrote to Cornelia five days after Asperti wrote to Propaganda, "as we were all working in the dark until he explained matters. But alas! I fear things at Rome are in a sad state, and that the Holy Father has more serious matters to think of than our little concerns."

He had. His official blessing of General Giovanni Durando's vanguard of the papal army led out of Rome on the same day as Charles Albert declared war (March 24) had been misinterpreted as an offensive gesture and not, as he intended, for a protective measure of defense against possible Austrian invasion of the northern frontiers of the Papal States. On April 29 the Allocution censoring the extremists of 1848 was published and the Pope and the Risorgimento parted company. The force that was to carry him to Gaeta was gathering impetus. But he did give Pierce some audiences through, one supposes, the mediation of Cardinal Fransoni. In fact, lulled by Pierce's sympathetic manner, and totally ignorant of the discrepancy between Cornelia's and Pierce's rules, as indeed at that moment so was Cornelia, the Pope gave the order his general blessing and even gave Pierce a small token present to be conveyed by Pierce to his wife on his return to England.

In May, before either Asperti's or Cornelia's letters written in hurried protest to Propaganda had arrived in Rome, Pierce left Rome for England. It was seven months since he had taken the children and fled, forbidding them to write to their mother. It was much longer, because of the school year, since she had seen them. "I have not seen either Mercer or Adeline since 1846, and I fear they are not allowed to write to me as my letters remain unanswered," wrote Cornelia to the Bishop of New Orleans.

Before following Pierce back to England this is, perhaps, the moment to return to Cornelia. When she agreed, in January, 1847, to Pierce's suggestion that Asperti should come over as chaplain to her community she made, though she did not know it at the time, a mistake whose consequences were to last all her life.

From the first mention of his name Asperti wrought distrust and disaster, most of it unintentional. He was one of those curious people who, with the best intentions themselves, fling everyone round them into a state of turbulent and perpetual disquiet—a catalyst who in size and appearance was as harmless and misleading as it is in the nature of a catalyst to be. He was a small unalarming person of great rotundity, but he began, long before he arrived, anticipating difficulties.

The first letter in which he does so is an unconscious and entertaining indication of character. He regrets that he cannot leave straightaway, certainly not before August, for he must visit the place of his birth and settle an important matter. He will not mind the appalling English climate, he was himself born in the icy plain of Lombardy, but of course a good fire is always comforting. He has been trying to improve his English and contemplating the idea of going from England to visit his father in America. He must have time to buy some suitable clothes to wear in the heathenish land he is visiting, where, he understands, priests are not allowed to wear their habits out of doors. He cannot afford the expense of the journey but he presumes this will be met, including some books he thinks essential and allowing for any "accident that may occur of sickness, or stoppage on the journey," etc.

The prospect was not reassuring but Cornelia completed her side of the arrangements without delay. But September passed and there was still no sign of Asperti. He was having trouble with his passport.

It was October, 1847, before he finally reached Derby. And, though his first duty on arrival was to visit Pierce and try to reconcile him to the idea of Cornelia's vows, the life that waited him was a peaceful one. The nuns and children were happy and settled, the parish priests helpful and kind—the only cloud on the horizon was that the convent buildings had not been paid for and that a large debt was owing to Mr. Syng, the priest who owned them. But this last was not a big cloud for, with sweeping and infectious optimism, Wiseman had just declared: "I have no hesitation in saying at once that I will take the whole convent and its liabilities on myself and trust to Divine Providence for the means of meeting all."

Into this well-ordered and tranquil scene burst the stout, tightly encased figure of Don Samuele Asperti.

The English, he exclaimed at once, were an apathetic race sunk ignobly in torpor and sloth. It was up to him to invigorate them. Thrilling sermons and threats of damnation were the means he chose. All his ardor was flung into the task. He was astonished to find the convent under the spiritual direction of the Jesuits. Had he not been sent for?

His activities caused so much disturbance that Cornelia had to appeal to Wiseman for advice. Curbed in this direction, Asperti turned his talents towards the parish. The parishioners were amazed to see little groups of village girls walking up to the convent in the evenings to attend pious Italian services that were as foreign as they sounded. The parish priests were infuriated by his tactlessness. And in defending and explaining the two points of view Cornelia was turned upon by both. She was not in a strong position to be attacked. She had introduced this violently pious foreigner into a peaceful community before even her own rule was confirmed in Rome and when there was still a debt of three thousand pounds to be paid on the convent; and more frightening still when Pierce, grown suddenly tired of stalking round his grievances, had removed the children from their schools and taken them with him to Italy.

At this inauspicious moment Wiseman was called to London and replaced by Bishop Ullathorne.

Ullathorne was, in spirit, a tory of the old school, insular and pugnacious. A straightforward man of immense practical ability, he had begun life as a cabin boy and had since become the Abbot of Downside. His mother was a lineal descendant of Sir Thomas More, his father a Pocklington grocer. This curious combination had provided him with a vein of poetry and idealism and a dogged obstinacy of character. He was a stubborn Yorkshireman without an H to his name and with an affectionate understanding of men and a real and attractive piety which made him the friend of men as different as Newman and Wiseman. He was to be Bishop of Birmingham for thirty-eight years.

But though he had thrown in his lot with Wiseman, he was

not necessarily committed to all Wiseman's ideas. He was later to support Cornelia at a critical and dangerous time, but for the moment he saw her with the natural prejudice of a Bishop for anyone causing trouble in his diocese. He must have viewed the situation with a sinking heart, and, having examined it, he did not declare himself on either side. It did not improve. Agitation succeeded agitation. Don Samuele regarded opposition as a test of his endurance. Mr. Syng began angrily to demand his debt and threatened alternatives, the parish priests refused their help, and Cornelia refused to dismiss Asperti. Her sympathies we know were not with "the gross-hearted English," and he had been extremely helpful to her over her rule and in dealing with Pierce's behavior. She felt a sense of loyalty to him personally and, perhaps, a desire to preserve through him some association with the peace of Rome, where spirituality and Pierce had been one.

While she was waiting and trying to decide what to do, Wiseman wrote to her. All the time that, as one of his minor tasks, he had been advising and struggling to support Cornelia he had been suffering from insomnia. He was writing in his private diary: "Seldom before have I felt more completely the peculiarity of my position in my total isolation as regards support and counsel as well as sympathy and concurrence in views and plans." From Rome, where he had gone at the end of 1847, Newman wrote: "There is so much discord, so much jealousy in England." Wiseman had barely time to answer Newman's letters. There were long periods when he could find no free moment. Cornelia suffered from the same pressure of events. "I have had for some days a long letter to you on the await," he wrote on August 28, 1848, "but it literally is being written sentence by sentence during such short moments as I have snatched from conversation."

Two days later the letter was sent. For a letter written in such circumstances it was extraordinarily lucid and comprehensive. The knowledge and care of detail gave no indication of how pressed for time he was. It covered many pages and was under three main headings. The first dealt with his new appointment "long before it was plainly proclaimed I knew of Dr. Ullathorne's appointment to this district yet I was not at liberty to reveal it." The second dealt with the troublesome Mr. Syng, who has "made the affair [of the final settlement of the Convent] one of too personal a nature with regard to myself, for me to be able to interfere as judge." He went on to say that he was trying to "neutralize Mr. Syng's violent opposition" towards both of them but that "the question is will you be able, even so, to remain where you are and do good in spite of the clergy there? Or will Mr. Syng forgo his legal hold upon the property and allow you to remain? Under all circumstances is it not better for the community to be where they are sure of peace, kindness, co-operation, and active assistance?" Arguing the case, he decided on the whole that a move would be best and that he had, with his usual enthusiasm, found the perfect spot; "the place to which I allude is All Souls, at St. Leonards on Sea, near Hastings. The house is built and will be quite complete by the end of September, suitable in every way for the progress of your order." It belongs to the Rev. John Jones, who "has been able through private munificence to purchase ground, and build on it first a house and now schools and a church and that he has put the whole at my disposal for any order or convent that I wish, and that on my naming yours, he has not only acceded to it, but he has expressed himself most anxious to have you or any of the religious on the spot, before he completely finishes the house, so that any alterations or improvements may be made.

"The ground consists of fourteen acres completely walled round in stone . . . the gardens are large with plenty of trees, vegetables, and even a hothouse. The land is situated on a cliff with nothing but a road and sands between it and the sea. The ground is secured beyond the road so that nothing can be built up in front. The house is solidly built and very large, one part is now occupied by Mr. Jones. Beyond and below is the convent, the largest room of which now forms the public chapel (with a separate entrance, etc.), but even so very extensive . . . the church and new schools are estimated at £13,000 with the finishing of the convent. . . . Such is the offer made to you for your community, and if the above has looked like an auctioneer's description I must in fairness mention the disadvantages, the house is not in a large town . . .

the situation is bleak and the air keen." But he does not enjoy the task of disparagement. "On the other hand," he quickly adds, "there is a great want of a house for education near the sea; the complaint is made that we have none; there is good sea-bathing almost at the gate. Dr. Duke, a convert physician quite at the head of his profession there, will give every attention to the health of the establishment. That the air is sound and not too keen will appear from the fact that an old lady of near ninety has made this her residence for several years and does not suffer for this case."

It was an attractive proposal, with no hint at the parts to be played by Dr. Duke and the chaplain in the years ahead. There was a lot to recommend it. As Wiseman's postscript suggested ("I have passed over many personal matters connected with this proposal"), it would make her more remote from Pierce, who had begun his attack upon her, while at the same time returning her within Wiseman's diocese and under his spiritual jurisdiction. She would be starting a new venture in a new place—and a growing one at that. For St. Leonards, which had only begun in 1828 when a large tract of land was bought from the Eversfield Estate, to the west of Hastings, and systematically laid out with polite houses and formal gardens, had increased its population in four years from one to thirteen thousand, a rise which merited a mail-coach to and from London which, by the process of evolution, soon became a steam engine. It could look forward with some complacency to a respectable future as a Victorian watering place within easy reach of London. As the pocket guide of 1850 insisted, with a warmth somewhat lacking in humor: "The fronts of the houses in few towns can compare with even the rears of the buildings in St. Leonards."

The following month Bishop Ullathorne paid a formal visit to the convent in Derby, listened amiably to the novices playing a charade upon his name, satisfied himself that everything was in good order, but decided nevertheless that the difficulties surrounding Asperti and the debt had provoked too many people too far and that it would be best to accept Wiseman's move.

Accordingly Cornelia, taking Emily Bowles, set off to inspect All Souls. The Rev. Mr. Jones was withdrawn but courteous. He was dressed, somewhat behind the times, in black silk stockings and smallclothes, a stand-up collar, frilled shirt, and flamboyant ruffs. He leaned with studied weariness upon a fine ebony cane crowned with silver and wore silver buckles on his shoes. He addressed the nuns as Dame, and never learned to vary the address. Later he was to call the children in their blue uniforms his bluebottles and to spend a large part of his time walking about beneath the scaffolding which constantly adorned the house, waving his ebony cane at the workmen and admonishing and directing their labors with more enthusiasm than knowledge and a bewildering desire to tear down today what he had advised the day before.

For the moment, however, he was persuasive and kindly. Cornelia did not know that she had already had six predecessors, six different communities that had failed to sustain Mr. Jones's approval for long and been quickly forced to leave. She was charmed by him and delighted by the house and garden. She felt a pleased sense of familiarity and homecoming as if she had known the house before and recollected it often since in dreams. She accepted Mr. Jones's offer, and on December 10, 1848, the first detachment of nuns left to take over. It is typical that in the middle of the move, at a time of intense activity, she insisted on a retreat for her nuns to support their spiritual equilibrium.

Pugin's "beautiful convent" was once more empty. In 1849 the Sisters of Mercy took possession but not for long. They found it unhealthful and inconvenient and soon left it for another site. In 1856 it was pulled down to make way for the breweries and malthouses which still stand there today.

Chapter 7

RIGHTEOUSNESS AND WRATH

WHEN PIERCE returned from Italy in May, 1848, Cornelia was still at St. Mary's in Derby. It was seven months before she was to go to St. Leonards, and she was still suffering from the shock of Pierce's dramatic departure with the children, as well as from the unrest caused by Asperti's misguided efforts to impose Italian customs upon an English parish.

In all that follows, and has just passed, it is impossible to understand her exact intentions. We have no insight into her personal motives and feelings during this crisis in her life. Those documents that existed were destroyed after her death. The explanations and letters that remain are all public and practical in the sense that they are the deliberate expression of policy and action. There is no clue beyond a vow she made on January 1, 1848, to tell one what one wishes to know. The rest must be guessed at, from between the lines of the other players who were perpetually accusing others and justifying themselves to each other. Throughout, Wiseman seems to have kept the most even keel, to have reacted most sensibly to the various scandals and accusations. It is he who puts his finger upon relevancy and keeps it there. Capable of general vagueness, he was not given to particular impreciseness. At first both Lord Shrewsbury and Dr. Winter were entirely on Pierce's side, and only persuaded to Cornelia's with time. It was to the former that Wiseman wrote in January, 1849: "What matters it now whether Sister C. or Dr. Asperti or Dr. Winter was to blame in steps the hideous results of which, as it turns out, no human foresight could divine. Who would venture to say, if such a given letter had not been written, or such a message had not been sent, the consequence most seemingly traceable to it would have been spared, while those consequences bear no human proportion to the cause, real or imaginary."

But at the back of so much of what happened was Cornelia's vow.

When she first learned that Pierce had taken the children with him and fled to Italy she was, as Pierce hoped, distracted. Legally and actually they were in his possession. Her only alternative courses of action were to give up the convent and go to him or to remain in hope and prayer. She chose the second course, and what it cost her we shall never know. But it was not merely a choice between two alternatives. She stamped her decision irrevocably with a vow. On January 1 she wrote: "In union with my crucified Lord and by His most Precious Blood; in adoration, satisfaction, thanksgiving, and petition, I Cornelia vow to have no further intercourse with my children and their father, beyond what is for the greater glory of God, and is His manifest will through my director, and in case of doubt on his part through my extraordinary [confessor]." The wording of the vow is of importance in interpreting a later event. It is also in spirit curious. Uncertainty is always hard to bear. But to turn aside from it, as Cornelia did, so soon and without external advice is as bewildering as the almost triumphant phrasing of "in adoration, satisfaction, thanksgiving, and petition." It is a spiritual commonplace among saints to thank God for disasters and to regard them as badges of merit, but in this context the idiom is peculiarly macabre. She would have been wrong to go but surely not wrong to effect, at this stage, a compromise. She had, until this moment, been exercising tact and discretion by letter to Pierce, and now, in startling contradiction, this determined vow. There is a loophole in "what is for the greater glory of God," but what is this to mean?

The motive behind the vow is obvious—to urge upon herself the irrevocability of her choice in agonized and wavering circumstances, in much the same way as Florence Nightingale was vowing, only two years before in her private notes, "Oh! God no more love. No more marriage Oh God," at the moment when it was hardest for her to do so. But Florence Nightingale was choosing between two modes of life. Cornelia was already wedded to both by strong ties of choice and responsibility. It was not really open to her to abandon one completely for the other. In absenting herself from the necessity to think out and decide upon each event as it occurred in this one final act of revocation, she was not in fact absenting herself from her responsibility. At the moment when she chose to act explicitly upon her vow (on Pierce's return from Italy) she set the stage for the last unhappy act of the drama.

In May, 1848, Pierce returned from Rome considerably strengthened. He did not know of Cornelia's recent letters to Propaganda against his innovations, and he was very conscious that as a founder he would find the same place in history, if not in present estimation, as a Cardinal. "Fortified," as he wrote, "with the authority of Pius IX to see Cornelia," and "with a present and the Apostolic blessing to give her from the Pope," he arrived in England. Unwilling to ask Wiseman for permission directly, but probably warmed by papal good will and wishing, this time, to act with propriety, Pierce asked Dr. Winter, his friend and ally, to get it for him. Dr. Winter wrote to Wiseman, but Wiseman had just been transferred to the London district and it no longer came under his jurisdiction. He should have handed the matter to Bishop Ullathorne, his successor. Instead he, too, relied upon delegation, for he was overwhelmed by the demands and business of his new diocese. He therefore merely sent a note to Dr. Asperti telling him "to look to the matter."

Pierce waited for a few days, heard nothing, and taking silence for consent set off with Dr. Winter as his chaperon. On June 3, 1848, he descended upon the convent, found Asperti, and demanded an interview with Cornelia. What steps towards "looking to the matter" Asperti had taken we will never know. What happened next is lost in contradiction and accusation.

According to Pierce, Asperti went to tell Cornelia and, coming back, refused to let them meet. Whereupon Pierce fell weeping on the sofa and for the next few hours remained in the convent parlor to rage and plead. He left in fury sustained by the outraged sympathy of Dr. Winter and loud in his recriminations of Asperti. From now on "very dear Don Samuele" becomes "that villain Asperti," and nothing is too low with which to blacken his name.

His rage was centered upon Asperti. Now and always he refused to consider Cornelia as a willing agent. She was trapped and enforced, imprisoned in the will of others. Nevertheless Pierce wrote to Asperti to apologize for his conduct.

Pierce was not alone in attributing the initiative to Asperti. The nuns agreed with him in this. They believed that Asperti had forbidden an interview on the grounds that as Pierce had already abducted his children he might also abduct his wife. They held that Cornelia was made miserable by his advice and that during the six hours of Pierce's visit she knelt at her *priedieu* in the chapel above the parlor praying for the courage to fulfill her vow (and do what her confessor said) while all her instincts urged her to go down and gentle him from his mood, to draw the venom from his rage lest it should grow cold and sour upon him and turn, as in fact it did, to desperation.

But this does not seem to have been the case. Cornelia herself, answering the note of sympathy that Lord Shrewsbury curiously enough sent her (since he was himself a firm supporter of Pierce), implies a very different attitude—the human resistance of a mother who refuses to be blackmailed.

June 16

My Dear Lord,

It is very good of you to write to me so kindly. I should have preferred going on in the same way with Mr. Connelly, letting time clear up all things. But now circumstances have made it my duty to take a decisive step with him, which will be more useful in the end, though at the moment he will be wounded. Every other means proved useless only exciting him the more. I have now destroyed every hope he may have of ever having any authority over the convent and shown it in the clearest way. I wrote also to Dr. Winter begging his assistance in the matter, and he will talk about it to you.

When this is done and Mr. Connelly has proved his sincerity by sending my little girl to me, he may then have the necessary intercourse by letter and even an interview.

This is not the letter of a woman acting upon the advice of her directors, and the Shrewsburys did not approve. They felt, as they continued to feel, that one interview between them would automatically banish certain prejudices. Months later Lady Shrewsbury was still writing: "He is now so maddened with jealousy and hatred towards the dear Bishop and good saintly Père Asperti that he is wound up to any desperate act . . . again and again I exhort you not to drive him to commit such a shocking scandal—and remember he will bring up his children in the tenets he may embrace. Were I so unhappy and unfortunate as to be placed in your present most trying situation . . . I would see Mr. Connelly for the last time and take that opportunity of telling him of all the scandal he has given by his unpardonable hatred and jealousy and censoriousness . . . if anything would stop him this might."

In the allegation drawn up under Cornelia's guidance for the Court of Arches in 1849 we have the definite statement that when Pierce "presented himself at the convent at Derby and then and there required and insisted upon an interview, with Cornelia Augusta Connelly, no preventative whatever to such required interview was interposed save by Cornelia Augusta Connelly herself, who declined to see Pierce Connelly and so communicated to him through the medium of Dr. Asperti." Ullathorne, writing to Lord Shrewsbury on January 3, 1849, confirms this view since he must have heard both Cornelia's and Asperti's original accounts, although since then each of the four parties involved—Cornelia, Pierce, Asperti, and Winter—have indulged in part or wholehearted recrimination against one or all of the rest. In an effort to clarify the situation he writes that Pierce "arrived suddenly and unexpectedly at Derby, and that Dr. Asperti saw him first. Thereon Mr. Connelly expressing a wish to see Mrs. Connelly, Dr. Asperti sent a message to that effect to Mrs. Connelly *remaining still in the room* [the italics are mine] that Mrs. Connelly sent out a message declining to see him that Mr. Connelly then threw himself in a passion of tears on the sofa and continued agitated all the while, that afterwards from Alton Towers he wrote a letter to Dr. A. apologizing for his conduct. That Mrs. Connelly continued to make it a condition of seeing Mr. Connelly that her daughter should be restored to her. . . . There can be no doubt that Mrs. Connelly was justified in declining to see Mr. Connelly if she had reasons and later events seem to intimate that reasons existed. . . . The entire spirit of the Church would seem to require that they should meet rarely and under certain restrictions. What the actual case is, and the extent to which Mrs. Connelly may have been advised by others, I am entirely ignorant of in fact."

A month before this letter was written Cornelia had moved to St. Leonards and come once more under Wiseman's jurisdiction. Physically she was at a greater remove from Wiseman's headquarters but in fact her move added fuel to the fire.

Pierce's instinctive apology for his breakdown at the convent had been bolstered too high by sympathy and understanding. It did not take long, by the process of self-pity, indignation, righteousness, and wrath, to become a full-blooded counterattack, the first step of which was a letter to Bishop Ullathorne accusing Dr. Asperti of gross immorality. Asperti, he said, had assaulted Cornelia and Pierce himself had caught him with a young nun in a bedroom. The accusations grew harsher, the stories taller, ignoring the fact that Pierce had had no opportunity for firsthand observation of the behavior he sought to disclose. Tactfully Ullathorne parried and Cornelia denied. Later Pierce published his accusations in several pamphlets, adding, in one of them: "My wife has not made any such denial" of such facts. Against this in Cornelia's copy of the pamphlet is an angry indented pencilling: "Positively deny that I ever charged any priest, confessor or otherwise with making such an attempt." (Hitherto her denials had been formal and impersonal.) Nothing would deter him. "Mrs. Connelly," he wrote to Lord Shrewsbury, "is in an atmosphere which, before God, fearless as I am of course of her bodily purity, I believe to be *worse* than that of a *brothel*." Even Wiseman's offer of St. Leonards was subjected to the same suspicions. "Wiseman," he insisted, "had the extraordinary purpose to withdraw your petitioner's wife from the ecclesiastical, natural, and legitimate Roman Catholic Bishop

[Ullathorne] and carry her with him to a place announced publicly as his future Marine Residence . . . the said dignitary, unrestrained by fear of God or man did, in December, 1848, thus carry off your petitioner's wife. That moreover he continued in surveillance over her the same Italian priest aforesaid [Asperti] though of well-known moral unfitness."

The virulence and injustice of Pierce's attacks on Asperti strengthened Wiseman's and Cornelia's defense of him and were partly responsible for Cornelia's refusal to accept the criticisms levelled against him by the Derby parish priests before she left for St. Leonards. She must not concur in reasonable criticism for fear of implying some truth in an outrageous one.

Asperti, for the time, remained. But Wiseman's wistful idea of a holiday sea residence in a wing of the convent looked after and comforted by the nuns was, on Cornelia's strong recommendation, and after a considerable struggle of wills, abandoned. It was not a moment to draw Pierce's fire upon Wiseman's morals from a public only too ready to manufacture a bonfire from such ragged wisps of smoke.

For a time Ullathorne preserved Pierce's confidence. It was to him that Pierce wrote on December 4, 1848: "I am a man, a husband, and a father before I am a priest and my first duties cannot be abandoned. Faith, fidelity, and honor I will never forsake, nor will I forsake the wife I vowed to protect for life, the mother of my children." Two days later he followed this profession with a set of propositions:

"The conditions upon which I am still willing to take no further steps to bring her back under my protection as her husband and the father of her young children.

"First. A solemn engagement (private) to have hereafter no communication by word or writing direct or indirect with Bishop Wiseman, Doctor Asperti or Miss E . . . B . . . or the nun whom I saw in Dr. Asperti's bedchamber.

"Second. Free intercourse with a sacred observance of the law of trust and secrecy, by letter and by personal visits in the presence of my children or some other person as at Rome after I was admitted to the holy priesthood with the express authority of his Holiness."

In vain Ullathorne wrote soothingly: "What I would beg of you, is to do nothing in a matter so serious and so liable to expose both Mrs. Connelly and yourself without advice, as you well know that in such matters, in which our own feelings are so deeply involved, we cannot always and at all times, even the best and wisest of us, be entirely prudent." In vain Wiseman wrote continually, and also to Lord Shrewsbury, who was still in strong support of Pierce, the Church's point of view. "The Church never sanctions a married man to be a priest without his wife *at least* taking a vow of chastity, but I think I can say *never* without her embracing the religious state; unless they stipulate to live in different countries. The old canon law, long before the Reformation, decreed this. Mr. Connelly had given his full consent to Mrs. Connelly taking vows (I have it in his writing) as a condition to his own ordination.

"In addition to this Mr. Connelly signed at Rome a deed of separation. . . . He has no rights as a husband whatever before the Church. A man cannot be half a husband, and your Lordship seems to think that he still was her husband and held rights as such. But the Church does not admit of the anomalous state of a husband's holding spiritual and moral rights and no more."

But argument had become academic, for Pierce had already gone to law.

On December 1, 1848, his solicitors, Messrs. Clarke, Fynmore, and Fladgate, wrote to Wiseman:

MY LORD,

I have been consulted professionally by Pierce Connelly upon the subject of his position with regard to Mrs. Connelly, and as to the proper legal measures to be taken to obtain a restoration of that lady to her right position as his wife and the mother of their children. The proceedings which I feel bound to take are necessarily of such a description as must lead to very great annoyance to the parties interested and will I fear bring great scandal upon, and do great injury to, the Church of which you are one of the representatives in this kingdom.

(An invitation to avoid scandal in informal discussion followed.)

But as a discussion with a mere lawyer may appear to you objectionable . . . I am authorized to say that Mr. Henry Drummond of Albury, Member of Parliament for West Surrey, will, as the friend of Mr. Connelly, be happy to accompany me in the hope that his mediation may assist in bringing the matter to a satisfactory close.

I have the honor to be, my Lord, etc.

Wiseman refused the opportunity and Lord Shrewsbury was dismayed and annoyed. In explanation Wiseman wrote: "Your Lordship is under the impression that his object was to prevent the matter going into court, and have it amicably adjusted. This was not, however, the case. He told Mr. Harting [Wiseman's solicitor] that he proposed an interview merely as a gentlemanly offer to break the roughness of his message, that he did not expect me to accept the offer but to name a solicitor, that he was glad I had not taken it for it could have led to nothing; as his instructions were peremptory, to proceed to law. I was then on the point of writing to Mr. Drummond to say that I had declined meeting a lawyer on such a subject (Mr. Drummond being only thrown in as accompanying him and not as a principal) but that I had no objection to confer with him, as a gentleman, about it, when Fladgate's second letter made it impossible for me to take the step. Sergeant Sheer and Mr. Bagshaw (counsel) have addressed us in the matter, and are both of the same opinion."

It was obvious that there was to be no turning back. On December 22 Wiseman wrote to Lord Shrewsbury:

MY DEAR LORD,

I enclose a letter from Mr. Fladgate, a solicitor, to me. Some time ago Mr. Connelly wrote to Dr. Ullathorne to intimate his intention of vindicating his rights and applying to the law to enforce them in regard to Mrs. Connelly on her removing from Derby to St. Leonards. He observed in that letter that "he was a man and a husband before he was a priest" and that this was a matter more clear than matters of dogma etc.

I sent my solicitor to Mr. Fladgate. This gentleman I may observe en passant is a low evangelical. I could say more but not by letter.

Mr. Harting, my solicitor, asked him what I wanted to ascertain, what was meant by "the restitution of that lady to her right position as his (Mr. C.'s) wife." If he had meant what the law understood by "restitution of conjugal rights." Mr. F. answered that this letter was written after an interview with Mr. C. at Mr. Drummond's and that he there told Mr. C. that the law admitted of no such quixotic idea as husband and wife living as brother and sister, and that he therefore asked him if "he was ready to go the whole hog," that is, state his desire and wish to cohabit, and that Mr. C. replied affirmatively, and that his instructions were peremptory to proceed.

In other words, Mr. C. is going into a Protestant, ecclesiastical court, being a priest bound by a vow of celibacy, to ask that his wife now, with his consent, a nun and bound by vow should be compelled to cohabit with him. Your Lordship will easily understand the scandal to religion, which even the first public step in such a matter will cause. I write, therefore, to put you in possession of the case as it now stands. It appears to me a madness and nothing else. But your Lordship will perhaps be able to prevent the mischief by timely interposition, or if not, prevent the scandal from acting perniciously upon your neighborhood.

I have only time to add my sincere good wishes and all the blessings of this holy season for yourself and family.

> Yours ever, my dear Lord,
> Very sincerely in Xt.,
> N. WISEMAN

Lord Shrewsbury wrote in distress to both parties. In the meanwhile the Bishops had taken no steps towards arraigning Pierce's powers of priesthood. They were hoping until the very end. On December 24 Ullathorne wrote to Lord Shrewsbury: "I would make a point of seeing Mr. C. but I fear that his mind is too much carried away. The position in which I am placed by the receipts of these documents as Mr. C.'s

Bishop will, of course, require me to warn Mr. C., that in the event of his pressing this suit it will at once affect his exercising of priestly functions." But three days later he adds: "I shall do nothing with reference to Mr. C. until canonically obliged to do so."

In fact, no further steps were ever taken. The Bishops were determined that the initiative should remain with Pierce and that he should have no opportunity for seeing himself as a martyr to his own cause.

Throughout, the Bishops preserved a calm that was all the more courageous since it was the eve of the restoration of the hierarchy and the prejudice against them was strong both within and without the Church. It was, moreover, only a few years since the scandal of Richard Waldo Sibthorp and the memory still rankled. When Sibthorp gave up his priesthood for a return to the Anglican Faith after what, as the Catholic press insisted, was an inadequate period of grounding and testing, Wiseman was so upset that he retired to bed for twenty-four hours. He was now to face a repetition of the theme in far less edifying circumstances. His integrity in never attempting to maneuver the situation is remarkable.

Behind the protestations of the leading actors, however, there passed private and somewhat anxious letters of conjecture and surmise between the two Bishops. They are reflected in a letter of Wiseman's to Shrewsbury (dated January 28, 1849): "Many circumstances lead me to fear that worse passions than appear on the surface have been at work. A lady told me the other day that when at Alton on a visit some months ago, she was quite surprised at Mr. Connelly's mode of talking to her about Sister C.—her *angelic beauty*, her perfection (outward) and made her go to see her as the finest woman in the world. Dr. Ullathorne told me that the way in which Mr. Connelly spoke of Sister C. was almost *indelicate*, and to his mind conveyed the impression that strong passions had remained in Mr. C. Your Lordship is perhaps not aware that what led to the determination (partly at least) to oppose his visiting the convent was a very imprudent expression which he used, in Sister Emily's presence, on his first visit, addressed to Sister C. as his wife. Sister Emily wrote to Mr. Connelly and he expressed great regret for it."

Whatever the truth in such suppositions, Pierce's tone remained one of uplifted sanctimony—"Always *inspired* in what he does and opposed by the devil," wrote Wiseman in exasperation. Physical desire may have lent impetus to his suit, but it did not altogether account for it. And, in all fairness to Pierce, restitution of conjugal rights was the only plea he could make in law. Throughout the long years of argument ahead he always maintained that this was the reason he made it. And in doing so he had, if his notes at the end of his petition to the House of Commons are to be believed, the support of Cornelia. She apparently "found means shortly after July 8, 1851," to write to him "denying that she ever suspected any other design on his part than merely to claim his former authority over her."

On December 28, 1848, Pierce wrote to Lord Shrewsbury a letter which showed that the noble Lord was in fact attempting an objective attitude. If he wrote reprovingly to Cornelia and Wiseman he had clearly done likewise to Pierce. "I only last night got your two letters. I think they are hardly as kind as you would be if I were near you or as in your heart you feel to me. The relations between us have more than anything aggravated the hardness of my trial. The letters kept me from closing my eyes last night, but thank God I never had a single misgiving. It is not the injustice of others that makes me act. I have not been precipitate. I vowed to God to do what I am now doing, if necessary, the day I waited six hours in vain at the convent in Derby. It is not that I have rebelled against anything but these worthless Bishops. It is here as in the idolatry of Faber, that Miss Bowles takes the place of the Pope and *The Tablet* of the Council of Trent . . . the gist of all my duties is to rescue my blessed wife from the hands of devils. . . . If I fail in the courts I will carry it into the House of Commons and will then make it an affair of the American Government. And in so doing I believe verily I am doing Truth and the Church better service, even though I break up every convent in England for fifty years to come. And I please and bless God that he has given me a clear head and a tranquil heart in the midst of this bitter trial."

Pierce had already left Lord Shrewsbury, presumably because he preferred not to put his host to the embarrassment of having him during the proceedings. He had gone instead to stay with Mr. Henry Drummond at Albury Park in the valley of the Tillingbourne. He had thus left one vast country house for another, for Albury's records dated back to 1042 and it had since passed from family to family, always increasing in wealth and position. It had been bought by Henry Drummond from the Earl of Aylesford in 1819, and, like Alton, had been subjected to Pugin's restoring hand. On the east wall of his construction he had left the pious sentiment NISI DOMINUS AEDIFICAVERIT DOMUM IN VANUM LABORAVERUNT QUI AEDIFICANT EAM, translating it himself "Unless the Lord build the house, their labor is but vain who build it."

It is no longer possible to discover where Pierce's children were all this time, when they were not at school. A pencilled note suggests that Adeline spent part of her holidays in Northumberland at Alnwick Castle, the home of Mr. Drummond's daughter, who had married the sixth Duke of Northumberland. Later she followed him to Albury, for one of his stratagems to get Cornelia concerned her. On December 21 he showed clearly in a letter to Lord Shrewsbury that he was hoping to frighten Wiseman, with the threat of scandal, into doing anything to avoid scandal.

"I now write to beg your Lordship to send a letter to Mrs. Connelly *here*, for Lady Harriet and Mr. Drummond to take to her when they go for her, that is in case Doctor Wiseman, to avoid the scandal, should write to recommend her to submit without the expense and disedification of force. We are all afraid of her being instigated to hold out. Mr. Drummond and Lady Harriet will go for her the moment Doctor Wiseman gives his decision and they think a letter to her from your Lordship would have great influence in prevailing on her to come here to Albury to settle everything—of course saying nothing about my being here. For my own part I am determined to go on cost what it may . . . *Dieu et le droit* and I will give up one when I give up the other and not before. I am sorry that Bishop Ullathorne will suffer but it is not to be helped. . . .

"I do not know if Cornelia is satisfied that I do not consider her a free agent and never will do so, nor hold communication with her until she is out of all control."

Wiseman's decision cancelled such a plan and the law took over.

During this period Pierce made his headquarters with the Drummonds, enjoying the notoriety which his unusual position gave him. In doing so he exchanged the grandeur of the Catholic nobility for the luxury of the Protestant. Pierce wanted to go into court as a layman, but Drummond advised against it. Pierce wrote: "That must not be said except in the last resort lest it should be turned against me (to keep me out of my functions)." But it was only the formality of his priestly status that remained. There was every sign that he was becoming a disciple of Mr. Drummond. In 1832 Edward Irving had started a new sect, the Catholic Apostolic, or "Irvingite," Church, a singular branch of the tree of Protestantism. The Irvingites looked for a second advent of Christ, in preparation for which they formed a sort of college of apostles, some of whom were held to possess gifts of prophecy. The apostles met at Albury, and their meetings were not distinguished by much austerity. Lady Shrewsbury was most anxious lest Pierce "either relapse into Protestantism or embrace Mr. Drummond's *awful* sect." Contrary to expectation, or rather the expectations of a young diarist, Adelaide Lister, a daughter of Lord Ribbesdale, "Mr. Drummond was a most cheerful and talkative host, more like the average country squire than the fanatic he was said to be. He made many clever and striking remarks on men and things; all tinged with theology as they must be expected to be seeing that he was entertaining, besides other priests, the apostles of the new communion."

Among such eccentricity Pierce was well able to hold his own. Adelaide Lister's casual description brings him flickeringly to life not as a protagonist, a candidate, or a priest, but as a man. "After dinner the floor was taken by a curious personage who did not please me at all. He had a broad clever forehead, and would have been good-looking but that his ears were placed so high in his head that they gave him an impish appearance. He was dressed, with great care, in semi-ecclesiastical costume, recalling that of the courtly abbés who appear in comedies of the Louis XV period. He was in fact in a very semi-ecclesiastical condition, having been, we were told, a convert from the established Church to the Church of Rome, from which he had apparently reverted to the Irvingite community. At any rate he appeared to be now under the wing of Mr. Henry Drummond, who listened with approval to the long and animating discourse he gave us on the curious ceremonies he had seen in Rome, among others those connected with the Boy Bishop who had only the year before been enacted by his own little son." . . . "This second Blanco White" did not greatly attract Adelaide Lister, and it was with relief that "the evening ended with a pleasanter sight than that of Mr. Connelly holding forth on the rug."

It was from Albury that Pierce directed his lawyers.

On January 25, 1849, a writ was served on Cornelia. She wrote at once to Wiseman:

> My Dear Lord,
>
> I received the enclosed citation this morning. A respectable person brought it. He asked no questions excepting to know if I were the person cited. Pray let me know what is to be done. . . . My dear Lord what shall I say or how can I make you understand all that I feel on this occasion. But you are my father and the heart of such a father can understand all. May almighty God reward you for all you have done and are still doing for me.
>
> Believe me to remain my dear Lord,
> > Your faithful and grateful child in Christ,
> > > Cornelia Connelly

Wiseman wrote at once—a letter of comfort and encouragement, adding: "You will be fully instructed what to do. No personal appearance will be required in this suit. I will look after everything for you. I never turn my back on anyone whom God has given to my care, especially in time of anxiety and trial."

But the prospect was most alarming—and behind it lurked the fear of Pierce's apostasy. The first rumors of this had reached Cornelia, to whom it was a great shock. She remained uncomforted by Wiseman's news that a priest, a friend of his, had noticed Pierce at the rear of his church during his sermon. Cornelia's love for the children was threatened by a new fear —fear for their religion. And all the time aggravating the situation were the solicitous, dramatic letters of Lady Shrewsbury and the general opinion that she was a cold, cruel-hearted woman and an unnatural mother. She was divided in herself as strongly, and far more agonizingly, than those who were divided against her.

Chapter 8

THE TRIAL AND THE AFTERMATH

THE CASE of Connelly versus Connelly came into the Court of Arches in May, 1849, before Sir Herbert Jenner Fust. In this ecclesiastical, and necessarily Protestant, court the plaintiff pressed his suit for restitution of conjugal rights on the ground that he would be liable for any debts that might be contracted by Mrs. Connelly. The defendant's plea was based on the legal separation effected at Rome. The judge, though admitting that deeds of separation decreed by proper courts abroad would be entitled to consideration in English law, did not consider a papal decree admissible. He rejected the defendant's allegation and gave judgment in favor of the plaintiff.

Pierce was jubilant. He wrote to Dr. Winter: "Wednesday last (31st) was the day Mrs. Connelly was summoned into public court. She made no appearance of course. The lawyer's letter in my hand says 'She may now be compelled by force to return . . . any agreement between you and her, or between either of you and any third person, notwithstanding.' They must now therefore know that force can be used, and most surely it shall be used." He suggested that Dr. Winter should take Cornelia to Albury at once, or else he would both publish and prosecute. Dr. Winter ignored the suggestion.

The only immediate result of Pierce's letter was to turn the tide of Shrewsbury's and Winter's wavering opinion finally against him. Two weeks later he paid a flying visit to Alton to pack up his belongings. He refused to see Winter. Writing afterwards to Lord Shrewsbury, who was away at the time, Winter explained that "he left his clothes in charge of the housemaid and his plate in charge of Mr. Doughty. But his books he left as they were." He had only to collect them. It was the end of his relationship with Alton.

Pierce was, in fact, unable to fulfill his threat of prosecution, in spite of the sentence of the Court of Arches condemning Cornelia to prison if she did not return to him. For Cornelia had immediately lodged an appeal to Privy Council against the decision of the Court of Arches—a move which automatically suspended sentence.

But the processes of English law are slow. It was nearly two years before the case came up for retrial. In the meanwhile, from every side, came persuasions to Cornelia to fly. The light yap of Lady Shrewsbury lay well in the lead of the deeper-throated clergy.

It was rumored that Pierce lay off the coast of Sussex in a yacht, waiting an opportunity to carry her off as he had already carried off the children. A neat pile of ordinary clothes lay always in Cornelia's cell for a quick getaway or a quick disguise. Inflamed, the situation seemed daily to gather momentum. Of all this the nuns, except the two in her confidence, knew nothing. They led the ordered existence of their rule. Cornelia herself had no intention of leaving them. "I think," she wrote to Lady Shrewsbury, "that you and dear Lord Shrewsbury must now see that nothing would have a good effect in England as the scandalous report is already widely spread. Indeed, on the contrary, by going abroad it would be more widely spread and, on return to England, no doubt greatly exaggerated. Besides, dear Lady Shrewsbury, a flight like this would be an acknowledgment of some *cause* for flight which would be contrary to the truth. We have nothing to fear. God and the truth are on our side."

It is not surprising that her equanimity was not fully shared, and it must have been an additional hardship for her that at this particular moment Wiseman was called to Rome.

He went, in September, 1850, with the utmost reluctance. His going, he knew, meant a Cardinal's hat and with it, as he thought inevitable, a formal residence in Rome. He was forty-eight and for ten years he had worked unceasingly for the conversion of England, teaching, administering, building, and educating; and with his exuberance and thrust, which con-

cealed so perfectly beneath its bulwark of "mountainous flesh"
the uncertainty, depression, and self-criticism to which he was
so often heir, he had won a huge section of the community
to his side. "The consistory," he wrote to Dr. Russell of Maynooth, "is to be held which binds me in golden fetters for
life, and cuts off all my hopes, all my aspirations, all my life's
wish to labor for England's conversion in England, in the
midst of strife with heresy and the triumphs of the Church."
Rome refused his plea to remain and he went, consoling himself that "I am sacrificing everything that is dear to me, and
perhaps destroying my own work in which too much of selfish
or earthly complacency may have mingled." But in spite of
the consolation, "the event depresses me, crushes me, nay,
buries me forever in this life, and so it *must* be good for me."

The Pope had returned to Rome in the spring of 1849.
Since then he had thought continually of his English dominion and had finally decided to restore the hierarchy. It was to
Wiseman, on September 13, 1850, that he confided the restoration. He was to be both Cardinal and Archbishop. He
was to be exempt from residence in Rome and to return to
England. It was in a mood of thrilled release, of triumphant
thanksgiving and Roman sentiment, that Wiseman wrote his
famous pastoral *From Out the Flaminian Gate of Rome*, and
dated it October 7. On October 12 he departed for England
by slow and dignified steps. It was the slow march of pomp,
the ceremonial progress of a Prince.

Cornelia, perhaps with her American disregard for convention, had suspected the outcome. She was one of the very few
to do so, and it was to her that Wiseman wrote at once before he left Rome: "You have proved a better prophet than
I believed as in the course of a few weeks I hope to be once
more in England. His Holiness has, in this day's consistory,
re-established the hierarchy in England and put me, however
unworthy, at its head, making me at once Cardinal and Archbishop of Westminster."

On October 30 Wiseman arrived in Vienna and dined with
the Emperor of Austria. He was beginning to think of his return. From Vienna he wrote to Cornelia: "I hope with God's
blessing to reach England about the end of next week. I shall

go at once to St. Leonards to stay quietly with you a few days. As that stove in the bedroom is of no use, I should prefer occupying the room within, and please to leave the chapel ready upstairs." As an afterthought dependent on his new position, he added the postscript, "Keep my coming quite quiet."

But there was no need. He never came. On his second day in Vienna he learned with horror that the news of his promotion had struck England. *The Times* of October 14 had greeted the Pope's decision "to erect the City of Westminster into an archbishopric, and to appoint Dr. Wiseman to that See," having conferred the rank of Cardinal on "this new-fangled Archbishop," with dismay and resentment. "If this appointment be not intended as a clumsy joke, we confess that we can only regard it as one of the grossest acts of folly and impertinence which the Court of Rome has ventured to commit since the Crown and people of England threw off its yoke . . . one of the most daring assumptions of power it has put forward in this country for three centuries." Five days later, in another leading article, it added: "Is it, then, here in Westminster, among ourselves and by the English throne, that an Italian priest is to parcel out the spiritual dominion of this country—to employ the renegades of our National Church to restore a foreign usurpation over the consciences of men? . . . Such an intention must either be ludicrous or intolerable—either a delusion of some fanatical brain or treason to the Constitution."

Wiseman was driving through Vienna in his carriage when he read *The Times's* first leading article. The qualms he suffered were intense. Only he could consider and suspect the effect of his pastoral letter coming on top of the announcement. He had already sent a copy to England, where it was about to be read aloud from every pulpit. It was, moreover, couched in terms of alarming and exuberant triumph. Hastily, he wrote a calm and reassuring letter to the Prime Minister, Lord John Russell, and prepared a more seasoned and reasonable explanation to send to *The Times*. He also speeded up his journey.

He arrived in London in the small hours of the morning on November 11 and, since his own house was being redecorated and painted, went to stay in Fitzroy Square with Mr. Bagshaw, his co-editor of the *Dublin Review* and close adviser over the matter of Pierce.

The country was already in an uproar. The pastoral letter had been published and in it, it seemed, their worst fears were realized. Under the heading *From Out the Flaminian Gate of Rome*, and beneath a highly colored and emotional picture of the historical importance of the new hierarchy, Wiseman had announced his own new appointment in the following disturbing words: "His Holiness was further pleased to appoint us at the same time the administration of the Episcopal See of Southwark. So that at present, and till such time as the Holy See shall think fit otherwise to provide, we govern and shall continue to govern, the counties of Middlesex, Hertford, and Essex, as Ordinary thereof, and those of Surrey, Sussex, Kent, Berkshire, and Hampshire, with the islands annexed, as Administrator with Ordinary jurisdiction." "How must the saints of our country, whether Roman or British, Saxon or Norman," went on this intrepid keeper of their inheritance, "look down from their seats of bliss with beaming glance upon this new evidence of the Faith. . . . Oh, how must they bless God, who hath again visited His people."

The English reacted at once, and in a traditional manner, to this "foreign lunacy" and to what *The Times* called "the strangest piece of mummery we ever remember to have witnessed." Priests were stoned and the Pope and Wiseman burned everywhere in effigy. Even the Prime Minister, writing by coincidence on the eve of Guy Fawkes Day, insisted, "I thought it right, and even desirable, that the ecclesiastical system of the Roman Catholics should be the means of giving instruction to the numerous Irish immigrants in London and elsewhere, who without such help would have been left in heathenish ignorance. This might have been done, however, without any such innovation as that which we have now seen." The Anglican hierarchy, with less restraint, complained of a "sinful," "indecent," and "audacious aggressor," the Archbishop of York of "a revolting and frightful assumption." The press loudly supported them. Even the throne was moved to proclaim the Queen's determination to uphold alike the "rights of my crown and the independence of my people against all aggressions and encroachments of any foreign power."

Wiseman's second public manifesto, a logical and more temperate explanation which he had planned in Vienna, was published in *The Times* and all the leading newspapers on November 20, and did much to allay the hysteria and suspicion which his first had caused. It went a long way, too, using the Prime Minister's own speeches in Parliament, to show how absurd was the suggestion that the Pope claimed territorial sovereignty over any part of England.

The English responded to the plea Wiseman made for fair play with their usual forbearance, and the newspapers, having had their headlines, sank gradually back into smaller print. But if it had reached a calmer and less vituperative stage, the battle still continued. And still Cornelia's case did not proceed. "The process," as Wiseman had said two years before, "is a very tedious one in the ecclesiastical courts."

On February 7, 1851, the Ecclesiastical Titles Bill was introduced into the House of Commons—a retort to the hierarchy. While it was before the House, the judicial committee and Lords of Her Majesty's most honorable Privy Council at last met to decide the fate of Cornelia Connelly.

It was not an auspicious moment for a stranger and a Catholic to have her incredible and unpromising appeal tried "before the most Protestant court of what was at that moment the most bigoted country in Europe."

It is all the more incredible, and all the more complimentary to British justice, that Cornelia won her case.

She did so by good luck as well as on a point of law. For although the Privy Council decided that Cornelia's allegation should be admitted by the Court of Arches they insisted that it should first be amended by the addition of some information as to the marriage law of Pennsylvania and the law of domicile in Rome. The appeal was therefore successful but the question still at issue. Pierce could have pressed for the amendment of the allegation and a new trial in the Court of Arches, but from this he was prevented (in spite of every kind of publication) by lack of funds. He was already liable for total costs, and even these he was unable to meet.

The case was dropped. But there is a parallel in the Gorham case, which had been pronounced upon, only a year before, on March 8, 1850. There, too, the Privy Council had overruled the Court of Arches—in their decision to uphold the Bishop of Exeter. The Bishop had refused to appoint a young clergyman, Mr. Gorham, to the vicarage of Bramford Speke because he denied the doctrine of baptismal regeneration. But though the Bishop had the agreement of the Court of Arches, the court of the Privy Council had taken precedence over the ecclesiastical. It was an ugly reminder that the ultimate law in the Church of England lay with the state and not the Church, and there was a general outcry. Among the Tractarians who protested most fervently against the Gorham decision were Archdeacon Manning and Robert Wilberforce. Both became Catholics soon afterwards.

For the moment, during the Connelly trial, the tension was relaxed and the dust of battle laid. But skirmishes of a different kind were soon to follow.

Where the law left off, the press, ably supported by Pierce, took over. Editors of opposing journals made good the excuse to conceal their dislike for each other in carefully partisan leaders; members of the bar and the aristocracy exchanged critical passages of arms in the letter columns of the national dailies, and throughout Pierce provoked, exhorted, and denied.

He had persuaded an impressive committee to supervise the raising of funds for the continuance of his campaign, but the names, among them the Duke of Manchester and Lord Winchilsea, were more impressive than the performance. Formidably, pamphlet followed pamphlet: *The Coming Struggle with Rome, Not Religious but Political; Domestic Emancipation from Roman Rule; Reasons for Abjuring Allegiance to the See of Rome.* Each set out to reveal the "detestable enormities of Rome," and each edition increased its girth with supplements and postsupplements, as letters from the press were included, refuted, repeated. Not all the pamphlets were restricted to Pierce's personal grievance. Arguing hotly from the particular to the general, he laid siege with assertive agility, and surprising dialectical skill, to the main bastions of the Roman Faith. On the legal front Sir George Bowyer, Cornelia's counsel throughout the case, waged war. On the intellectual front, and Pierce's arguments were by no means negligible when it came to the delicate interpretation of canon law that he had learned at Rome and could now twist to such neat effect, Wiseman engaged battle in the *Dublin Review*.

Pierce himself showed a genius for improvisation. It was easy enough to translate the Latin *dicta* of the third century to suit his purpose, but not so easy to quote exact contemporary support. In 1852 *The Cases of Conscience* by Pascal the Younger were conveniently published, very much along the same lines, to prove the essential wickedness and immorality of Catholic doctrine. With forceful rhetoric Pierce quoted chapter and verse from "this irrefutable authority" to a public which was too entranced to care, had it been given a chance to know, that Pascal's other name was Pierce Connelly.

On every hand, no punches were pulled. The *Morning Herald* was delighted at the chance to brood gloomily over the insidiousness of Rome creeping so dangerously into English life, even through the strong doors of law, to paralyze and undermine. *The Tablet* was pleased to be able to call Pierce a "miserable old man struck down by ignominious and conflicting passions" and through his disgrace to attack Lord Shrewsbury. Everywhere the name of Pierce Connelly was wielded triumphantly as the stick with which to beat a chosen enemy.

The public responded with avidity and the reviewers did nothing to raise the tone. "It is one of the most important and truly *awful* books we ever read . . . we conclude by again *entreating every Englishman* to read this extraordinary and most important pamphlet of Mr. Connelly," wrote the *Morning Herald*, reviewing *Reasons for Abjuring the See of Rome* in July, 1852. "This is one of the most instructive and remarkable pamphlets which has appeared in modern times," said the *Bulwark*, reviewing the same work. "It is written evidently by a man of intelligence and determination. It should be showered over the country in thousands."

It *was* showered over the country in thousands; the nineteenth edition at one shilling had been conveniently followed by a cheaper repeat "to go by post for one penny and one guinea a hundred."

But among all this professional hatred, and somewhat shoddy harangue, there were both the hallmarks of sincerity and the arguments of truth, "though my allegiance to the Church of Rome was a delusion and a culpable delusion—for it had its origin in carnal-mindedness and pride—it was most sincere. At the time I made those sacrifices they were the almost involuntary expression of my passionate love to the church of my imagination and my hope." And indeed what more probable than that "from the moment I accepted infallibility I never examined one single doctrine of the Church of Rome with any other view than to be able to defend it against heretics and other infidels."

Moreover, in spite of the Bishops' earlier suspicions, Pierce insisted throughout that he was not motivated by passion. He did not wish to enforce his physical rights as a husband. He had pleaded this in law because it was the only legal plea he could use by which to obtain the authority over Cornelia he wished. He missed her, he wanted her, he may even have occasionally desired her, but he convinced Cornelia and himself, as he convinces his readers today, that he missed her for her sympathy and her strength and he wanted her as the necessary reflection of his glory. He saw her not as a mistress in love but as a companion in power.

In spite of the sales, in spite of the fascination of learning that a "Roman Catholic may any day have the duty of shooting his sovereign imposed upon him," that "he may choose an agreeable director who will indulge him in poisoning his own father, which according to the Church may occasionally be innocent and lawful," and that celibacy was a "myth without basis in Catholic dogma or fact," the public, who deliriously shared his views, did not succeed in raising the funds that Pierce required. At one point he would have been threatened with a debtor's prison had not Cornelia, strongly advised by Wiseman, refrained from suing him. "You will observe," he wrote to her on March 12, 1852, "that your proctors have two accounts, one recoverable from Mr. Connelly and the other not. If you make them an advance on the latter, you do not in the least prejudice your, or their, rights to recover the other part from Mr. Connelly. The way in which this would be done, would be by suing him, and he might be thrown into prison. This would at present be an odious proceeding and make him a martyr with his present friends. It seems they will not pay for him, as his own proctors who trusted to Mr. Drummond are equally unpaid. It would be better to let them move for payment, and then you will be justified before the world for having resisted his attack. I would therefore advise a payment, to be made on account, of the extra judicial expenses, without prejudice to your right of being paid for the rest by Mr. Connelly."

This was presumably the outcome of a letter from Cornelia's, and Wiseman's, solicitor, J. Vincent Harting informing her on March 9 that "an order has been made on Mr. Connelly to pay Thomas and Capes the total cost of the proceedings on your part up to this time. He alleges his total inability to pay . . . he is moreover liable to be arrested and imprisoned for the amount at any time. Under the circumstances, Messrs. Thomas and Capes have applied to me for instruction and I have promised to write you on the subject, and shall be glad to hear from you."

Pierce was not thrown into prison. But since his friends and his finances proved unable to support him in reinstituting his case in the Court of Arches, he wrote a petition to the House of Commons. A debate arising out of the form of this petition decided it was improper and indecent and the petition was laid aside.

Cornelia's supporters were convinced that Pierce had gone temporarily insane. It is interesting that Pierce had reached the same conclusion about Cornelia. He was, at the time, writing frequently to John Bowen, Cornelia's half-brother, in order to obtain money from him with which to educate the children. The money was technically Cornelia's, left in trust to the children, but John Bowen, with her consent, arranged to have it freed and sent to Pierce when he learned of his circumstances. "You know," Pierce wrote to him, "I suppose that every penny of what I invested in Natchez is lost—except indeed the Arkansas land from which, however, I do not think I have ever received, for sales or otherwise, enough to pay even Mary's shares of the taxes and other expenses. . . . My persecutors here have a bill of costs of £250 or £300 hanging over my head . . . whatever is to become of us God only knows. I have kept out of debt, but am unable to educate my children, or indeed to do anything more than barely live, as you may suppose, with £80 in England." Pierce was, he went on to say, "without even the money to buy books" necessary for the education of "Ady and Frank, both of whom I have at home" (at Albury). He was quite unable to leave Cornelia out of his correspondence. Her name occurs frequently. In a letter he wrote to John Bowen on March 27, 1851, while waiting for her appeal to come into court, he said: "I always believed that she was not a free agent. But I begin to fear her heart is wholly with the devils who have made use of religion to root out of her all that ever made us love her as woman rarely has been loved." Sixteen months later he was writing to Bowen: "I am sorry to say I have no news to give you of your poor sister. I do not even know if she is in England. It is quite evident they fear her making revelations of sacerdotal villainy and one object of getting her out of this kingdom would be the greater facility of poison. But her pride, which she is made to believe is sanctity, is so wholly engaged in her present greatness that one spangle on a priest's vestment is of more moment to her than the life or death of all of us. Blessed be God the children she has left us are all she ever was in our old happy happy days to me the greatest of all consolations and that you would love with all your heart to be a friend of as ever you were of their poor mother."

In spite of these letters, Pierce wrote once more to Cornelia, in 1853, to beg her to return to him. She refused, and he never saw her again—although he did see, and remained friendly with, one of her nuns, Sister Theresa, who was appointed as go-between. For years Sister Theresa wrote to the children and sent them presents and, with the strange illogicality of the case, remained their confidante.

In the year 1853 Pierce returned to Italy with Adeline and

Frank. He had recently seen a great deal of his old friend Bishop Otey, who had been on a visit to England and had expressed his longing to receive Pierce back into the Episcopal Church in terms so extravagant that Cornelia scribbled beside them with affectionate scorn (when they were published in one of Pierce's pamphlets), "The old donkey!" It is more than probable that Bishop Otey was responsible for the present move to Italy. Delighted that Pierce had left the Church of Rome and that, after his short-lived flirtation with the Irvingites, he was showing a prodigal desire to return to the American Episcopal fold, Bishop Otey was unlikely to allow his talents to lie wasted. Pierce had spent quite long enough, as a layman, in vigorously attacking the Roman Faith and in proving his emancipation from it. It was quite time he was back in active harness.

Four years previously a small American Episcopal ministry had been founded in Florence. Its future was unassured, its living a vacancy. Pierce spoke excellent Italian and he loved Italy. He was just the man to set it on its feet.

It was, therefore, to Florence that he went with Adeline and Frank. (Mercer had already left England two years before to find work in America.) There, in the Piazza del Carmine, on the corner of Via Santa Monica, facing one of the largest Catholic churches, he began his new ministry. It thrived and developed. Into it he emptied all the energy and inspiration for which he had failed, in Catholicism, to find the proper scope.

For the rest of his life Pierce remained the American Episcopal Minister in Florence, exchanging the patronage of the ancient Catholic aristocracy for the intinerant Protestant aristocracy of Europe. They came to Florence as they came to Rome, and there to greet them was Pierce—as always in his capacity of adviser and friend. Today his apartments in the Piazza del Carmine have been replaced by a modern Gothic church and presbytery in Via Bernardo Rucellai. But the serried ranks of Rolls-Royces, the green-liveried chauffeurs, the *Tatler* on the presbytery drawing-room table, the velvet cushions, and the soprano so exquisitely interpreting the Scriptures are evidence of the same tradition.

The children were together, and if they learned in time to blame and reject their mother, they at least had found a home and some semblance of family unity. They were no longer apart in alien English schools but with their beloved father, to whom they were almost hysterically devoted. They never wavered in their devotion. Cornelia's love and respect for Pierce survived twenty years, his children's their separate lifetimes.

In 1853 Frank was still a red-cheeked, stout-hearted boy of twelve. Adeline had become a timid, frightened girl. Her love for Cornelia had turned into an obsession for Pierce. Her features were a pallid replica of her mother's; her small share of spirit, blown upon by her father's fanaticism, spurted now and then into rude resentful letters to her mother. She clung to her piano playing and her femininity. A photograph at this time shows her in a tulip crinoline, but leaves her in its mist without carriage or confidence. She was "Papa's daughter" and there her status and her desires began and ended. For Pierce's large ambition and his extraordinary talents had shrunk to the circumference of Victorian fatherhood. He became the sun around which his children moved entranced. Lord Shrewsbury and Prince Borghese had withdrawn their financial assistance towards the education of his sons, but he had learned enough from tutoring other people's to make good the loss.

His enthusiasm, gaiety, and knowledge made Pierce a fascinating father, his egotism and possessiveness a bad one. In 1860, eight years later, Adeline went to America to stay with her uncle, George Connelly. His spirit of independence was horrified. He wrote at once to Pierce: "I confess I am greatly disappointed—at the age of twenty-five instead of a dignified ladylike woman with some knowledge of the world I find a gentle, affectionate, ignorant child with no practical knowledge—and if suddenly left alone in the world not so capable of taking care of herself as an infant . . . you have utterly sacrificed her to your own selfish enjoyment of her company . . . when I am asked what you do now I shall be obliged to answer you lead a life of idleness. Ady on her arrival had not a cent nor sufficient clothing. God grant you may so bring up Frank that when old he may point to something done."

His brothers had always been forthright, and Pierce responded now, as before, with the same uplifted reproach: "I dare say you meant to wound me as deeply as you did."

Adeline returned to Italy and to her life of gentle, thankful dependence, pouring out love on her father and on her brother, who had grown so quickly into a tall young man with a long face, cut in half by a luscious mustache, and a heavy, rounded jaw lightened by a rather fine forehead. At twenty it was the sort of face one would expect to see, and not to notice, beneath a straw boater—had boaters been the fashion. The love of painting that Cornelia had shown all her life became in him a burning passion. He learned under good masters and he became, towards the middle of his life, a well-known sculptor who found no difficulty in obtaining commissions from the Italian and English aristocracy and, later, from a larger and more appreciative American public.

In 1871, when he was thirty-one, two busts, one of Lord Percy, the other of Mr. Drummond's son-in-law, the sixth Duke of Northumberland, were accepted by the Royal Academy Exhibition of that year. Five years later, at an exhibition in Philadelphia, he was greeted by the critics as "one of the most significant among American sculptors." A bronze group, "Honor Awaiting the Triumph of Death," which had been begun in 1866 and had already been exhibited in Florence, won him special attention. It was, like his other compositions, romantic and elaborately detailed.

Nearly all his works tell the same story, whether they represent Leda pressed crushingly upon the feathery bosom of a swan, the young lover stretching towards the reluctant nymph, or the mother cradling her replete son. They are passionate exaggerations, in terms of noble sentimentality and meticulous physical accuracy, of human love.

Frank never forgave his mother. His father never made up to him for her loss. He lived to be an old man who died just before the last war, but in spite of his affection for his father, his success, his comfort, he was always ready to inveigh against the irreparable damage he suffered from being motherless, and he preserved to the end a touching romanticism about the power of love.

Both he and Adeline visited Cornelia when they were grown up, but the visits were not a success. Adeline timidly refused to be drawn into affection or argument. Frank, who felt the loss of his mother with an intense personal resentment which Pierce had done nothing to allay, went to see her twice, but only to plead his father's case and to express his own hurt anger.

The first time he came to the convent his pacing footsteps and loud impassioned voice were heard by the anxious nuns below. For the second, it was arranged that Cornelia should meet him for a few brief moments at the local station where he was forced, by the journey he was making across England, to change trains. The two nuns who accompanied Cornelia to the station left her alone with him in a compartment and retired to wait at a discreet distance down the train. Twenty minutes later they returned. But Frank had already gone. And his mother, who was wearing the newly invented mackintosh cloak of which she was so proud, sat quite unmoving. Even allowing for the exaggeration of Victorian sentiment, it is impossible to dismiss part, at least, of their testimony. They were shocked to see that the tears that Cornelia had shed lay still upon her lap, where they had formed a dark and shallow pool.

Late in life, Frank had a daughter, Marina. By a strange coincidence she married Prince Marcello Borghese, a descendant of the same family who had sponsored the Connellys in Rome. After the death of their father, Frank remained the center of Adeline's life until her own reconversion to Catholicism. For in the end, and largely owing to the influence of the Holy Child nuns, she returned to the Church of her Baptism.

Cornelia never lived to know of her daughter's reconversion. And if she had suffered through the attitude of Adeline and Frank, this did not compare with what she was made to suffer over Mercer.

When she wrote to Mercer in the autumn of 1847, distracted over the failure of his examination, she had no idea that she would never see him again. But shortly afterwards Pierce had taken him to Italy and, on returning with him to England, had refused to allow him to see his mother. Not long afterwards, at the age of eighteen, he went to the United States to find work, the idea being that he should go to one of the family farms. His aunts and uncles on both sides welcomed him. But a letter which he wrote to John Bowen, Cornelia's half-brother, on September 25, 1851, from New Orleans, where he was staying with his uncle George Connelly, shows the trend of his opinion:

My Dear Uncle,

I hope you will forgive me for not having written to you before. Believe me, dear uncle, it might have been through negligence but not through indifference or of want of reflection, you surely would not believe me so ungrateful as to forget so soon all your kind offers to Papa on my account, and for my well-being. I have not as yet learned, dear uncle, to be cold-hearted and I hope I never may be so, I have not forgotten the instructions of my parents. I had a letter the other day from Papa in which he tells me of his having been to see the Great Exhibition with Ady and Frank and that they had enjoyed themselves very much; he gives some unpleasant news from Mamma. I suppose you heard that Papa's case came on before the Judicial Committee of the Privy Council June 28. I send you *The Times* newspaper in which it is all contained and which I no doubt [sic] you would like to see. Dear, dear uncle I beg you will forgive me and in future I promise to write and also to answer your letters as soon as possible.

Uncle George has gone to the North, but is expected back every day, from last accounts he is very well. Uncle John and aunt are very well, but bitterly opposed to Papa and take every opportunity of making me feel their displeasure. Uncle George is very kind to me and I love and respect him with all my heart, and try as well as I can to please him.

Good-bye dear uncle,

Ever your affectionate nephew,

Mercer Connelly

PS.—I only received your letter today. It was fifteen days coming.

When she learned that Mercer was in America away from Pierce, Cornelia could not resist the thought of getting permission to visit him. She wrote to her old friend the Bishop of New Orleans and tried to sound him out. But his reply, in his awkward transliterate English, was adamant. "I entreat you to guard against the temptation. I have not the least doubt, but so soon as Mr. Pierce Connelly would hear of this move on your part he would be here soon himself, and I am equally sure that what he has attempted in vain in England he would obtain in this country. This is the opinion of Mr. John Connelly, whom you may continue to regard as a true friend." Ironically, Pierce's brother, who remained Catholic, continued Cornelia's friend. Members of her own family, some of whom had not embraced Catholicism, regarded her for the first time with hostility as an unnatural parent and were, possibly for the first time, in sympathy with Pierce.

The Bishop did not spare Cornelia. He had seen Mercer, who was by now a firm Protestant and convinced the Catholic Church had been unjust to his father. The Bishop went on: "I see no inconveniencing in your writing to Mercer, though I doubt of any good remitting from it . . . his prejudices shall ever be in favor of his father and rather adverse to you, that is he will range rather on his father's side, whom he considers as victimized."

In 1853, the year that Pierce took Adeline and Frank to Florence, Mercer died. He had contracted yellow fever. He was not yet twenty-one.

The hour he died, it is said, the bell tolled in the convent chapel. Told by her nuns that there was no ringer, Cornelia first made sure and then replied: "We should look upon this as a call to prayer. Let us pray for whatever soul may be in need."

A short time afterwards the news of Mercer's death arrived. It coincided with the ringing of the bell.

The grief was almost insupportable. "I cannot help it," she said in explanation of her tears to those who witnessed them. "You do not know what it is to be a mother." For the only time in her life she feared a breakdown. She was suffering from rheumatic gout at the time and could not absorb herself in action. And yet she dared not think. She sent for Burchett's *Geometry*, which had just been published, and set herself a certain number of problems to solve each day. Superficially it was a successful remedy. She recovered and she did not speak of him again. But she carried the lines of his death upon her face for the remaining years of her life.

Pierce himself outlived Cornelia by four years. At eighty he was still game for an argument. In 1880 his pamphlet *Cardinal Newman versus the Apostles' Creed* was published. It remains an eloquent apologia, as competent as ever, with translation and quotation, to unseat the opposition; as determined as before to admit the idea of a visible church while affirming that Catholicism is merely the visible church of human invention and "not of Holy Writ." He interprets the twelve articles with the loving care of an untroubled faith. It is an attractive and a powerful essay written "during my late long and nearly fatal illness and already past my three score years and ten, [when] these thoughts lay heavy on me and the object in what I have to say today is, so far as in me lies, to try and restore to the Apostles' Creed its primitive significance."

He had returned to the basic comfort of Protestantism and it had steadied his bitterness. When, in 1879, he learned of Cornelia's death, he wrote the kind, untouched letter of an acquaintance to Mother Theresa in condolence.

Four years later he himself was dead and Adeline wrote to Mother Theresa of how peaceful in his faith he was and how happy in his last communion. He had proved himself an insoluble mixture of vanity and affection, sincerity and affectation, fanaticism and compromise, as extreme in his failures as in his triumphs, as complete in his essential faith as in his irreverence. Lovable, incorrigible, and, for a time at least, wicked in determination and guile, he must rest at last in the words of his daughter Adeline to the Reverend Mother who replaced Cornelia on her death. He had not been afraid of death, only of pain and long illness, and when, in the end, he died from an attack of bronchitis it was to the last in anxiety "for strength to write once more to say all he had to say on the immortality of the soul, for the infidelity of the times was distressing to him.

"... He enjoyed every bit of fun to the last, his strength was failing visibly but his bright spirit gave me hope he would be spared to me for a little while. I was hurrying away to get the medicine for his heart, he opened his eyes and said in his sweet cheery voice, 'Where are you scampering to?' I gave him, what he always had of a morning, an egg beaten up with some coffee, and I added some brandy for he was getting colder and colder. I got alarmed and sent for the doctor but he could do nothing. Dear, darling Papa had got warm when he had arrived and had gone I thought into a sweet sleep and I did hope he would wake stronger. He never woke—but I had his hand in mine when he breathed his last gently as a little child . . . he was my work, my life, my happiness."

Part Three

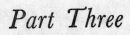

Chapter 9

THE BOOK OF STUDIES

THE LAST years of Cornelia's life covered such a wide field of activity, and included so many events that overlapped, that it is not possible to record them chronologically. If, in the chapters that follow, time often runs parallel it is because they are concerned not so much with the succeeding years as with the difficulties and achievements that filled them.

From the time of her trial until the end of her life, Cornelia suffered so much through petty disagreement and trivial circumstance, as well as through her own personal unhappiness, that it is surprising to find in everyone's description of her the common denominator, "her calm," "her tranquillity."

She gave no evidence of her private thoughts and feelings. She never wept—or, if she did, the tears, as she jokingly told a young novice who had accused her of never suffering from homesickness or an overwhelming sense of loneliness, "run down the back of my throat." "I must not dwell on deep sorrow," she had written in her diary, "for I am without the power of remedy. I can only cause distress to others by my tears; useless tears unless they move the heart of my Lord to pity."

To understand this seeming indifference, this imposition of courage, it is necessary to follow a little way the progress of her spiritual life, a difficult task since she never consciously revealed it except in the ardor with which she expressed her love of God and in the time she gave to Him, and insisted upon her nuns' giving. It was her will to found her spiritual life upon our Lord's life at Nazareth, of which nothing is known except that "He was subject to them." Cornelia, normally never at a loss for words, was spiritually devoted to the virtue of silence.

The current which caught at the surface of her life and pulled it irresistibly onwards in constant turmoil was no reflection of her interior life. Her soul had left "the valley of the shadow of death" when she left the Trinità dei Monti. The agony, the reluctant unwilling submission of the soul who fights as hard against its love as for it, she had experienced already. This had been replaced by that peace with God which is so complete that "whatever her trials or labors, the center of her soul is never moved from its resting place" and where "the accustomed movements of the faculties and imagination do not seem to take place in any way that can injure the soul or disturb its peace." She was drunk with love; or, as St. Theresa puts it, "You may fancy that such a person is beside herself and her mind is so inebriated that she can care for nothing else. On the contrary she is more ardent than ever in all that concerns God's service . . . such a one suffers much during this life, for whatever work she may perform, her soul has energy for far greater tasks and goads her on to do more, so that all she can perform seems nothing to her." (*Interior Castle*, 7th Mansion.)

She had been constrained by suffering into a freedom of spirit that only suffering obtains. As a poet deliberately imposes upon his inspiration the steel discipline of form, so God imposes upon His saints the self-denying discipline which, by restraining, gives, in the end, the finest release.

Cornelia echoed her experience in her teaching. She recommended to those of her disciples who were capable of understanding her, the deliberate practice of interior death, to be followed by a spiritual resurrection—by which she meant a voluntary detaching of the soul for a long time from indulgence in natural joys and self-will, until, loosened from all bonds of this world, it could rise to a new life and see everything from a supernatural point of view. Then, she thought, it should relax something of its austere self-discipline and become a child again. When the soul has given up all things and lost the taste for everything but God, then "all things else are given back to it in a new way, and it may use them all fearlessly for Him."

She had found her spiritual balance and nothing again disturbed it, which was fortunate as there was more to trouble her than Pierce and the loss of her children.

The urbanity of Mr. Jones's drawing-room manner, the comradely jollity with which he twitted nuns and children alike, was not to last for long.

At first he became uneasy because the scaffolding and the building did not progress. But as the workmen complained, with despairing gestures, what could you expect when what they were told to put up one day they were asked to tear down the next; "his Reverence always gets a better idea." Indeed, he usually did. The next upset was on the subject of the children. Why were there not more? Did the Reverend Mother think he had asked them to come simply to enjoy a rent-free building and garden produce? They were a community of thirty with only thirty pounds between them as covering funds, he understood. When were they going to expand? His hearing was growing worse, and with it his temper. He was convinced that the nuns took advantage of his deafness, and Cornelia must have grown to dread the tapping of his ebony stick along the passages; the loud explanations to be poured down his silver ear trumpet with so little opportunity for soothing intonation and tact. It was not, she said, the time for expansion with the scandal about Pierce not yet cold and with her own nuns so young and untrained. She was determined to give them a chance to consolidate their vocation before rushing them into the activity of school. She was, besides, appalled by their ignorance. Before she would allow them to teach others, she would first teach them.

And this she proceeded to do—and in doing so was forced to realize the magnitude of her task. In an age when women were not only uneducated but considered barely worth educating, and when the education that existed followed the dreariest routine, the destructive practice of hours of repetition and memorizing, she inaugurated the unusual and stimulating theories which she later turned into a handbook for her nuns and printed in 1863 as *The Book of Studies*.

To appreciate her ideas fully, it is first necessary to realize her attitude to children.

She came into the arena armed not with the conventions

and intellectual enthusiasms of Miss Beale and Miss Buss, the great Protestant pioneers of female education in the nineteenth century, but with the practical knowledge of her own American education, and the lessons taught her by her own children. She was not an enthusiast longing to test out theory in practice but a practical woman concerned with putting into theory for her nuns and their successors all that experience had taught her. She was, it must be remembered, entirely satisfied with her own upbringing. In this she was very different from Miss Beale, who forged her decisions from a burning resentment towards her own inadequate education and saw the problem always from the standpoint of one who had suffered from it. It is therefore all the more interesting that both women reached so many of the same conclusions.

Cornelia had the greatest sympathy with the restlessness, the ceaseless activity of children. She knew the misery of sitting still, of staying too long in one place until minutes become hours and tedium an agony too great to be borne. On an awareness of this characteristic she based all her methods. Like Miss Beale, she found the school day that already existed not only too long but too solid. When Miss Beale was a child, "the following was the arrangement of hours. Rise at seven, lessons till eight, breakfast consisting of bread and butter with extraordinarily weak coffee, lessons till twelve, luncheon consisting of bread and butter or bread and jam and 'turns' till one o'clock. These 'turns' consisted in going round and round the garden; they could scarcely be accomplished unless the luncheon were carried round in the hand and eaten en route. Lessons from one o'clock until three forty-five, dinner four o'clock and 'turns' in fine weather immediately following, as after luncheon. Lessons until eight, then tea and bed at nine." The lessons were in periods of an hour, but the timetable was far more formidable than the work, which was shoddy, piecemeal, and uninvitingly dull.

Cornelia's day was only an hour shorter for children of the same age, but the afternoon was always devoted to games and recreation and she insisted on half-hourly periods. Moreover, between each period there was always to be five minutes of fresh air and freedom. In later copies of her book, the space for these breaks has been resolutely crossed out by her successor. But in her lifetime she always maintained them. In the same way she believed that every lesson should make use of, if not inspire, "the love of activity so natural to children." The children were always encouraged to move about in class; "one child can pin on the board, another place the letter in the letter-case, another point to it on the reading card." All their lessons were based on games and stories, on drawing and acting—methods that today are the commonplace of child psychology but in her own day were unrecognized. Like Miss Beale, who founded Cheltenham Ladies' College, Cornelia was appalled at the amount of learning by heart, of soulless repetition. Poor Dorothea Beale had found herself, though at a school "much above the average," being taught history "by committing to memory little manuals." Both she and Cornelia insisted that "an explanation of every lesson to be learned should be given before the memory is taxed . . . always making use of the blackboard that the memory may be assisted by the eye," and made it a rule that nothing was ever to be learned by heart that had not been first clearly understood. Cornelia found to her distress that her nuns were as bad at reading aloud as her children and wrote emphatic rules for both. "Faults of manner, drawling, rapid, pompous, inflated, timid. Reading should be slow but not drawling, distinct without loudness, impressive without affectation." Each part of *The Book of Studies* (for it is divided into subjects and discusses each detail minutely) begins with a firm emphasis on the need for explanations and "a clear and spirited description of persons, scenes, and things calculated to excite interest in the subject" (in this case geography). Always, she underlines the importance of imaginative teaching: "the first lesson should be given to them in the form of simple tales, to excite their curiosity and rouse their imaginations" [religion]; "the object of this exercise [reading] is to excite interest"; "all exercises [grammar] should consist of sentences not mere strings of words"; "the first lessons [always] to be about familiar things," and the aim always to "inspire the pupil's imagination." The examples are endless, and again and again she stresses the need to combine the other senses with that of hearing. "Never forget," was her maxim, "that the memory may be assisted by the eye," for it was her fondest belief that observation is a habit of value, "the only habit by which knowledge generally can be obtained." Every word that was wrongly spelled in an exercise book was ruthlessly scratched out so that it could not be remembered wrongly. A single line was not enough to erase it. In the same way her insistence that arithmetic be taught partly as a game with a "box of bricks, box of cards, weights and a few plain figures capable of being taken to pieces" was to capture not only the imagination but also the eye, for "as children come by their first ideas of number through the medium of objects so their whole early training in the principles and processes of number must be based on an observation of objects. They do not use numbers for their own sake but for the sake of the things numbered. They count by sight and are not able to abstract number from the things. It is with number as a property of bodies like color, form, etc., and not with the science of Arithmetic that the pupils should be occupied in the first lessons." In the same way she felt it more important to read before they spelled because "the eye must be familiar with the forms before the pupils are required to reproduce them." Familiarity was an introduction she valued in all lessons. Everything could be made more exciting by comparison and contrast with what was already known. In geography, place names were not enough. The children "must learn what a map is and how to use it. They should begin by drawing plans of (1) the table, (2) the schoolroom, (3) the playground, (4) the neighborhood." And, most important of all, the classes must be related to each other. She disliked the idea of subjects being taught in isolation and was careful to tie them up with each other so that the children could get some sort of perspective and a sense of relationship and continuity.

But behind such carefully woven theory was the firm conviction that the lessons to be learned must be short and within the capacity of the child. She did not share Miss Beale's fear that it "is a worse fault to teach below than above the powers of a child." Yet she was careful to discriminate and to protect any sparks of individuality and inspiration she divined in any of her pupils. Justice, she found, did not lie in equality of treatment, and she felt, as Blake had done, that one yoke for the lion and the lamb is tyranny. "We must encourage our children to bring out their original ideas and put a check on this seeking to copy," she was constantly repeating, although never at the cost of accuracy. "Be accurate" was her favorite advice. But throughout her instructions to her teachers runs the thin vein of hope: "It is well not to be too severe in the criticism and correction of the compositions. We are not to expect a perfect composition from a child. It is easy to correct redundancy, but a barren genius has no remedy."

She refused to consider, as her contemporaries did, that drawing was "an extra or superlative art" but, on the contrary, regarded it "as a Christian art, and one of the most important branches of education, second only to that of speaking and writing, and in some respects even beyond the languages, as in itself an universal language, addressing itself to the ignorant as well as to the most refined. Nor is it to be considered as an accomplishment, but as an art which has its own philosophy as well as its poetry."

In the light of such high artistic aspirations Cornelia's own minute instructions to her nuns have a charming naïveté. "It is necessary to have a moist surface in order to prevent hard lines in the sky. It is necessary to have an old cotton stocking, or cloth, to absorb the water when too much is put on and also to vary and soften the sky." This is followed by several pages on how to achieve certain effects, and the stocking plays other parts. It is not asked to help in creating sunsets on trees or in painting walls, high lights, and old roofs, but it must be used to put in distant buildings "with purple madder, or gray"; and here the tone becomes peremptory: "soften with the cotton stocking."

Yet school is not all soft soap and sentiment, and Cornelia could, on occasion, be a hard taskmaster. She hated slovenliness and vagueness, and she was as instant in the dismissal of a girl with a bad influence as Miss Beale. This did not cover the ordinarily naughty child, who was generally her favorite, but those curious, and fortunately rare, children who distill an atmosphere of discontent and who, in a bewilderingly short time, can undermine the peace and spirit of a community with their restlessness, their belittlement, and, most frightening of all, their scorn.

It was never in Cornelia's character to fear difficulties or turn aside from unpleasantness. In the same way that she allowed her malefactors no third chance, though usually a second, she refused to teach watered-down versions of unpalatable facts. In Church history she took note of Christ's warning, "It must needs be that scandals come"—an unblemished account was not only false but unhelpful. Someone was bound to provide the blemishes sooner or later. Better to learn everything and see how, in spite of scandals, the Church persevered. "Judas," she said, "with his terrible example has probably done more good than St. Jude with his Catholic epistle." It was a far cry from the day, twenty years ago, when she wrote to her sister with anxious dismay of the scandalous behavior of the Roman Church which so worried her when Pierce was feeling his way towards conversion. Like Newman, she did "not deny the superstitions in the Catholic Church." She shared his view of the case, that "they were inevitable incidents attendant on the historical growth of religious belief among corrupt men. Tares grew with the wheat," but the Church "was the witness to, and preserver of, the spiritual truth once imparted by God to man, keeping it alive and operative by the preaching of her ministers, symbolizing it by her rites, guarding it by her dogmatic formulæ." Newman had divided converts into "those whose main anxiety is to discover how little it is possible to believe, while yet remaining orthodox, and those who think that there is some peculiar merit in believing as much as possible." Newman himself adopted the second to start with but veered with time towards the first. Cornelia took a more moderate course. She did not accept superstition without reserve, but she had a weakness for relics which, on one occasion, landed her into difficulty with the Customs. She had been sent the remains of St. Theophila in a sealed chest, as a present from Rome, but the Customs would not part with the chest unless Cornelia gave them permission to open it. This she would not do as the contents would be invalidated if the seals were broken before the chest reached her. The Customs remained convinced that seals meant contraband—and only the intervention of the British Consul at Rome resolved the situation and obtained the chest for Cornelia.

But in teaching, truth, whether trivial or philosophical, was Cornelia's aim—and if her ways seemed devious to her age they were never so in fact. She trusted a lot to imagery but never false idols. She was, in fact, afraid of allegory and cautious even of analogy, or parable, for on the one hand "under the appearance of making it teach a great many things it will teach nothing in particular," and on the other "overstraining the analogy results when the story is pushed so far into detail as to cause distortion of the spiritual truth in carrying out the parallel between them."

She preferred the language of logic to that of metaphor and insisted on her pupils being grounded in it. "It would much assist in forming their judgment and reforming and abridging their language if they could be instructed a little in the art of reasoning." Writing to a prospective parent, it was her proud boast that her girls also learn "fractions and cube root which is generally thought too difficult for girls."

Some of these ideas did not encourage the parents of children who already had reason to fear Mrs. Connelly's unorthodoxy. Apart from the day poor schools which Cornelia started before, or simultaneously with, her boarding convents and which were taught along the same, though simplified, lines, Cornelia never had more than sixteen pupils during the first sixteen years. In spite of Mr. Jones's grumbles and the anxiety of some of the nuns who were worried about future prospects, Cornelia remained undisturbed. "Weigh your subjects, not count them," she joked, refusing to be upset by gloomy foreboding and prophecies. She would not consider altering her policy and, in any case, was grateful for the time in which to establish her nuns, try out her ideas, and allow the school a slow growth to maturity. In fact, the Gorham decision had precipitated a great many more converts from among the Tractarians into the Church, and Cornelia soon benefited from the influx. Emily Bowles's friendship with Newman was one contact with these and Cornelia's with Wiseman another. Even the litigation in which she was constantly involved helped. Nearly all her lawyers sent their children to her; Sergeant Bellasis sent three and Sir Charles Russell four. Once the tumult of Pierce's publicity began to die down the numbers began to increase.

But the old Catholics were more cautious than the new. Her convent was "worldly," "ridiculous," "a vain and foolish attempt," "a failure," and she herself an American adventuress all out for fame. The more sedate were shocked by her modernity. Was it generally known, they inquired of one another, that Cornelia actually imported male teachers? Cornelia did not give in. The children were always chaperoned by a nun in the classroom, and in many cases men were far better than women. The parents registered dismay and some of the "professors" took gross advantage of the situation. Suspecting that Cornelia would be only too anxious not to make public any more disagreements, one of them, a music master, claimed payment for a number of lessons he had not given and cited Cornelia before the local court. The surprise and embarrassment was considerable when Cornelia appeared in court. It was also fortunate, as the judge pronounced unhesitatingly in her favor and added an unwelcome homily to the professor.

Humor and tact waged perpetual war with prejudice and convention, and on no subject more strongly than upon acting. For Cornelia had imported the extraordinary notion that acting was a good thing, and a stage essential. Only the children at first appreciated the novelty. The nuns complained that the children who played the leading parts were vain, that those who did not were jealous, and that everyone identified themselves too strongly with the less desirable traits of those they were portraying. It was a waste of time and made discipline impossible. Many of the parents supported them, and at one of the early performances at a school concert the Bishop was forced to remonstrate when he noticed that the leading male part was played by a girl wearing "bloomers" outside her dress. Somewhat formal and pompous letters were exchanged on the subject and a compromise was reached about the bloomers, though not about the stage.

It was an age when children went home only for six weeks in the summer and had only two weeks' holiday at school for

Christmas and Easter, and they could not be expected to work all the time. In acting Cornelia felt they had an activity that was exciting and enjoyable as well as one that, incidentally, taught them courage, grace, and deportment in addition to the words of the great plays. She liked them to treat the whole thing professionally and, under direction, to look after the entire production. The first attempt was Milton's *Comus*, and Cornelia was actor-manager, choreographer, dresser, and designer. She herself painted the river scene and dressed Sabrina. The play was a success. Corruption had not set in. Sabrina was later to become a nun, and so were three others of the cast. To those of her nuns who still grumbled of vanity, jealousy, and inordinate love of display Cornelia retorted that vanity and other faults were not created by the plays but merely revealed by them and that it was easier to correct children during rehearsal when they were eager to accept criticism than at any other time. Reluctantly the nuns agreed that the children seemed to tolerate correction with remarkable good temper, and acting settled into a regular feature of the holidays spent at school and of the school term.

Cornelia's audacity was not always so successful, although she got away with importing one of the earliest sewing machines, with bringing a real donkey onto the stage for a religious tableau, and with processions outside, in spite of the gaping Protestant public, who were both astounded and disapproving. The school choir, which she herself trained to sing in the Italian manner, became eventually a source of local pride, and so did the school uniform, the bright blue of which was later replaced by crimson, colors chosen by Cornelia because she disliked somber clothes for children. But an attempt to install a private printing press and another to get the nuns taught modelling—so that they could make as well as paint their statues—failed, the latter largely because the molds were so heavy that the nuns could not lift them. Two puny statues, eighteen inches high, of St. Aloysius were the only tangible results of a Signor Regali's instruction, and Cornelia uncomfortably reflected that "if we can't do it ourselves, we at least know how it is done." Like Signor Regali, a Doctor Pic and his craft had also to be abandoned soon after his introduction.

He had rashly undertaken to "improve memories" by a system which was more or less the forerunner of Pelmanism.

It was for the children a life of humor and fun as well as of work, for Cornelia had found that a happy child is, with very few exceptions, a good one. And happiness enabled her to introduce her system of mutual responsibility in which each class voted for its own "badges" and the badges met to decide the policy of the school. Trust begot trust. There was to be no constant supervision. "Watch over not watch them" was the guide.

Although Cornelia strove diligently to instill the principles of ladylike behavior and maintained that no girl was educated who, on leaving her, could not read *The Times* leader with intelligence, it is comforting to find, from her list of transgressions, that the nature of children varies little from one generation to another and that ladylike qualifications were as difficult to achieve with Queen Victoria on the throne as they are now: "It is not allowed to drink with their mouths full, nor to put their knives into their mouths instead of their forks, nor to bite off the bread instead of cutting it . . . nor is it allowed to sit in a lolling position with the feet stretched out . . . nor to quarrel, nor wound by cutting words, nor to bring up superiority of family, nor to depreciate the family of another, nor to use college boys' slang, nor to jump over the benches, nor to push one another, nor to call across the school hall, nor to run past the sisters, nor to answer back when reproved, nor to go out in the garden with thin shoes, nor without hats and gloves, nor to rush into the school hall in disorder." The list flows on to the first generation of her children. A less meticulous hand in later editions has substituted "unruliness" for the lot. But apart from the infringement of certain strict rules, Cornelia did not like punishment. "Let not the mistresses be too hasty in punishing, nor too eager in seeking faults, but let them dissimulate when they can do so without injury to anyone, and not only must they never use corporal punishment, but they must abstain also from any abusive words or actions." It was her belief that "the children's faults are the sisters'." "Know your children," she urged, "take the trouble to study the character of each child."

But in any system, however careful, a crack sometimes appears. It is impossible to be completely fair. Cornelia was quick in sympathy and laughter for the small child who bellowed at her with shrill fury, "You don't love me because my hair is red. It isn't red, it's golden." But she remembered too the temptation to become too involved in the love of small children. "Love your children with a true Christian love, a self-sacrificing love. Love the soul you cannot see, more than the body that you can see. Lead the children to God, not to yourself," she told her nuns.

It must be remembered that behind all Cornelia's theories and innovations, and her determination to stick to them, was no deliberate eccentricity or search for novelty but the firm conviction that she was preparing her children for God in the best possible way. In His service she was adamant, and if she rode her charges with a light hand it was nevertheless in the one direction that she took them.

Of course she made mistakes. She was too quick in introducing certain of her methods, too slow in abandoning others. There was still too much dictation, copying, and learning by heart, and lessons were too often couched in the familiar form of Question and Answer so favored by Miss Mangall and her contemporary authors of *The Child's Guide* and *The Universal History*. The school day remained too long in conformity with other schools, and the syllabus was both too ambitious and too wide. To the first school advertisement which read "English and French, Writing, Arithmetic, Geography, History, Grammar, Singing and the principles of Church Music. Drawing, Plain Needlework and every kind of embroidery, tracing, point-lace, stitch, together with the cutting out and making up of vestments" was added "Philosophy, Logic, Astronomy, Geology, Architecture, and Heraldry as well as Latin and Greek." But against this it must be remembered that Cornelia was not tied down by examinations and the need for specialized education, and that not only were her girls with her nearly all the year but, when they left, they were not destined to earn their own livings but to take their place in society. It was her aim to give them a liberal and broad education, and beyond that to teach them how to concentrate and how to think for themselves.

It is a tribute to her system that it remains very much the same today, altered only by those details which bring it up to date and which it was her desire should be always changing to "meet the wants of the age." She disliked rigidity and saw very clearly that every age produced new problems and demands that must be met as they arrived.

In spite of opposition, she was quick even in her own day to gain approval from official sources. Already in 1853 the Government Inspector was able to report on the poor school attached to the boarding school at St. Leonards: "It is impossible to witness without admiration the results obtained in this very interesting school, in which consummate skill in the art of teaching, unwearied patience and the most persuasive personal influence have combined to accomplish all the rarest fruits of Christian instruction. The school is now one of the most perfect institutions of its class in Europe."

In 1858, Barbara Charlton, the forceful and buoyant autocrat who had been so stringent a critic of Mother Barat and the Sacred Heart Convent in Paris, arrived with her daughters Fanny and Amy in "the midst of holidays and plays" and "was much pleased with what I saw." She remained delighted with "Mrs. Connelly and the nuns, who seemed not to have thrown off all common sense with their worldly raiment." Like many others whose children had been taught by the Holy Child nuns, Barbara Charlton remained their fond admirer, and urged her family and friends to send their daughters to St. Leonards.

Today in England there are five Holy Child boarding schools, two direct grant grammar schools, two preparatory and sixteen parochial schools, one university hostel, and a training college. The houses and schools of the order in America, Ireland, Italy, France, and Switzerland, as well as the missions in Africa, have followed the same pattern of expansion over the years, but in each case the principle has been the same—"to meet the wants of the age."

Chapter 10

MR. JONES

In 1851 Cornelia's equanimity about the scarcity of pupils still failed to reassure Mr. Jones. For the moment, however, he contented himself with angry asides and veiled threats. His architectural activity still continued. Deciding, with some cause, that Pugin's chapel, which he had planned and begun some years before, was unlikely to be ready for years, he built a temporary chapel to hold nuns, children, and a small local congregation. The nuns remained behind a curtain and out of view, and the rest of the limited space held a strange assortment. The exiled monarchs of Europe, whose absolute rights had been swept away by revolution—Dom Miguel of Bragança, Queen Christina of Spain, King Louis Philippe and Queen Amelia of France—jostled with organ-grinders, gardeners, Irish coastguardmen and fishermen from the port. It was there, in 1849, that the Requiem Mass for the Duc d'Orléans had been said and where, on one of her visits, Queen Amelia was delighted by the children chanting with flustered enthusiasm their demand for a blessing, *"Daignez nous baigner!"*

But gradually Mr. Jones's threats gave way to action. He refused to allow them the full use of the garden produce, demanded that they give up some of the rooms he had allotted them, and began to talk openly of revoking his gift and bestowing it elsewhere. With this in view he got in touch with Colonel Townley, the nephew of Lady Stanley of Puddington, the original benefactress of All Souls, with whom in the first flush of enthusiasm he had begun preparations two years before to establish the nuns in ultimate possession.

Since Cornelia and her nuns had only their own small dowries, the income from sixteen pupils, and what they could do with the produce of the garden still allowed them by Mr.

Jones, they too were forced to make plans—once more for departure. It was a bitter disappointment, but Cornelia accepted it with surprising unconcern: "If the Society is the work of God it will endure in spite of opposition; if it is not, the sooner it is brought to an end the better." Putting the matter straight to the test, she started her nuns on a novena to discover God's will. He left them in no doubt. The novena was started on February 14, 1851. On February 21 Mr. Jones, with commendable rapidity, fell ill and died. It was with some awe the nuns learned of such an alarming manifestation of Divine Providence.

Mr. Jones, however, had conducted the finale with dignity as well as dispatch. Sending for Cornelia, his last words were a plea for forgiveness and the promise that his old will, which he had threatened to destroy, was valid and in the library.

But no will was found, although the libraries of All Souls and of Mr. Jones's London house were both ransacked. It had been arranged that the will would be read aloud to all concerned in three months' time. For three months the nuns searched, with no success. The whole incident of Mr. Jones verges on farce. Once more the nuns fell to prayer and once more their prayers were answered. On May 24, the day before the will was due to be read aloud, Cornelia went for the last time to the desk where she was convinced it must be. Inadvertently her hand slipped, carrying her weight with it, and pushed with unexpected force at the prim Corinthian pilasters that fronted the top. They moved forward, in the manner of their period, revealing a thin cubicle behind. In it lay the neatly folded will.

On May 25, in the presence of Wiseman, Colonel Townley, and the nuns, the will was read aloud. Its terms made Colonel Townley heir and sole executor of the entire property but with the understanding, expressed in a letter, that he would carry out the charitable intentions of the deceased. No opposition was made at the time and the nuns remained in possession.

But the possession, snatched as it were from the jaws of death, was not an easy one. From the beginning it led to discord and dislikes which were to last for thirteen years.

The dispute fell into two main phases. The first phase, 1851–54, which also included controversy with Wiseman, coincided with Pierce's litigation and subsequent pamphleteering. The second, from 1861 to 1864, came after a lull of some years due to the painstaking meditation of Bishop Grant, who relieved Wiseman of the Southwark district, to which St. Leonards belonged, in 1852.

The trouble arose over the building and land which had been bequeathed to Colonel Townley on the nuns' behalf (with the probable object of avoiding the technical difficulties involved in bequests for religious purposes) although it had been half committed elsewhere. Mr. Jones enjoyed dispensing largesse. He had dallied with other forms of charity and had even solicited and received, as well as endowed, contributions towards the erection of a parish church and schools. Some of this money had already been sunk in the All Souls buildings which, at the moment of his death, included the convent boarding and elementary schools, a chapel that was shared by nuns, children, and the local congregation, and a space in the convent for a boys' school for the village. The property fell into two divisions, the convent and "the mission," as the parish part was called. But there was no mention of the mission in the will, perhaps because, at the time when it was made, the situation between the two had been too nebulous to define and Mr. Jones must have assumed, if he considered the future prospects at all, that the convent would care for what rudiments of a parish there were. This the nuns proceeded to do, but on terms which did not suit the parish.

What Mr. Jones had not allowed for is the capacity for misunderstanding among people of thoroughly good intentions. Florence Nightingale was astonished by the sectarian bickerings at Scutari and was even moved to write to Mrs. Herbert in 1855: "It would be very desirable to diminish disaffection. The wisest thing the War Office could do now would be to send out a few more of the Bermondsey nuns to join those already at Scutari and counterbalance the influence of the Irish ones, who hate their soberer sisters with the mutual hatred which, I believe, only nuns and household servants can feel towards each other." Florence Nightingale's experience was extreme, but it is a sad fact that, ever since St. Paul's quarrel with St. Barnabas, opposition between holy men has often been the more determined because of the strength of their convictions. Few saints reach Heaven without suffering the persecution of just men, and only time, and God, can decide which side of the case was the better.

Dr. Duke, who represented the parish in the fight ahead, was himself a generous and passionate devotee of the mission. It was in his ear that Mr. Jones had poured so much of his irritation and disappointment about the nuns and, no doubt, hinted at promises of the legacy going in Dr. Duke's direction.

In any case Dr. Duke had expectations and the will came as a severe shock to him, followed, as it closely was, by a letter from Colonel Townley, inspired by Cornelia, saying that he considered a boys' school within the convent unsuitable and suggesting that as "the most influential member of the congregation" Dr. Duke might like to express his views on a proposed alternative site to which the convent would contribute £150. Dr. Duke replied that the parish could not afford to build a boys' school and suggested that Colonel Townley should build a school and priest's house on the property of All Souls. To this Colonel Townley replied: "I have received your letter and I assure you I duly appreciate your feeling as regards the boys' school at All Souls. But there is an insuperable difficulty. *It is utterly impossible for me to build either a boys' school or a priest's house as I have not* a single shilling to build them with. Poor Mr. Jones frittered away so much money that the funds left in my hands will scarcely finish the convent, and perhaps get the roof onto the church. With what money remains, I mean to make the convent, the girls' school and infants' school as efficient as possible, and this cannot be done without removing the boys from the room they at present occupy. And therefore if a room can be hired for them for the present at Hastings or elsewhere I should not mind contributing from the building funds a small sum, say £7 or £8 per annum for three or four years, as a temporary substitute. If this cannot be done the best thing is to give up for the present till the congregation are able to re-establish them. But they cannot remain in the convent."

The war was on and Dr. Duke engaged with a letter of great length explaining that not only was Mr. Jones's real intention to preserve the mission, and to invite a religious order of men to work and aid it, but that he had appropriated money that Dr. Duke himself had raised towards a parish school and church and incorporated it in the All Souls buildings. It was therefore reasonable to presume "a confident assurance that the church and schools would always continue as they had been led to believe them to be, really mission church and schools; and that they never would become the absolute property of an order of religious on which the congregation had no claim as a matter of right but only of sufferance."

Dr. Duke had good grounds for his grievance but no legal support, as Townley pointed out by return post, and continued to point out regularly for the next few years. "I received your letter with much surprise. I have before me now (in Mr. Jones's own handwriting) the views he [Mr. Jones] entertained regarding the convent of St. Leonards and the disposition of his property there and elsewhere, and they directly contradict every word of the first six pages of your letter. Mr. Jones's sentiments, as expressed to me during his life, exactly correspond with those he left in writing. You must therefore excuse me if I choose to follow the directions Mr. Jones has left in regard to his property in his own handwriting, which he distinctly expressed during his life to my father, my aunt Lady Stanley, and myself in preference to your version of them."

In legal terms the situation was simple: "The late Rev. J. Jones left Mr. Townley the whole of his property in fee simple." He could have sold it or converted the proceeds entirely to his own use had he chosen to do so. Instead, he chose to interpret Mr. Jones's wishes and the effort cost him thirteen years of strife, although it was against the nuns that the main offensive was directed. For, on finding Colonel Townley adamant and the law an unlikely vehicle, Dr. Duke openly declared that the nuns had taken unlawful possession, had misappropriated funds, and were "relentless adversaries of the mission. Of the money they have confiscated they have spent not a shilling on the mission. Mrs. Connelly's zeal for the interests of the convent has blinded her to those of truth and justice."

This ignored the fact that Cornelia was carrying the whole financial cost of running the church for the laity as well as for the school and that by this time, 1852, she had, independently of Colonel Townley's recommendation, also built a school for the boys who had been turned out of the convent. The Poor School Committee found it very suitable, "well arranged and of ample dimensions." Dr. Duke declared it a miserable shed and stopped his subscription. Since his enthusiasm and financial support had been far greater than anybody else's, the school dwindled and emptied.

Altogether Cornelia contributed over two thousand pounds to the mission. She had been forced to provide a second chaplain, Mr. Foy, to look after the parish interests, in addition to the convent chaplain, and the expenses of altar linen, candles, wine, etc., were quite large. But having learned from her lawyers that Mr. Jones's will was irrevocable and Colonel Townley its only legitimate interpreter, she would give no ground in the matter—she was willing that the congregation should share her church but she was *not* willing to build them, at her own expense, a separate one. Nor would she abandon her claim.

It is the weakness of the biography that, over matters like this, it imposes a false perspective. For the sake of clarity, problems, which in fact lasted interminably and straggled untidily and intricately through other affairs and events, must necessarily be explained briefly and in one place. They are thus isolated from their context and assume at once a less disturbing mien. But for Cornelia the St. Leonards dispute was, for thirteen years, a source of endless distress. And the worst aspect of it was Wiseman's reaction.

Wiseman's letter of 1848 had made it quite plain to Cornelia that he considered the St. Leonards property in the nature of a bequest to the convent. But after Mr. Jones's death in 1851 he changed his opinion. As Bishop of Southwark, which he still was, he was perhaps annoyed that Mr. Jones, a priest, had bequeathed the property independently of his

Bishop. But his change of mind was due, in part at least, to another cause.

Only a short time before he himself had added a fresh complication by demanding a part of the convent buildings for conversion into a seaside residence for himself and the priests of the Archdiocese of Westminster. Against this Cornelia had been adamant. She had suffered too much already from rumors about her moral laxity and she was not putting herself in the way of more. Moreover, Pierce had already heard of the proposed "marine residence" and was bruiting it abroad as fresh proof of the iniquities of convent life. But when she refused to give way to Wiseman over this, Cornelia laid herself open to criticisms which had begun with Asperti and which were to gather alarming force during the next few months and to prejudice the whole of her case during the St. Leonards dispute.

Wiseman was annoyed. He took refuge in the hurt sensitivity which so often overtook his moods of elation and triumph. While he continued to support her against Pierce and his admirers in public, he showed her his gravest displeasure in private. His disappointment over his seaside villa assumed a significance out of all proportion to its importance, and precipitated him into a curious course of action. In fact, without the relevant documents which, if they exist, do so in that part of the Southwark Archives which is sealed off from the public pending investigation into Cornelia's cause, it is unaccountable.

He began by sending down workmen to St. Leonards to do alterations that had already been decided against and which Cornelia, on their arrival, forbade them to touch. The workmen returned disgruntled. Wiseman became, in consequence, more irate. Unable to persuade Cornelia to change her mind and aware, for the first time, that her charming manner hid a resolution as great as his own, he refused to give his stamp of approval to her order, or to speak for it in Rome. The effect of this decision upon a newly founded order, which had begun in the most unorthodox circumstances and been followed by the most distressing events, was great. The nuns were torn in their allegiance before they had even settled into their new life. For the Cardinal lost no opportunity in making his views clear to them. In the beginning of August, 1851, he sent a priest to the convent to give a retreat and to express his disapproval of Cornelia. Wiseman himself arrived the following Sunday to preach a sermon in the convent chapel. The subject he chose was the Pharisee and the Publican, and he left immediately afterwards without speaking to anyone.

It is obvious that he was beginning to regret the impulse which had led him to ask Cornelia to start an order, and to wish that she had never entered his life. From the moment that she did so she brought in her wake complications and publicity of a sort which he most disliked and which might threaten the uncertain, delicate peace he had established with the Government, the press, and the Anglican Church after the restoration of the hierarchy and his own overconfident announcement of it. The least she could do, he felt, was to remain inconspicuous and preserve a proper modesty and respect for authority. Instead, she had proved herself unwilling to obey him about his beloved project and was sticking to her refusal in a manner ill-fitting Victorian womanhood.

Rumors now grew about the convent—it was said that it would be suppressed—and Wiseman did nothing to allay them. In fact, he must be held partly responsible for the dislike which all priests began to feel for Cornelia, including Father Foy, the mission chaplain, and, though unknown to her as yet, her own convent chaplain, Dr. Pius Melia. It is strange that during her life as a nun Cornelia kept the admiration and affection of all lawyers but few priests. It is impossible to avoid the suspicion that the latter were affronted by her sex in conjunction with such mental shrewdness and firm purpose. She was spoken of as "that bold woman," and Dr. Duke found, in Wiseman, a willing listener to his complaints where, a few months before, he would have received short shrift.

Melia, who had replaced Samuele Asperti as convent chaplain in May, 1850, when it became clear that Asperti was likely to offend the parish of St. Leonards as grievously as he had that of Derby, was Wiseman's protégé and a lover of intrigue. He was an exiled Italian Jesuit of great charm and wit, an able supporter of Cornelia's singing and artistic ventures, and very helpful in translating the rules of the Society into Italian for the benefit of Propaganda. He was a good confessor and theologian and a lively orator whose speeches were adorned by sweeping gestures and malapropisms which delighted his audience more than they distressed them. His exhortation to "plaster the congregation" and his suggestion that on rogation days "we will run about the fields" caused less dismay than his remark in a Sunday sermon that he had seen "ladies taking ass rides on the sands," but he remained confident that he would be understood in spite of a language that was "too stout to be masticated." At first he had been in charge of both school and parish, but, after the preliminary skirmishes, it soon became evident that two chaplains were needed, and might even diminish the difficulties, and Mr. Foy was appointed. They did not, in fact, do so and it was with a sense of shock that Cornelia learned from Sir George Bowyer two years later that a great many troubles had emanated from and been aggravated by Melia, whose good faith she had never doubted. The revelation was unkind but it explained a lot. As Bowyer wrote from the Temple on March 30, 1854, "for the last two years Dr. Pius Melia has to my certain knowledge been trying to have you removed from St. Leonards, and the Cardinal's feeling against you which I have heard him express is all derived from Dr. P. M. . . . I have said nothing of certain particular charges which Dr. Melia made to me against you, for no one would believe them. I refer to matters in the house which if true would show an utter disregard for decency. I never believed them myself, and indeed they first began to open my eyes to the real character of the man. But I have said that to my certain knowledge he has been a bitter enemy of yours, with the Cardinal especially. . . . I trust this will be a favorable turn in your affairs and that it will show how ill-used you have been—by unmasking your principal enemy. Dr. Duke is still entirely under the influence of Dr. P. M. He wrote a letter a few months ago which I did not condescend to answer, in which he warned me against you."

In the same words, Sir George Bowyer, whom Wiseman thought "most timid, takes always the darker view, and has great awe of the majesty of the law," seconded Cornelia to

Monseigneur Talbot, the papal nuncio, and tried to neutralize the letters that poured in against her from Dr. Duke to the Holy See and to Propaganda.

But before the situation reached this stage, and before Cornelia went to Rome to plead for her rule, which she did in 1854, the future looked dark. Once again Cornelia faced the prospect of resignation and departure. And then, at the eleventh hour, the situation was retrieved. News came from Rome, in the spring of 1852, that the district of Southwark, to which St. Leonards belonged, had been withdrawn from the jurisdiction of Westminster and Dr. Grant appointed its Bishop. Relieved of the property as a diocesan responsibility, Wiseman relented slightly towards Cornelia and wrote, in answer to her suggestion of a visit of reconciliation, that he hoped to come later "to show how little anything that has occurred has altered my feelings towards the community to which I send my cordial blessing." But the relationship was never the same and Wiseman could not resist the parting injunction to Cornelia in the same letter: "The more you adhere to the principles of the Church in what regards obedience, discretion, and close adherence as between religious and their superiors the more you will flourish and be blessed." With some aloofness he maintained that "as to myself I have, and have had, no personal feelings in anything that has happened. I have been anxious about the house, feeling much responsibility for the share I have taken in its foundation. But about myself I have remained indifferent." But it was clear that he was hurt, and he continued to place implicit trust in Melia as a mediator as his letters to Manning from 1861 to 1862 show. It was for him a period of ill-health and ill-temper. He complained of his own fretfulness over trifles, his loneliness and overwork, of being generally misunderstood. His capacity and enthusiasm for his various projects was, however, unimpaired and he accepted Manning's stricture, in December of 1863, on another matter with a good grace: "Happily our Master takes better care of you than to give you your way in everything." Unfortunately, his attitude to Cornelia was not improved by Sir George's efforts. He was still writing angrily in 1862, as a letter he wrote Manning from Leyton shows. "I must solemnly

make my protest if I write to Propaganda against the scandals
likely to come if visitation and correction by a stronger hand
than the Bishop of Southwark (at whom Mrs. C. laughs and
who seems afraid of her) and of the Bishop of Birmingham
(whom I understand she boasts of having twisted round her
fingers) be not soon made. In June the convent, if not barred
by the Holy See, will have most unjustly seized what Mr. Jones
intended for the mission. Can you not rouse the Holy Father
about the Matter [Manning was in Rome]. He abhors such a
state of things so much."

It was a strangely unbalanced letter for Wiseman to write
even allowing for the fear of scandal he had come to dread
and for the personal irritation he now felt towards Cornelia.

By this time (1861–64) the war was in its second stage under the calmer auspices of Dr. Grant, the new Bishop of Southwark. Grant was a gentle and scrupulous man to whom any
decision was an agony. At one time he was so racked by doubts
of his motives and duties that he went to confession several
times a day. He was a scholar and an introvert who inherited
few of the physical traits of his father, who had been a sergeant in the Seventy-First Highlanders at Waterloo. But he
bore with great humility and cheerfulness his physical sufferings from neuralgia and pains in the chest as well as the tor-
ture of his own scruples. It was only just before his death that
the pernicious form of cancer from which he had suffered all
his life was discovered. His indecisiveness irritated Wiseman
on the one hand as much as it worried Cornelia on the other.
"Dr. Grant as usual suggesting some verbal emendations,
mostly if not all wrong," Wiseman wrote testily to Manning.
To Cornelia he was a man not slow in delegation but, worse
still, slow in authority. His exacting desire for detail, his meticulous interpretations, his deliberate justice often caused her
weeks of unnecessary waiting and suspense. He was, too, in-
clined to be forgetful and on one occasion she wrote impa-
tiently: "You are mistaken in saying that I named the 29th,
I have your Lordship's letter before me dated December 11th
to Mr. Wenham in which you say 'Will you write to Reverend
Mother to fix December 29th and 30th as the days for the
Queens Scholars.' Everybody has been expecting Mr. Wen-

ham all day as it is the 29th, but we shall be equally ready next Monday. . . . Secondly, your Lordship is also misinformed, or mistaken, in saying that I left three letters unanswered. I left *one* unanswered because I *could not* answer. . . ."

But far from laughing at him, she loved and admired him. As a Bishop he was a cause of worry and anxiety, but as a man a source only of courage and the love of God. Ullathorne was still Bishop of Birmingham and he was not a man to be lightly twisted round anyone's little finger.

Dr. Grant and Richard Roskell, Bishop of Nottingham and "the best Bishop in Europe," according to Colonel Townley, were two of the original trustees to the Deed of Trust drawn up by Colonel Townley on his inheritance in 1851. With the years, Grant veered in the direction of Dr. Duke, who never ceased trying to convince the Bishops that Cornelia was a selfish autocrat out to undermine parish work in England. Dr. Roskell remained all along on Cornelia's side, and it was in fact he who won the final battle for her.

In 1858, Grant, with his genius for choosing the middle way, suggested to Cornelia that the most tactful way out of the St. Leonards dilemma, since neither side was willing to yield an inch over their claims, was to volunteer to build a separate church for the congregation. For seven years Cornelia had refused to contribute towards such a project. During those seven years she had built a presbytery to house the convent and mission chaplains and had supported the existing chapel and mission priest to the tune of £1,500—an amount which exceeded the sum originally sunk in the All Souls building by Dr. Duke's subscribers. She doubted if a congregation mostly made up, now that royalty had dwindled, of laborers and summer visitors, could afford it. "If the boys' school cannot be kept up for want of funds, how are all the expenses of candles, wine, washing of church linen, repairs, the sacristan's wages and choir, to be kept up—costing not less than £200 per annum?"

But time, the growing success of her order which brought with it financial compensation, and the desire to be out of the impasse weakened her determination. She suggested a site to Grant and offered to contribute £500 towards its building.

Her offer was not accepted by Dr. Duke, who was not out for compromise, or acknowledged by Propaganda, to whom she also sent it.

Dr. Duke, in spite of the fact that he had chosen to send his own daughters to All Souls, now took up the cudgels in earnest once more. In January, 1859, he appealed to Propaganda against the Deed of Trust because "upon the strength of the Deed the religious have made themselves masters of everything . . . they have alienated the property to uses of their own never contemplated by the late Reverend J. Jones." Propaganda ignored this petition—as it did its successors sent in October, 1860, and May, 1861. Used to English quarrels and wary of interfering in them, Propaganda had found that a policy of nonintervention often provided the best solution.

In refusing Cornelia's offer towards a separate mission church, to be built on a site beside the presbytery she had already built for the two chaplains, Duke was refusing any agreement whatsoever short of total capitulation.

In 1862 the joint-occupation clause was due to expire. This was a clause inserted in Townley's Trust Deed, and one which possibly Dr. Grant, as one of the trustees, had introduced, since it did not meet with Colonel Townley's own approval. It specified a length of time in which the convent and the mission were to share occupation of the conventual property so as to give them plenty of opportunity for reaching an amicable agreement about the future.

This they had failed to do. Dr. Duke now doubled his efforts and censures and helped lodge an appeal to the trustees to extend the period of joint occupation for another five years. Cornelia wrote to Grant to say she was praying that the extension would not be given and promising him that "you shall have much more for this mission than this grant of extension would give you. You seem to think we do not care for the mission. But my Lord you are wrong. We have always had the mission at heart, and when matters are depending upon our good will you shall indeed prove the truth of our sincerity." "How," she adds, "your Lordship can suppose that we can love

God and not care for the good of the souls around us, I have never understood."

Dr. Duke's last petition was before Propaganda, and the Cardinal was inauspiciously in Rome. On July 10, 1862, Propaganda declared "it is obliged to finish the church with the goods proceeding from Mr. Jones, etc.," and sided unconditionally with Dr. Duke. Colonel Townley published a rejoinder to say such a decision had no validity as the property was his. Bishops Ullathorne and Roskell supported him.

Cornelia's efforts at compromise had been repeatedly turned down. As a last bid for peace she wrote to Grant in September, 1862: "If we ourselves offer to build a church by the east side of the presbytery, not as an act of retribution, but as a gift to the diocese, would it be accepted at Rome? If you think it would be accepted will you make the offer? Or if your Lordship doubts the acceptance as a *free gift* will you know for certain whether it would be accepted or not? I think there would be no doubt of our being able to build a church that would be double the size at present required, for £1,000 or £2,000. Our present chapel cost £600." She did not wish the church built near the convent with easy access to the town; young men were already lolling against the outside convent walls on Sundays, smoking and, no doubt, leering at the girls. With this provision, that it be built as far away as the borders allowed, she would offer, as well, "an annual sum of £30 out of whatever income or donations we may receive" to meet "the additional expense which would fall on the mission" by separation, and promised to supply "vestments, altar linen, and plate."

Her offers were ignored. Her letters to Propaganda remained unanswered. She felt she could no longer bear the disapproval of her ecclesiastical superiors and wrote to Colonel Townley: "We are quite willing the property should be sold and the community transferred elsewhere rather than continue in our present state incurring the dissatisfaction of Rome, subject to constant misrepresentation and most injurious persecution here."

But once more, at the last moment, relief was forthcoming. In 1864 Bishop Roskell went to Rome and laid the case history before Propaganda. Having considered all the facts, Propaganda reversed the decision of 1862 and accepted Cornelia's latest offer. What delighted Cornelia was that "Propaganda says that no obligation whatever rests upon you [Colonel Townley] or the nuns to finish the church or to provide in any way for the mission . . . so . . . whatever you or we do in carrying out our offer is done freely and we become benefactors by our deeds." There would be no more doubts about her motives now.

Only the matter of Mr. Foy, who had reviled Cornelia steadily over the years (the only fact we know about him), remained. Dr. Melia had been recalled in 1854 for another post. Cornelia would have preferred Mr. Foy removed, "since it is no small matter to have to serve a priest daily in the sacristy for six years who has been acting openly as well as secretly against the reputation of the community." But this she knew the Bishop would not tolerate. For the rest she wanted no public apologies, beyond having the new decision made public as soon as possible. This was done and the struggle over. But the seeds of distrust were too deeply planted to wither away completely.

In May, 1866, the new mission church was consecrated by Dr. Grant and an impressive sermon preached by Manning. But Dr. Duke was not there to see the church in which he was so painfully interested. He had died in 1864. Four years later, in 1868, the convent church was finished and St. Theophila safely laid to rest in it. Although the mission church was, as Cornelia desired, at the edge of the convent boundary, only a road served as protection against the lolling youths and separated the two churches—a lasting symbol of the split that had brought them both about.

Chapter 11

A WIDER FIELD

AT FIRST there was never a shortage of poor schools to take over, or children to educate, outside St. Leonards. The only difficulty was to provide the nuns.

Newman had written in the autumn of 1849 asking the Holy Child nuns to help in Birmingham, and had even proposed sending several suitable young women as postulants to help swell the numbers. Cornelia could not accept the offer. It was not in the spirit of her order to accept candidates from expediency and with no facility for testing their vocation. She felt, too—as she did so often in the early years—that the work would be too active for young nuns and give them too little time in which to practice their spiritual life. Having no older nuns to spare, she was forced to refuse—"for two years at any rate." "I am afraid you could not possibly wait two years for us. It is not likely nor reasonable that you should."

But by 1851, when Wiseman asked her to send a contingent to help his Gate Street schools in Lincoln's Inn Fields, she was able to agree—although the Reverend Mother would only be twenty-two and the life extraordinary. The convent was to be housed in a narrow, dingy London house, and the nuns were to live in the attic and basement, for the six floors dividing them were already occupied by classrooms. Cornelia took her first volunteers, chosen with some difficulty since her entire order volunteered for the job, to London to settle them in. They left St. Leonards on February 27, after a parting speech from Father Pius Melia, who exhorted them not to expect "a house like your castle in the sea."

His warning, if curiously worded, was apt. The nuns, who had only a small allowance on which to live, given them out of the convent treasury, were often too poor to eat much more than a breakfast of bread and dripping, weak tea or coffee, and, on most days, a lunch of the same. But their zeal was undeterred and their venture a success. Their numbers had soon to be increased, for requests poured in for their assistance. And though Cornelia had to refuse many of these, she did consent to two other schools of a similar nature in Bunhill Row and Baldwin Gardens—and later on in the fifties to three other schools, as well as to a day school for young ladies in Bentinck Street. But the main body of nuns still lived in Gate Street and went out daily. As they could not afford bus fares, this meant they had several miles a day to walk. And to do so they had to abandon their habits and put on civilian clothes, for, in those days, to wear a religious habit in the streets of London would be to merit anything from a flow of obscene language to a pelting with mud and stones.

As there was no money with which to buy extra clothes, the nuns had to fall back on combining the most useful garments they could muster from among those they had all arrived in as postulants. The old-fashioned, ill-assorted, and oddly shaped clothes they went out in provided the only light relief they were likely to get. One extravagance Cornelia insisted upon—boots and mackintoshes. She worried about their long, cold walks in fog and snow. "Let me hear how you are and what you are doing about your cloaks, etc.," she wrote. "I think you will do much better to see at what price you can buy black waterproof cloaks ready made." But they were young and pioneering and she could not quite trust them to take care of themselves. Sending for samples of all the various makes of gabardine, she sent them her conclusions: "The enclosed is much the best, and it is waterproof. I have tried it for an hour and a half, pinned up double with a teaspoonful of water, which it held without being damped on either side." She wrote endless letters of comfort and advice, not only about their religious life but about their daily one. They were to be merry about their poverty but not careless about themselves. Their meals might be frugal but at least they could be hot and well cooked. But she disliked hampering her delegates with too many minute instructions and regulations. She provided the basic plan and encouraged them to develop it on their own initiative. "Pray about it and then let me know what you think." "Use your own judgment in this matter and write to me when you have decided." They must work hard and uncomplainingly, but never for too long. "If you feel able to run down to St. Leonards, come and get a change of air and plenty of good food. A fortnight here would set you up for the winter. Of course I do not say you *are* to come in obedience, as you are the best judge of your present state and of what would be best for you," she wrote on one occasion, and on another: "Send them down here for a week's rest as soon as the term is over. I will pay the fare if you cannot." The invitation was a frequent one.

In the early days, when money was always a great problem, Cornelia's delegates often tried to keep their financial worries from her. But she usually discovered them in the end, and once, when she did so, wrote: "Always be frank with me. Never leave me in the dark. If any still remains unpaid let me know at once, and what amount. Let me know also whether you are all sufficiently clothed for the winter, and if not what you really need." Another time she sent long, careful instructions on the best methods of banking and added, at the end: "I can assure you that the want of business knowledge but little becomes the heads of a Religious Order, and an indifference or carelessness on such points would be positively wrong."

Applications for more help continued to arrive—requests for schools in Blackpool and Preston, as well as for other schools in London. Some had to be turned down; others were accepted. They were all, to start with, poor schools, for, as Cornelia had encouraged Emily Bowles to write to Newman, their order was pledged to the Poor School Committee, which later became the Catholic Education Council. They were also in the experimental stage.

Preston was one of the first requests. It came from the Jesuits there as far back as 1848. But it was not until 1853 that Cornelia was able to send out a colony under the exceptionally able administration of Mother Lucy, a young woman who combined intelligence and calm efficiency in equal measure.

In November, 1852, a year after the first London founda-

tion, and before the Preston one, an application from Canon
Newsham of Liverpool for the nuns to take charge of the mission school, St. Anthony, promised greater scope. Cornelia decided to send her brilliant, delightful, but impractical Emily
Bowles, who shared with her the daring notion of one day
starting a training college. The idea was in its very first stages,
an embryo without basis in fact or likelihood, but a comfort
and an ideal in the rare moments of frustration and depression.

They had both nursed and enjoyed the prospect, but it had
come to assume for Emily an importance of which Cornelia
never dreamed.

Emily's first year with her five nuns in Liverpool proved as
successful as those of her contemporaries in London. Her
numbers were increased to seven and she was asked to take on
another local school. But success had come too soon. Without
Cornelia's restraint to temper her quick ambition Emily was
lost. She moved her community to too large a house, accepted
two more parochial schools, and began a school for young
ladies at the same time as, moving towards her dearest ambition, she asked Mr. Stokes, a Government Inspector, about
the possibility of establishing a training school. His approval
was given and the plans were begun.

But before they were completed disaster had set in. Cornelia, who had been given too optimistic reports, came on a
visit and saw that things were not as good as they should be,
administratively or financially. Emily, however, was as confident and plausible as always and, after discussion and a few
changes, Cornelia returned to St. Leonards. But there was still
too much work for the nuns to do and too few to do it. Something was bound to be neglected, and the examination results
of St. Anthony's proved it had been. Canon Newsham, furious, asked the nuns to withdraw. Emily, appalled by such
quick failure after such apparent success, fled to Cornelia for
advice and comfort. She was restored and sent straight back.
After her departure Cornelia wrote: "You wasted £5 in a useless journey here. Our feelings ought never to govern us. You
asked leave to come. But remember you came before it was

possible for me to answer your letter—only two hours before the post which brought it."

The withdrawal was a painful one, and Emily, impatient to make amends, begged Cornelia's permission to go ahead with her plans for the training college. As always her arguments were cogent and appealing. With many provisos Cornelia agreed to let her look for a suitable house, which on no account was to exceed £3,000, of which £1,300 would be guaranteed by Cornelia. She impressed upon Emily that the Society was poor and would have to borrow money for the purchase and pay annual interest upon it. It was always her maxim that the amount of any money borrowed (which did not belong officially to the community) should never exceed the value of a possible mortgage, and that individual responsibility should always be avoided. Several houses were considered and turned down, and it was at this stage, in 1854, that Cornelia was called to Rome to put her rule once more before Propaganda. She left Mother Lucy, who was also her Assistant General, in charge of the English houses.

It was unfortunate that her going coincided with Emily's craze for house-hunting and with the discovery of a particularly large and imposing building called Rupert House. It was the embodiment of Emily's dreams. It was also unfortunately in need of repairs which would bring its total cost to £5,000. But surely, Emily felt, it was the principle that counted, and if she undertook the transaction in the spirit Cornelia had advised an extra two thousand pounds would not matter so terribly. Convincing herself, she convinced Mother Lucy. Permission was granted and, acting joyously and immediately upon it, she borrowed £5,000 from her brothers on what was virtually an IOU, and purchased the property in the name of the nuns, who neither signed nor witnessed the deed, nor supplied a penny towards it. Emily herself paid several instalments of interest at four per cent to her brothers.

Cornelia, on her return after a weary and inconclusive visit, was alarmed and angered by such direct disobedience. She had failed to have her rule ratified, and Church law applying generally to convent property in England was not yet clearly defined. Uncertain of her position, she consulted Bishop Grant

and Emily's confessor. Both of them advised her that she had
no responsibility in the matter. She was not answerable for
what amounted to "a private act" between Emily and her
brothers.

The advice was sound but its effect was immediately spoiled
by the Bishop's urging Cornelia to patch up the peace and
preserve a working arrangement.

There seemed only one way of doing this, since Emily was
one of her nuns and was, in fact, already running Rupert
House as a training college—by not disclaiming the transaction
and by allowing Emily to go on with the college. But this
Cornelia felt she could not do unless Emily's brothers were
given some security for the money they had advanced merely
on Emily's written promise to pay. She therefore agreed that
Rupert House should be conveyed by mortgage to John
Bowles in order to secure the debt. But, because of the peculiar circumstances, the only personal liability she would allow
the nuns to incur was for payment of interest for one year.
Emily willingly agreed to this and a mortgage deed was
drawn up on this understanding and signed by both parties.

Under Emily's intense government the training college
lasted only two years. Troubles and debts increased. Emily's
disappointment, the second misfiring of her excited plans to
prove herself, and Cornelia's disapproval were too much for
her. With a sense of grievance she asked for a dispensation of
her vows and left the Society. When she left, the Sisters of
Notre Dame were asked to take over the training college, and
Rupert House was presumably sold to them for £2,000, since
Emily's original debt of £5,000 becomes £3,000 in the storm
ahead.

For Emily's departure was not the end of the story. Shortly
afterwards, urged on, somewhat unwillingly, by their sister's resentment, the Bowles brothers threatened proceedings
against the convent for the sums of money they had spent on
Rupert House.

It was with some dismay that Cornelia learned that they
did so on what she could only describe as "an inconceivable
dishonesty" on Emily's part. The mortgage deed which Emily
and the nuns had signed two years before, on the agreement

that the nuns would pay one year's interest, had contained an all-important error in Emily's favor. It was upon this error that the Bowleses' claim now rested. For the mortgage deed had not expressed the original agreement. It had contained instead a covenant requiring the nuns to pay principal and interest on the property in the usual way. (This covenant was normal procedure. The alternative to which Emily had agreed was exceptional.)

Cornelia was incensed, and with some justice, at Emily's behavior. The Bishop's advice had been that the original transaction was "a private act" between Emily and her brothers. She felt that her later attempt to give Mr. John Bowles some return for his loan was in fact founded upon a false representation and in consequence refused to pay the £3,000. The only sum she would agree to pay was the £1,300 she had originally agreed to guarantee for investment in real property for a training school.

But in this the Bishop would not support her. Worn out by the St. Leonards dispute, and constantly aggravated by minor disagreements which poured between them ("I see your Lordship has marked *Aikin's British Poets* as prohibited. As we are obliged to use it *daily* for the schools I have not withdrawn—am I to do so? It is not read by the children but simply for dictation and extracts"), he could not face the prospect of a further long-drawn-out legal squabble. For unless Cornelia publicly announced in court that the mistake in the deed was deliberate she was prima facie liable for the £3,000. In any case he felt that she was responsible for the debt since she had, however unwillingly, agreed to the transaction after the event and had, moreover, used Rupert House for two years.

It was ironic that the Bishop's desire for peace when Cornelia first returned from Rome, and her own desire to see justice done to Emily's brothers, had led her to such an impasse. She herself entirely failed to see or share the Bishop's point of view. She could not understand the reasoning that constituted his change of attitude from that of two years ago. Again and again she argued and pleaded her case. Why should she be liable for a debt which had been incurred against her wishes in the first place and been settled against her by a dishonest trick in the second?

But a decision had to be made. The Bishop finally refused her plea and ordered her to pay the debt in full. The convent was saddled with a heavy debt which was not finally paid off until 1871, and Cornelia with yet another black mark against her administration.

During all this time Cornelia's language was strong and decisive, her final submission to the Bishop an immense effort of will in the face of her conviction—which never altered to the day of her death.

To an outsider it is obvious that there were two points of view. And one cannot avoid the suspicion that the whole situation could have been avoided if only Cornelia, or her solicitor, had read the mortgage deed with sufficient care. But oddly enough, this suspicion does not appear to have occurred to the Bishop in his arguments against her, or to her lawyers who supported her desire to fight the case. Perhaps there was some circumstance, the details of which, like so many in this case, are lost and irretrievable, which accounted for such apparent carelessness.

In one event, at least, time proved Cornelia right—Emily had behaved very badly. For seven restless years she sought her vocation, first in another order and then in various good works among the poor. At the end of them she wrote to Cornelia, acknowledging her fault and begging for readmission. Cornelia was grateful for her letter, and for the chance of reconciliation, but she would not have her back, although she did not leave her uncomforted. "You have two great means of serving and pleasing Our Dear Lord, your works among the poor and your writings. I have just packed up a case of four dozen of your *History of England* to send to America, where it will be much relished." It was not an ungenerous acknowledgment considering the years of loss, anxiety, and damage to her reputation that Emily had caused.

It was the end to one of the most exacting phases of expansion, but it came at the beginning of another. For Emily's plea to return arrived only a few months after Cornelia had refused to admit another, and more august, candidate, Louisa Catharine, Duchess of Leeds.

The Duchess was a compatriot, a granddaughter of Charles Carroll of Carrollton, the last surviving signer of the Declaration of Independence. She had come to England in 1825 with her two beautiful sisters, and together they were soon known as "the three graces." Not slow in following a pattern familiar to beauties from across the Atlantic, the sisters all married English peers—the Marquis of Wellesley, Lord Stafford, and, at one remove, the Duke of Leeds. For Louisa Catharine's first marriage had not only been outside the peerage, but regrettably tainted with bad taste. Sir Felton Elwell Hervey Bathurst, Bart., had shot himself at breakfast one morning after remonstrating with his wife, with singular lack of success, about her frivolity. She considered his plea—that she should never dance with anyone but himself—remarkably ungracious, and so, in the course of time, became the seventh Duchess of Leeds. Her second husband was devoted to her, and even to her staunch brand of Catholicism. He put down one of his lucky escapes in the hunting field to a holy medal she had given him and some time later was received into the Church by Manning, whom he helped to earn, by becoming another tick on his list of converted aristocrats, the title of Apostle of the Genteels.

But the Duchess was soon left a widow for the second time, and in 1860 she and her sister, Lady Stafford, came down to St. Leonards to get some sea air. She was anxious to make the acquaintance of Cornelia, of whom she had heard a great deal and to whom she felt a curious attraction.

They met and, each recognizing in the other the same national characteristic of forthrightness, quickly became friends. The Duchess lost little time in asking to become a postulant. The picture of the autocratic old lady in the short-veiled youthful dress of the postulant was a slightly incongruous one, and not only the dress was incongruous. Cornelia explained to the Duchess how little suited she was. The Duchess replied that she would prove herself to the contrary and promptly embarked upon a most rigorous routine, rising at the same early hour as the nuns and obeying to the letter the routine of the day. The letter of the law was not, however, enough and the Duchess's idea of convent life decidedly *outré*. It took her some months to dismiss her coachman and carriage, which she kept at livery in the town, and longer to become reconciled to visiting her various charities in a hired cab.

A compromise was reached by which the Duchess did not become a nun but was allowed to live in a suite of rooms in the convent, from which she paid occasional visits to Hornby Castle, her home in Yorkshire. If she could not become Cornelia's disciple she would remain her patron, and it was in this role she saw herself—a role she played with a consistent mixture of generosity and eccentricity. She amused the nuns with her stories of the past, of how the Duke of Wellington once fell in love with her, and of the night she spoiled her complexion by eating too much ice cream after the heat of the ballroom. She thought nothing of ordering a tradesman back and forth from his shop seven times in an afternoon, or of rewarding him with an order for £70 at the end of it, but she was extremely shrewd about small expenses. "Don't call me Your Grace," she hissed in the ear of a small lay sister who accompanied her on a shopping expedition. "It'll put up the price."

She knew of Cornelia's desire to start a convent in America, which had become more pronounced since Cornelia's niece, Catharine Duval, had visited her a few months before, and the idea appealed to her. At the time Cornelia was negotiating with the Bishop of Melbourne about a foundation in Australia, but this would have meant the nuns' becoming farmers, and though Cornelia entertained the idea with her usual enjoyment—"We might purchase for a small sum 50 or 100 acres where they could raise their own sheep and supply their schools with butter and milk, and gradually build their convent"—it was not a very practical one and had to be abandoned. Reluctantly Cornelia put aside a book she had discovered which told her that "land could be purchased at 5s. or 10s. per acre" on the supposition that "this is only the wild parts of the country which will not do for a convent."

The Duchess's alternative was an attractive one. She had heard from her agent in Philadelphia and was able to offer the nuns a gift of 2,000 acres in Lycoming County and 150 in Towanda, Pennsylvania.

The American Civil War and Dr. Grant now intervened. Praying in the first case for "a just separation of North and South, being of such opposing interests," and in the second for a change of heart, Cornelia decided "to give up all intentions of going to America until the war is over."

But reports from the Duchess's agent sounded so idyllic, the property specially chosen for the convent perfectly situated and surrounded by Catholic families who, if poor, were numerous, the site four hundred miles away from the war and unlikely to be disturbed by it, that Cornelia's resolve began to weaken. The war might be ignored but not, unfortunately, Dr. Grant. Once more she set about changing his mind. "Do you think it reasonable My Lord to doubt the capability of supporting the community of five sisters, with a garden and fruit of five acres and two farms . . . our own property not an offer made to us." But his Lordship did. He viewed all Cornelia's enthusiasms with extreme caution, and this one in particular. He could not make up his mind. He did not want the nuns to travel alone; he did not want Cornelia to go with them; he did not think it wise with the war on and without their knowing exactly the conditions to which they were going; he was not altogether convinced by the agent's promises to fix furniture and prepare for the school and chapel, nor by Cornelia's foresight in ordering "about fifty dollars' worth of timber to be on the premises and dry, so as to be fit for use at the time of the arrival of our sisters."

The nuns had their trunks packed and were ready to sail before the Bishop finally made up his mind. As some American Bishops were returning to their sees by a convenient boat and could act as chaperons, he decided to let them go.

His caution proved well founded. The glorious welcoming picture painted by the Duchess's agent had no basis whatever in fact. The five nuns were introduced to Father Carter, the Vicar General of their new diocese, in Philadelphia, and it was he who drove them, curious and expectant, to Towanda. He left them with his blessing and some dollars. He had become at once their friend and supporter and without him they could not have survived. The land was unfertile and unused, the buildings old and neglected. The "mansion" of which the agent wrote so proudly was not as big or in as good condition as his own stables. Miserable and broken down, it was a frame building two stories high beneath a slanting and unplastered roof that had been for years the home of rats who were slow to relinquish their ownership. There was the minimum of furniture, no tables, and, downstairs, only one chair. The walls were unpapered and the foundations so unsafe, having given way in several places, that the workmen who were repairing the house were afraid every morning when they came to work that they would find the occupants buried beneath its ruins.

The nuns had meant to open a school at once, but instead they were obliged to spend the first weeks cleaning, painting, papering, and carpentering. They were amateur and clumsy and their efforts not only took longer but were not always successful. Their trestle table fell to the ground the first time it was called upon to bear any weight. But at last they gained a breathing space and were able, in a room lent by the agent, to start their parochial school of eighty boys and girls from six to sixteen, ignorant but eager to learn.

The convent school provided greater difficulty. It was opened but not a single child appeared. The nuns, nothing loath, went from door to door to find them.

There was little or no money—for the large income promised was as far from reality as the rest—and the poverty extreme. Father Carter's kind dollar bills pressed into the hand on a quick visit could always find a better use, in the nuns' view, than food. They went towards textbooks and improvements, and the staple diet remained thin pea soup.

The winter of 1862–63 was an unusually bitter one and the nuns were unprepared for it. The snow fell through the holes in the roof; the tears that ran down their cheeks from the intense cold on the way to daily Mass froze into tiny globules, and the wine in the chalice turned to ice.

But of this nothing, at first, reached Cornelia. The nuns joked and made light of their privations. The schools increased. A further contingent of nuns was sent for, and in 1863 set out. Father Carter wrote to Cornelia suggesting they should leave Towanda, but his, and his Bishop's, praises for what they had accomplished were so great that Cornelia, ignorant of the extent of their sufferings, wished them to remain. So did the Duchess, who had not yet learned of her agent's perfidy and was personally affronted by the idea of their going.

But in 1864 Father Carter could bear to watch them no longer. He wrote sternly to Cornelia to say that the convent at Towanda was "a miserable shanty far inferior to your stables and cow-houses in England." His sympathy with these women who had been gently nurtured in the soft, upholstered nurseries of Victorian England was great. "With regard to the sufferings and privations of the Sisters at Towanda during the last winter and part of this," he wrote, "God knows it was worthy of the Christians of the first ages of the Church. They have borne them with patience and resignation and never did I hear the least complaint, but they always carried cheerful and smiling countenances. I knew they could not be very flush for means, and for that reason I gave or sent them occasionally some little assistance. But it has only been within some few weeks that I began to suspect that they were deficient in necessaries. When I inquired I ascertained (not from the sisters) that some mornings when they got up they did not know where their breakfast would come from, and with regard to their bedding, they had to use their habits, cloaks, old pieces of carpet, etc. And even since, when I put the plain question on the subject, I got a smiling evasive answer. But I got sufficient and this determined me what course to pursue." Their health was failing and he must have replacements, for he did not wish to lose the benefits they had brought with them. Cornelia was unable to let him have replacements at that moment, but she agreed at once to let them leave Towanda and join a few of the number who had already started a new venture in Spring Garden Street, Philadelphia. The move did not come quite soon enough. Mother Mary Xavier became very ill indeed, and Mother Stanislaus Gray, one of the second detachment from England, unable to bear the severity of the winter, died of consumption.

Father Carter could not do enough for those who remained.

In May of 1864 he bought a beautiful old Quaker house at Sharon Hill in Delaware County, about six miles from Philadelphia, so that the children from the city could be educated away from it in the country, and gave it to the nuns.

In 1867 when Cornelia went on a visit to America, her two convents and their parochial schools were all doing well. She herself was able to open yet another in West Philadelphia. There was no longer any pressing need for replacements from England, as several Americans were already wanting to enter. Of the children Cornelia spoke to at Sharon Hill nine later became nuns there.

While Cornelia's pioneers were struggling to make good in Towanda and Philadelphia, in London and the North of England, another opening suddenly occurred. Like so many large events, its beginning was trivial and haphazard. It was the children who unwittingly brought it about. Clamoring to know where their annual Whit Monday picnic was to be, and eager that Cornelia should accompany them, they persuaded her to bring out a book of sketches of the ruins of Sussex, and to choose one. Her choice fell upon the Old Palace, Mayfield, the ancient country seat of the Archbishops of Canterbury. Its history stretched back into the tenth century, when St. Dunstan built a wooden church there to help civilize the swineherds in the surrounding forests. It was said that when he performed the ceremony of dedication he noticed, to his annoyance, that his church lay outside the line of sanctity— that it did not stand due east and west. Pressing it, therefore, with his shoulder, he moved it into the proper line of orientation, "the which that he easily effected," his awed chronicler remarks, "no one can doubt except he would incredulously oppose the words of Christ by which He promises to those who have faith as a grain of mustard seed, that they should transplant a mountain with a word." It was at Mayfield that St. Dunstan fought his many astounding battles with the devil, winning from him, on one occasion, the solemn promise that he would never enter any house where a horseshoe was hung outside.

It was St. Dunstan who conferred episcopal status on the church, and succeeding prelates added to it in size and splendor. When, in November, 1545, it was surrendered to the King by Thomas Cramer it was a rich and desirable gift. Afterwards it passed from hand to hand. Its first secular owner, Sir Edward North, sold it to Sir John Gresham, and there he entertained Queen Elizabeth. The curse on the spoliation of church property was, in this instance, remarkably effective. The Old Palace was sold again and again, crumbling with the years into disuse and ruin.

Cornelia first saw it on a sun-pricked summer day. The straggling village crowned with the ivy-covered broken walls appealed to the romantic in all the picnickers, the majority of whom had been nursed in the tradition of Gothic ruins—and Gothic the remaining walls showed themselves to be. Even Mr. Searle, Cornelia's present chaplain, professed himself delighted and, on their return, the Duchess was drawn into the general excitement.

A few months later the Old Palace farm of 119 acres, with a house of ten rooms, was announced for sale. The coincidence was too great. Cornelia, backed by Mr. Searle, begged permission to bid for it. Without hesitation the Bishop refused and, without temporizing, Cornelia obeyed. For once he gave her his wholehearted approval: "Your prompt obedience will be blessed by God."

But they had reckoned without the Duchess. Thanking God that no Bishop could interfere with her, she ordered her agent to secure the property at any cost. She had, however, no intention of sharing her prize with Cornelia, who was not, for the moment, in her good books. She had transferred her main affection to Mother Catharine Tracy after Cornelia had allowed her to take three of the nuns to Hornby Castle only on condition that they heard daily Mass, and had recalled them instantly when she learned they had not been given the opportunity to do so.

The Duchess quickly found herself in possession of the Old Palace farm, and in the unfamiliar, unpleasing circumstance of being a farmer. Dealing out weekly wages, instructions about livestock, and hop gardening soon began to pall. She looked round for a likely tenant but even among the religious orders she next solicited could find none who were willing to take on a property which included enormous ruins and a clause insisting upon their preservation. At last she appealed to Grant. It is easy to assume that his sense of humor got the better of him. Enjoying the reversal of normal procedure, he refused the gift and suggested she should offer it to Cornelia.

The Duchess returned to the convent to brood. Pious, peremptory, and capricious, the Duchess did not take kindly to persuasion. But after giving the matter some thought she decided to act on the Bishop's advice and hand over the Old Palace to Cornelia. She would make only one condition: that Cornelia should not be content with preserving the ruins—she must restore them. A reconciliation was effected and the property transferred.

It was not the only reconciliation it effected. For Wiseman, on hearing that Cornelia meant to begin the restoration at once, was delighted. The restoration of the ancient shrines of England was one of his favorite ambitions. Letters of congratulation and suggestion flowed in once more. In spite of the Sussex Archæological Society, who resolutely opposed the idea, Edward Welby, son of Augustus Welby Pugin, was invited to design the restorations. Happily, for their liking was instantaneous and mutual, he and Cornelia settled into discussions of architecture and niceties about cornices and her wish to avoid the cloisters becoming a "rope-like looking thing."

As usual, money provided the great difficulty. How to raise enough? Bazaars and sales of work only touched the fringes. The Home Secretary was approached and agreed to a glorified form of raffle called A Drawing of Prizes for which eighty thousand tickets were issued and sent all over the world. The answers were so many that the local postmistress was forced to toil up the hill with a wheelbarrow every day. Wiseman suggested that the nuns should beg for alms in Europe, and during the holidays Cornelia sent her nuns through Holland, France, Belgium, and Spain. She was surprised at their success. Gradually, the restoration progressed and the convent filled.

But the Duchess's good works did not stop with Mayfield.

Before her sister's death she had bought two other properties in Sussex which she intended to become orphanages. One of these she had entrusted to the Xaverian brothers for boys; the other she wished Cornelia to run under Mother Catharine. Cornelia agreed in spite of Lady Stafford, who, on the eve of death, roused herself to say: "Mother Catharine, have nothing to do with Lou's orphanage, or your hair will turn gray before its time." This was to be the Duchess's pet project, and she brooded over it with an intense and personal interest. Under her sovereignty nothing but a sense of humor could have survived. The housekeeping might have been invented by Lewis Carroll for another story. Always anxious to be generous, the Duchess was equally concerned with not being made to appear a fool. She refused all counsel and advice. Asked for pepper, she would order a hundredweight but forget the bread; she ordered salt in such quantity that it was built into a wall which reached the ceiling and extended the whole length of the kitchen. She quickly became suspicious on hearing that the nuns had gone out to buy a few cents worth of caraway seed for a picnic cake and to prevent a repetition ordered a ton of spices which was still being used in 1907. Refusing to allow more than two packets of sewing needles for the entire establishment, she would exact a minute account of their use. When the orphans suffered an attack of scarlet fever she forbade the local doctor to go on attending them as she considered his first bill too high. Instead, she sent for a resident doctor at more than double the cost. About chickens she felt particularly strongly. Although at St. Leonards she kept five hens and a Dorking cock to ensure the freshness of her morning egg, she did not like the orphanage to keep hens. They might constitute a slight on her housekeeping—the orphans "will only eat my food." Before her visits the few recalcitrant hens were stuffed quickly away in a box. But on one unforgettable occasion she saw a hen stalking slowly across the yard at the boys' orphanage and her rage was great. Whether it put an end to the brothers' secret activity, it is now too late to learn.

But to the orphans themselves she was kind and gentle,

although she had a weakness for a pretty face and always made their good appearance a condition of entry.

After her death it was discovered that the money she had promised to leave for the upkeep of the girls' orphanage came nowhere near what she had promised. It was so little that pupils who were not orphans had to be accepted, and gradually the nature of the orphanage changed and so did its site. It was moved first to Mark Cross and later to Combe Bank, near Sevenoaks, where it survives today in its altered form.

When Mayfield and Mark Cross settled into running order Cornelia turned her thoughts to France. This was to be her last adventure, and it began in the winter of 1867, when she was sent by her doctor to Hyères to recover from a serious illness. Cornelia had always wanted to have a house in a Catholic country "where the blood of martyrs has so lately been shed, and where there is so strong a spirit of fervor and zeal," and she looked upon Hyères with the eye of a prospective inhabitant. But it did not prove suitable, and while she was there her attention was directed towards Toul. A house was duly rented in Toul, and a small group of nuns moved in in July, 1870.

But their first efforts at establishment were a failure. A contingency for which they had not allowed interrupted them—the Franco-Prussian War. The nuns were forced to leave and, though they returned in 1871, the convent did not prosper. It started, for the second time, with difficulties when the nuns had to travel there from England via Belgium, instead of Paris. For it was early in 1871 and the Paris Commune, strengthened by the declaration of its manifesto in April, was defending Paris house by house, street by street, against French troops of the National Assembly, whose numbers had had to be increased, with Bismarck's permission, from 80,000 to 150,000 men. The bloodshed and smoking ruins of a fierce civil war, conducted under the sardonic gaze of the Prussian occupier, provided a strange comment on the courage of a people who had withstood a four-month siege only a few weeks before and eaten the rats in the sewers, as well as the elephant in the Zoo, rather than let the aggressor in.

The Toul convent, shaken in its beginnings, never got properly under way. The war left little prosperity in its wake and pupils were not forthcoming. Cornelia decided to withdraw.

It was not until the third opportunity presented itself, five years later in 1876, that she achieved success. It came, innocently enough, in the form of an advertisement. An old dusty envelope was discovered one day in an unused mailbox in the house where the nuns were living and brought to Cornelia. It contained a description of a property for sale in Paris. By a coincidence the property was still for sale. It was the Petit Château of the Duc d'Orléans, a curious mixture of royal splendor and dilapidation, housing the room where the Comte de Paris was born and the underground passage from the Tuileries through which Louis Philippe made his escape when he left the throne of France in 1848. More recently, in 1871, the tops of the trees in the garden had been shot off by the cannon from Mont Valérien during the siege of Paris. And in the polished oak floors of one of the downstairs rooms were holes made by the troops of Prussian horse. The Petit Château and The Pavillon were all that remained of the once magnificent Orléans Palace. The Grand Château had been burned to the ground during the war, and the estate sold in building lots.

Cornelia managed to rent the property for a period of three years, since the price asked freehold, twenty thousand pounds, was far above the convent means or the possibility of a loan. It was not until after her death that the price was reduced to nearly half the original sum, and the nuns were able to buy it.

The Petit Château at Neuilly was not only Cornelia's last personal foundation but her favorite. She had only one regret —that, unlike its counterparts in England, it had no poor school attached.

In January, 1877, Cornelia helped a group of her nuns to move in and take possession. She remained for three months before returning to England and the last years of her life. They were three months of new ideas and hard work—a combination she always found irresistible. When she had left, frequent injunctions to struggle on with the French language, and more particularly its verbs, flowed back to her nuns in Neuilly. She missed it sadly, her beloved Paris, for, as she wrote, "Paris is full of life and energy, the most beautiful place in the world."

Chapter 12

THE REVEREND MOTHER

THE YEARS after 1850 seem to have been so full that, reading through old letters, the impression is one of long and constant struggle, of endless skirmishes over housekeeping and chaplains, of litigation over finance and property. So much so, in fact, that one is not surprised to learn that Cornelia's spiritual notes, her encouragement and consolation, were written on any small scraps of paper that came to hand and often most incongruously. It is only surprising that so much could have been fitted into the life of a woman who, by rule, spent five hours a day in prayer and, by choice, was known to become so absorbed in meditation during extra visits to chapel that she had to be reminded to lead her nuns out.

And yet she was seldom disturbed by activity. She never appeared hurried or anxious. To the hundred minor interruptions and irritations of the day she presented an imperturbable calm; to more important calls on her sympathy and advice, in loneliness, doubt, or sickness, she gave her complete attention. Those who came to her "were made to feel as if she had nothing in the world to do but attend to their concerns." Those in her schools knew nothing of the frequent controversies which were concealed by her apparent calm, the defense and explanations she was forced to give to her Bishops; of the depth of the mistrust and, in places, dislike in which she was held; of the uncertainty about her rule which shadowed her last years and which, as it was slowly played out between Southwark and Rome, kept her in suspense until the day of her death.

It is curious how great the discrepancy was between the opinion of those who knew her within her convents and those who saw or heard about her from without. To the inmates she was a mother, a counsellor, and a friend. To those outside she was a tiresome, bold woman who gave no quarter and expected none; who was ruthless in her will and resolute in obtaining it.

About one thing, however, both would have agreed. Cornelia was not, and never had been, introspective. She did not know the paralyzing effects of doubt, the fearful hesitancy of choice. This was her strength. To others, who did not share her strength of purpose, it often smacked of obstinacy and pride, but they ignored her simplicity. She was a woman for whom, in spite of an excellent intelligence, life, in the light of God's love, was very simple and any abasement which was not true humility, false. She did not understand the humility of pretense, the mock self-deprecation which so often passes as a substitute. This made her a stern critic, of herself and others, but never a sentimental one. As she grew older she would often say, "I have changed my opinion," and her sigh of relief was almost audible. She was glad to be able to change her mind, delighted that another conviction had superseded her own and that, in obeying it, she was more likely to be doing God's will. When this happened she was as quick in apology as to make amends. But each occasion was judged on its merits by her shrewd precise mind and she was not always confident that she had reason for apology. "I was astonished at her calmness," wrote one of her nuns, "when I had repeated to her some very strong statements, which I believed were correct, about something she had done. After listening quietly to all I had to say, she replied, 'Well, my dear, on looking back over the circumstances I think if they occurred again I should do just the same.'"

She could be, and often was, a stern disciplinarian. "Mother Connelly looks as if she must be obeyed," wrote a gay, beautiful, spoiled young woman, Annie Laprimaudaye, staying with her parents in Rome while Cornelia spent her first visit (in 1854) pleading for her rule. But like so many others she fell under Cornelia's spell and, feeling that same thrilled desire to please her, joined her order and maintained her affection.

Kind, and sometimes overindulgent to both nuns and children, Cornelia was instantaneous and exacting whenever she sensed a deliberate evasion or denial of duty. One of her young nuns, who was both amusing and fond of being amused, hated the ending of recreation in the afternoon and would try to draw it out over the hour. Not, however, for long. One afternoon in summer when they were having recreation out of doors Cornelia called her as the nuns filed into the house and asked her to stay behind in the garden, where she would return and speak to her. Three hours later another nun reminded Cornelia that she was still in the garden, waiting where she had been told: "Mother have you forgotten Sister X?" "No," she replied, "I have not forgotten, but I wish you all to remember." It was the same with another of her nuns who produced for her pleasure a beautiful piece of pointlace she had done during the hour for tatting (a peculiarly dull form of lace-work which had been temporarily revived). "Who gave you leave to do this instead of tatting?" she asked, and the quietness of her voice would have warned those who knew her better. But the nun was young and undismayed by protocol. "Oh, nobody," she answered, and stood by, her nonchalance waning, as her careful, precious lace was thrown into the fire.

Severities like these were the exception, not the rule. "Stiffness and rigor," Cornelia wrote, "will not bring forth love, and these are not the spirit of the Holy Child," necessary as they sometimes might be, in starting and maintaining a new order, to instill the principles of obedience. Her own obedience to her ecclesiastical superiors, and her attitude to authority, seem to have been the same as Newman's to the governing body of the Church—to fight to the last ditch, as Newman did over the definition of infallibility, but in the final instance and in the face of an absolute definition or command, to accept. Clear-sighted, determined, and sometimes angry, Cornelia argued and denied, but she always obeyed. In argument it was her peculiar and unfeminine trait to present both sides of a case so clearly that, until the summing up, her audience sometimes did not guess on which side she would come down. And it was this quality that appealed to her lawyers and, in the end, to several of her adversaries who came over to her side, although it was often her great personal charm that finally persuaded them. As is true of all leaders, Cornelia's personal influence was great. She exercised over a great number of people a fascination which even those who disliked her found hard to resist. "If you listen to the Superior, instead of to facts," wrote Dr. Duke angrily in 1854, "she will persuade you out of your senses as she has done others." Cornelia recognized her own powers of persuasion and, over religious matters, feared them. She would refuse to interview any possible candidates until they had already been seen by someone else, and whenever a possible vocation was discussed, as discussed it would be among women whose life it was, she would say at once: "Leave her to God." In the same way, once she had gathered round her a nucleus and was able to make her own rules of entry, she disliked choosing the very young and preferred them to have done other things or to have remained with their family for as long as they were needed. For marriage, as an alternative, she had the highest respect. "I am much interested in poor Sybil," she wrote of a girl whose engagement had just been broken, "but I do *not* believe in her religious vocation. Why not go to India and marry again?"

For those she allowed to join she had certain basic standards, and, curiously enough, and unlike other superiors, good health was not one of them. She felt that the delicate had often a stronger will towards good and startled one of her sisterhood by asking one day: "How often do you thank God for being delicate?" There was no reply since the thought had never occurred, and she went on: "My child, you have the help of a constant reminder that you are on the way to God." She had no great regard for unusual talents—Emily Bowles had foundered upon hers—and it was her belief that given willingness and a sound judgment anything could be accomplished. "Test the vocation, not the talents," she advised her superiors. Writing about one candidate, she says she may come if she has "good common sense as well as piety." In spite of her own leanings towards the artistic—which went to the length of disliking ugly toys for the children—she had "constantly in view that our novices must never forget that the vineyards of the Holy Child Jesus require ardent and earnest laborers and not devout statues." She was frequently surprising her nuns with new ideas which she was at once confident they could put into effect. Usually her confidence inspired them to succeed. She never allowed a beginner to feel herself a failure. That would be to multiply useless members in the Society. If, after encouragement, a nun proved herself no good in a particular capacity she was transferred to another, but not before she had been helped "to succeed a little better first, to restore her confidence . . . we must not make her failure the evident reason of the change." Her nuns must be humble in the eyes of God but they owed it to Him to have confidence in themselves. And yet behind Cornelia's love of progress and her sense, which she shared most strongly with her age, of a new and exciting world unfolding, she was no muddled enthusiast. She was meticulous in defining and distributing the duties of each office, and was often heard to say that almost all disturbance in a community could be avoided if each member of it knew clearly what work was expected of her.

At first Cornelia herself was everything, prefect, infirmarian, cook, laundress, and in fact till her rheumatism crippled her she helped with the weekly laundry, dusted the stairs, and served at table. She liked all her nuns to help in the housework even when their numbers had increased and enabled them to hold individual offices. As cook, in the days of large, farinaceous meals, she wrote out careful lists of balanced sensible diets and superintended the kitchen closely. In the early days, when many of those who entered her order had never even boiled an egg, and before there were as many lay as choir nuns, she wrote out instructions as full as those for her classrooms and underlined them in her decisive hand, "*Salt meat* should *never boil*, it should *simmer briskly*, this will make it tender." Again and again she urges that, however poor the nuns, the children must always be properly fed and the nuns themselves eat pleasantly even if frugally. The dishes must always be hot, the saucepans properly "scoured with vinegar and salt immediately before being used," and the tea freshly made. "It is not allowed to boil tea, nor to put fresh tea on old leaves." Her instructions overflowed into her letters, and in 1872 she was writing to Sister Dunstan "regarding the meat, I told you that the fat is bad and only fit to make night lights. But the meat and the jelly make excellent soup and curry on rice." To her superiors she insisted that "a religious *may* become not only immortified but even gluttonous if not checked in the love of eating, but all that is *necessary* for *health* and *strength* we are bound to secure for them." There is a faint still echo of the *Ancren Riwle* in the first half of this sentiment.

Infirmarian was the job Cornelia liked best. She was intensely interested in the medical and psychological aspects of health and herself a confirmed homeopath always ready with a small remedy to give or send to her nuns. "I wish you could tell me that you are taking Calcarea Carbonica and sulphur, alternately every three hours, and if in pain with your swollen cheek take four globules of Pulsatilla. I am sure you would soon drive out the Erysipelas from your blood," or to Sister Dunstan about one of her lay sisters, "If you rubbed her with a Belladonna lotion mixed with chloroform it would relieve the pain almost immediately." Somewhere in a medicine chest she had pencilled one of her brisk notes—"Brandy only for sickness"—but she was as great a believer in wine and brandy as recuperative agents as she was in fresh food and air. To Sister Dunstan in 1871 she wrote: "If you would try the cod liver oil three times a day with Sister Edward and leave off all study, letting her walk out in the garden, and take two fresh eggs for breakfast and watch over her in this way, perhaps she might get rid of her cough." Poor Sister Dunstan, to whom so many of these letters were written, was not of a practical turn of mind. When another nun had left a pillow behind on a visit, Cornelia, on her return to St. Leonards, wrote: "Mother Theresa is expecting the little pillow by post which she left—you can tie it up tight in a roll and then put paper around it with ends open." If genius is attention to detail, then Cornelia had it in large measure.

In the field of medicine it received special scope. All her sickrooms were to be light and full of sun and flowers. Cornelia visited them as often as she could when she was not herself acting infirmarian. She was as quick in detecting a real sickness, of mind or body, in her nuns as she was slow in noticing a feigned one and would immediately suggest a change of air or occupation or a proper cure. To those who were really ill—and several suffered and died from the prevailing disease, consumption—she gave her whole time, often sitting up all night or, on one occasion, bringing a young novice to sleep in the room beside her so that she could hear her coughing and sleeplessness and comfort her. When any of them died she was always with them at the last with her queer mixture of vigor and gentleness which, in another context, describing to her nuns what she wished them to achieve, she called "loving in strength rather than in too much sweetness."

To achieve this there was much to learn beyond discipline of the flesh and of the desires. Meditation and prayer have their own complicated and extremely delicate mechanisms. Cornelia was sympathetic with those who found they weighed too hard upon a spirit that longed to soar. She was able to say to a novice bewildered by the mechanics of meditation, and anxious to know if she could begin the colloquy sooner than the book advocated: "Make it all colloquy, my dear child, if you like and follow the leading of the Holy Spirit." But she had a horror of unenlightened devotion. Her discourses were carefully prepared from St. Thomas Aquinas, St. Francis of Sales, St. Ignatius Loyola, and others of the great saints. She was meticulous in basing her spiritual teaching on the great masters of the Church and, curiously, in this field she lacks originality. "She wrote," as her first biographer, a nun of her order, said, "hastily on any small scrap of paper, putting down in un-self-conscious and homely phrase just what she wanted to say and no more. Sometimes a sentence stands out almost epigrammatic in its conciseness and exact expression of a spiritual or psychological truth; at other times thought outruns expression and the sentence trails confusedly off. And sometimes it must be confessed, the influence of the florid or sententious Victorian idiom makes itself felt." It was as if here she felt herself in all humility a disciple inheriting the vast treasure of the Church to which her own lately acquired understanding would have added little. It was her business to interpret and paraphrase the Fathers of the Church, and if she did so unimaginatively her notes bear testimony to the fact that she did so with all her customary vigor.

Now that she was a Superior, in charge of a growing order, she felt, as Bishop Flaget had felt in her regard, a terror of restraining the ardent, of spoiling because of the many the chances of the one. "Be careful," she wrote to one of her superiors, "not to thwart in others desires for higher things. You may be thwarting the Holy Spirit. This is one of the great responsibilities of superiors, who have souls to answer for as well as bodies."

Her spiritual life was based, to a large extent, on the belief that "Martha and Mary are sisters, not enemies," and that their two ways of life were compatible. She would advise her nuns "to sit in silence before Our Lord and be more ready to listen than to talk," but she sturdily opposed "the prayer of indolence and reverie," just as she distrusted spiritual introspection or what, in another context, she called "twining round self like woodbine on a stick." Throughout her spiritual notes runs the theme of self-denial allied with joy—and it is not perhaps too fanciful to see in her choice of the Holy Child as her emblem the personification of this ideal. In Him the austerity of self-abnegation was lent the charm, simplicity, and pure abandonment of a child. In Him the crib and the cross were one and the way of man to God was made joyful. This was not to deny the purpose of Christ's command, "Deny thyself, take up thy cross and follow me," but to transfigure it. The sufferings still remained and, most difficult lesson of all, the choice of suffering did not. Cornelia was long familiar with God's habit of bypassing a chosen form of suffering for a totally unexpected one. To her, and to many, the hardest part of the virtuous life is acclimatizing the soul to shock, "to take the cross *He sends*, as it is and not as you imagine it to be." For all that, she besieged God with the same tenacity as she besieged her Bishops—and occasionally with the same results. But on the whole a contract with God is not, as it sometimes appears, a one-sided one. If those who love Him give up much they also receive a great deal.

Directness was the keynote of Cornelia's relations with both God and man, and during the most active part of her life she must have covered many sheets of paper, however scrappily, in her firm, decisive hand. Her intelligence covered a tremen-

dous field and her vitality drew strength from living always in
the present, for as she said, "it is a waste of time and grace
to dream of the future or brood over the past."

She could write severely to the town clerk that "if he is
unwilling to supply the school cistern with water on the same
terms as he supplied the Presbytery, that is at £3 per annum,
he will please to cut off the pipes immediately. Mr. Clerk perhaps forgets that the cistern is half supplied by the rain water
which is introduced from the roof of the school," because she
had given the matter considerably more thought than the usual cursory harassed glance of the householder. The amount
of energy she put into problems of this sort can be deduced
from another occasion when she had been asked by one of
her superiors for advice on a similar issue. "I think the sum
enormous for the draining," she wrote. "You ought to have
taken the number of pipes (per thousand) and the number
of rods. I should have said that £25 would have drained the
whole. I will tell M. Angelica to look at her book where she
will find prices per thousand 2-inch drainpipes and prices per
rod for laying them. This is the only fair way to get the work
done."

She waged constant war with builders, and Grant was called
in to mediate again and again. The first plans for restoring
the St. Leonards chapel were drawn up by an architect called
Goldie, but Cornelia did not like them and persuaded her
nuns in chapter to turn them down. Goldie answered Cornelia's request to let her know "the sum which I am indebted
for your drawings" with a furious demand for a large sum,
and Cornelia retorted: "I am advised that the amount due to
you is 2½ per cent on the value of the work ordered. Our
present contract amounts to £2,965, making your rightful demand a little less than £75 for drawings and time spent. I think
you will remember that you applied for tender on your own
account much to my surprise and before I had seen the drawings and been charged for tender." She would send him a
check for £75 but not more since she had not estimated for
more. But Goldie would not accept the check, and Grant, in
spite of Cornelia's permanent plea that "the real value of a
contract" was lost on her as she was never allowed to abide

by contract but had always to give way in order to preserve the diocesan peace, intimated that he would not support her into chancery. An unsatisfactory compromise was, as usual, struck and the encounter ended, in consequence, with weapons still drawn. "I certainly did not expect so ungentlemanly a pressure on your part," wrote Cornelia to Goldie, "though your letter proves that I ought to have expected it."

With Goldie's successor, E. W. Pugin, who was also responsible for restoring the Old Palace at Mayfield, Cornelia hedged herself round with every precaution. As she wrote to her lawyer, Stonor: "You know as well as Mr. Hodgson [the builder] and the workmen that I have most positively declined anything being done without an especial estimate." But even so arguments occurred. Mr. Hodgson stopped his workmen and forbade them to go on until he was paid on account. He, Pugin, and Cornelia exchanged cold comparisons and estimates. All three advanced upon Grant, who wrote back with slightly querulous tact. Pugin, it appeared, had insisted on Hodgson's presenting a price on each of his very rough drawings. When Hodgson refused, because the prices were bound to be inaccurate, Pugin worked out his own estimates and took them to Cornelia, who accepted them. The hapless Hodgson was thus persuaded to "take on a £5,000 building for £3,000," and disgruntled both by Pugin's haphazardness and Cornelia's demands ("The work does not seem to be too good for Mrs. Connelly. She requires everything to be most fully carried out even though perfectly aware of the position") he decided to stage a sit-down strike. Cornelia's appeal to Stonor began: "You will give me credit for not teasing you with letters during the last six months but now I am obliged to begin again." This time, however, the breach was mutually healed and the building went on.

Pugin and Cornelia understood each other. Their arguments and fierce discussions were based on good-humored regard and the insults which flowed amiably between them were carried on in the knowledge that they would be mutually stimulating and provoking. They exchanged ideas continually as the building progressed: "We should prefer the east window long to take in a beautiful stained-glass design," she wrote thoughtfully, and then, gathering impetus: "The entrance from the infirmary to the tribune is not drawn, perhaps you have forgotten it . . . of course you observed that your drawing in the choir windows on your section are not the same as those shown on the south elevation. Did you intend this or was the south elevation an afterthought?" Their friendship allowed room for gibes, and some time later Pugin retaliated, with somewhat cumbersome jollity, by describing her drawings for a proposed concert hall as "a diabolic invention of an infernal mind."

Cornelia's faith in the efficacy of the British law courts was, in fact, put to the test less often than she wished, although, from the number of times she was involved in litigation, this is sometimes difficult to believe.

Two occasions stand out in the second half of her life. The first, although it provided a legal decision in her favor, did her reputation considerable harm; the second, nothing but good.

The first concerned a young girl called Annie McCave, who, as she has come down to us, is no more than a name in the legal jockeying for position which followed her indiscretion—the not unusual one of failing an exam. She was a young pupil teacher who had come to Cornelia in 1860 to join a training college that Cornelia had opened four years before in St. Leonards.

This training college, whose life was as abortive, if not quite as short, as Emily Bowles's training college in Liverpool, had been suggested to Cornelia by the Government, advised, no doubt by Mr. Marshall, a Government Inspector, and by Mr. Allies, Chairman of the Poor School Committee, who thought so highly of her methods. The Government had shown itself willing to aid the college provided that the majority of pupils were there on Government grant. Cornelia, having gladly accepted the offer, provided the buildings and the staff, and made the strict rule that no one failing their examination should enter her college, which was opened in 1856 with nine Queen's Scholars. The numbers quickly increased and at first all went well. But then, after a faint disagreement over the amount of ironing the Queen's Scholars did for themselves, the Government got scent of an unorthodoxy and the fat was in the fire.

It was all over Annie McCave, who had failed her examination before coming to Cornelia. On this occasion, as the girl had come to the college as a privately paying pupil and not on a grant, Cornelia had waived the rule. To prevent a precedent she called Annie McCave by her mother's maiden name of Kavanagh.

Why she did so we do not know. For, in spite of the endless correspondence and legal complication which ensued, there is no mention of what Cornelia's personal motive was in making such an exception of Annie. What circumstances, pathetic or otherwise, induced her to sympathize with Annie McCave to the extent of bypassing a college regulation we shall never discover.

Cornelia, as Mr. Allies's letter, later laid before the Investigation Committee, proved, had already discussed the matter with the Government Inspector, Mr. Stokes, who had advised her against accepting the girl. She had, at the time, made it quite clear that she did not agree with his advice.

Mr. Stokes was a friend of Emily Bowles and the same inspector who had supported her training college. Whether this friendship had anything to do with the attitude he now adopted, at a time when Emily was still feeling very bitter about Cornelia, it is impossible to say. But when he learned that Cornelia had chosen to ignore his advice he wrote angrily to Dr. Grant about Annie McCave's presence in the school, and complained that she had been presented at an examination in June, 1861, under the name of Kavanagh. "The Government," he added, "in paying yearly hundreds of personal grants is at the mercy of the fraudulent if payees may be personated. Any individuals disgraced for copying or other cause might escape the penalty in the same way."

After a great deal of discussion, in which Dr. Grant played his usual conciliatory part, the matter was laid before a Committee of Investigation in Whitehall.

Mr. Stokes claimed loudly that Cornelia was a liar and a cheat; Cornelia protested that the very absence of secrecy proclaimed her innocence. Throughout, Mr. Stokes behaved with

the complacent clumsiness of an amateur sleuth. He was forever piecing together evidence and detecting guilt. It was this
that especially annoyed Cornelia, for, as she wrote to Allies,
not only had Annie never been entered for the examination
under a false name, which it was never Cornelia's intention
that she should be, she used the name of Kavanagh only during term, but "how could he have anything to *detect* even had
she been presented to him knowing the fact before he went
to the school." For "it was before he had set his foot within
the training school that the conversation took place in the
parlor, where I assured him that Annie McCave's name had
not been presented and that when sent in officially that her
own name was to be given and not that of her mother."

Allies comfortably informed Cornelia that he had dug up
a "judgment of the late Lord Chief Justice Tindal" that would
"defeat the enemy," even had Annie been presented for the
Christmas examination under her mother's name. But there
was no need, fortunately, for it. Subsequent discoveries proved
beyond doubt that Annie was never presented in the June
exam, that the exam she did finally enter for involving a grant
was under her own name, and that Mr. Stokes had introduced
the whole matter with no written evidence whatever.

But though the law found Cornelia right on every point,
the moral problem still remains. Why did she do it? There
was nothing particularly heinous in calling Annie McCave by
another name during term-time, provided there was no intention of doing so in an exam, but what was the point? Especially since, as Mr. Stokes says in one of his letters, there were
other girls in Annie's class who had been with her at a previous
college and who therefore knew her real name. Without knowing any of the personal facts, the whole affair must remain a
mysterious one. Cornelia's letters show that she herself was
bewildered by the fuss over what to her seemed no more than
a most minor point of etiquette—making an individual exception from a rule of her own contriving.

But rumor was not slow to take advantage of the case. It
had been an impropriety and a foolish one. It was to be responsible for the downfall of the college. Mistrust grew and
multiplied. The McCave incident had been investigated in

March, 1862. In June, Cornelia was writing to Grant: "When a priest has recourse to another to know whether it is true that I am excommunicated we must expect consequences that are most hurtful to the community and injurious to me personally." It was no moment for prolonging battle. Cornelia offered to resign the college. "It seems to me," she wrote to Grant, "that it would be much better to withdraw my name (with any amount of injustice) than to risk the loss of the training school. The one is a personal matter, in which the charge has been refuted, while the latter would involve the loss of a great charity." In fact, at this juncture, Mr. Lowe's revised code of "payments by results" was extended to training colleges. The payment of grants for students was to be deferred till after they had left college for more than a year, and was even then to depend upon how well they had done in school. Without endowment or assistance it would be impossible to carry on. In 1863, therefore, the training school was closed—and before the year was out its useful buildings beside the convent had been turned into that Victorian hybrid, a middle school, which catered for the children of the middle and professional classes who could not afford the fees of an upper school but who wished the same opportunity and education. It was run successfully, for twenty years, by which time there were a great many replicas up and down the country and the buildings were urgently needed for a junior school. It was therefore turned into one and remains the same today. The educational authorities had remained the least affected by discrediting rumors. In 1873 Cornelia was again requested to undertake a Government training school, this time in London, and it was only the difficulty of finding a suitable house, and the general inconvenience of the moment, that prevented her from doing so.

The second occasion on which Cornelia faced legal investigation during her last years was after Grant's death, when she herself was sixty-eight. For once, although Bishop Danell, who replaced Grant, was not a sympathetic man, she received the wholehearted support of her Bishop. The case concerned one of Cornelia's nuns, Sister Mary Frances Kenworthy, who had died after being only four years professed. As she was an heiress to something like forty thousand pounds and had left a considerable part of this sum to the convent in her will, her relations were somewhat upset and, the following August, entered a caveat stopping procedure in the proving of her will on the plea of undue influence. They protested that the will and codicil were not executed in accordance with the Wills Act.

The case could not have come up, from the point of view of the press, at a more opportune moment. For the country had already been roused by attacks on convents by men like Pierce Connelly and Hobart Seymour, who drew an alarming picture in which the unhappy inmates either cowed beneath exacting tyranny and pined away into early death or else led lives of fantastic avarice and immorality. "It appeared a few months ago," wrote Wiseman, "that the safety of the Kingdom depended upon two measures—the suppression of convents and the extinction of Maynooth." In 1870 *The Times* of March 30 announced that a Mr. Newdegate had obtained a majority vote which directed a select committee to inquire into the "existence, character, and increase of conventual and monastic institutions or societies in Great Britain, and into the terms upon which income, property, and estates belonging to such institutions or societies and the members thereof are respectively received, held, and possessed."

Mr. Gladstone, voting against the original motion, had suggested a compromise—that a committee should inquire into the "state of the law with regard to conventual and monastical institutions," leaving out the words "the existence, character, and increase," and depriving Mr. Newdegate of his salacious burrowing into any and every scandal that rumor brought him on the wind.

The Times, in gloomy but more uplifted parenthesis, echoed Mr. Newdegate's sentiments and assumed that the point at issue was whether a law should be passed establishing a permanent system of visitation of all convents by Government inspectors. Its correspondence bore the heading Inspection of Convents. In 1877, when the Kenworthy case came up, the hunt was still on and had, in fact, just entered a new and energetic phase.

At this inauspicious moment Cornelia went to law representing her Society, which, since procedure had been stopped on the will, had to act as plaintiff. The best lawyers were enlisted, among them Sir Charles Russell, later to become Lord Russell of Killowen. Several nuns were served with writs and the street posters bore the promising legend, GREAT CONVENT CASE. FORTY NUNS TO BE IN COURT. In fact, only sixteen were summoned and their friends sent carriages to convey them to the courts at Westminster, which were packed. The press and the public waited in pleasant suspense, and the judge, Sir James Hannan, took his seat to a thrilled murmur of anticipation which, as it turned out, was doomed to disappointment. For there were no proceedings. Counsel at once retired for consultation, and half an hour later returned. The counsel for defense rose to say it afforded him the greatest pleasure to be able to inform his Lordship that the defendants had unanimously and entirely withdrawn the plea of undue influence. The charges had originally been placed on record in order, by that means, to try the merits of the case and the circumstances under which the will was executed. And, moreover, he was bound to say that, looking at all the facts in his possession, he would not have been able to prove undue influence. Finally, arrangements had been made by which the court would not be troubled with the hearing of the case, which would have occupied a considerable time. All that was now necessary was to prove the will in solemn form, and Sergeant Bellasis's daughter, now a Holy Child nun, got to her feet to describe witnessing the will. The public, thoroughly disgruntled, straggled out, and, apart from the satisfaction of knowing themselves vindicated, the only tangible result for the Society was that Sir Charles Russell sent his four daughters to Holy Child schools.

But in his day, and throughout most controversies, Grant steered a cautious, uneven course. The house chaplains at St. Leonards succeeded each other with rapidity and were, with few exceptions, difficult men who came to the job for reasons of health or because they were generally unsuited to a more robust post, and they viewed it with prejudice and remained only as long as they could have their own way. One of them,

Mr. Richardson, refused to entertain visiting priests at Cornelia's request, although this was part of his purpose and she provided for the extras. He complained that his stipend was too low and advertised in the local paper for a lodger to supplement it. Mr. Stonor confided to Colonel Townley that he thought Richardson "a very bad style of lunatic," and both of them upheld Cornelia, who wrote to Grant to explain that "this is the first time we have had the right of sending priests to the presbytery (as guests) questioned or refused. . . . My Lord, I was sure before Mr. Richardson came to us that we should not go on well, and if your Lordship will remember I expressed this opinion to you. Mr. Richardson may be more happy and contented in some place where he may receive £300 per annum," which is what he claimed he could get. Dr. Grant's uncertainty, and his inability to pick out the salient point and stick to it, is manifest in his letter to Stonor. Ignoring the fact that Cornelia provided the extras, that Mr. Richardson knew the sum he was to get before he came to St. Leonards, and that it was he who raised the complaint in the first place, he writes: "I really don't know what to do at St. Leonards. Mr. Richardson receives £100 a year for everything, and his predecessor, Mr. Bamber, when times were less dear, had £120. He says he cannot live on this money and wants a lodger to help him. Add to this a fresh situation raised by the Reverend Superior, who asserts her rights to send visitors without any arrangement with Mr. Richardson, whose servant has additional work and he additional expenses on these occasions. I am quite willing to tell him to have no lodger, but I do not know how his salary is to be made up."

Mr. Richardson did not, fortunately, stay long, but Cornelia had been made aware once more of the annoyance and worry she was to Grant. "How many times have I said that we hope in our humble way we may yet be of some consolation!" she had written sadly to him some years before. "Yet even in this we must resign ourselves to being a trial to your Lordship's patience which is not limited." In all her dealings she was forced to put aside her vanity, to remember that it did not matter in what opinion she was held, that she must always do what she sincerely held to be God's part for her—

and if this colored her relations so strongly with her superiors, it conditioned also the lives of those under her. "We have given ourselves to God in religion," she wrote, "not to be anything less than perfect religious, not to be housekeepers, nor dressmakers, nor artists, nor musicians, nor schoolmistresses, nor authoresses, nor superiors." It was, after all, their vocation.

Chapter 13

THE RULE

It is impossible to overrate what her rule means to a nun. It is not a mere codebook of regulations restricting her inclinations and freedom at every turn. It is a delicate, finely drawn map of her relationship with God in the particular vocation to which she is called—a rubbing freshly made from the inspiration of her founder and bearing the marks of her founder's individuality as well as of the will of God.

When she joins an order a religious voluntarily surrenders her liberty. It is a gesture of finality, a wholehearted abandon which is strange, and rather shocking, to an outsider. But though the gesture is complete, it is not chaotic. It demands a minute working out to trace the expression of God's wishes upon every detail of her life. "This expression she finds in her rulebook, the manual of her individual holiness, her textbook in the art of union with God." What she feels for it is necessarily only a shadow of what her founder, who gave it life, must feel. Although St. Ignatius had calculated that the time it would take him to resign himself to the annihilation of his Society, the Jesuits, was ten minutes, this is, perhaps, a measure of his sanctity.

When Cornelia came to England in 1846 as a woman of thirty-seven she knew her rule to be incomplete. She did not worry for she felt it essential, in this as in her schools, to found theory on practice and to wait and see what she would learn from experience before committing herself too definitely to paper. She came fresh to a new job in a strange country and without even the familiarity of being already several years under religious rule. Few founders can have come so casually to their task. As she herself said many years after: "Had the

Society been *my* work I should long ago have given up all and retired into some corner to pray."

Comforted by Wiseman's support during her first years, she continued roughing out her ideas in the notebooks she had begun, for a different purpose, as far back as 1835. Here and there she jotted down odd points that occurred to her at random from studying other rules. Under one of these, *Enclosure*, she scribbled: "(5) Walls high and in good repair (6) Double grates in all the parlors six or nine inches apart from one another." The first of these she eventually used, the latter she did not.

But while she worked on her rule, a preliminary draft of which had already been submitted to Propaganda before she left Rome in 1846, Pierce's behavior began to deteriorate. His eccentricity soon became public knowledge, and it was not long afterwards that Wiseman's support gave way beneath the St. Leonards dispute. Letters of dissatisfaction from him, and from Dr. Duke, began to reach Propaganda, until, thoroughly disquieted, and only too aware into the bargain that their files were out of date and incomplete after the revolutionary years, they sent for Cornelia to come to Rome.

This was the year 1853, and Grant, playing a familiar role, refused permission. He knew Pierce to be in Italy and was nervous of the consequences. He proposed, as a delaying action, that Cornelia should remain in England until the rule was translated into French, as the international language. The Sacred Congregation of Propaganda Fide, unused to having its invitations declined, sent a more imperative summons: "It would appear that I have not sufficiently clearly expressed in my first letter how expedient it is that you should come to Rome soon." Cornelia showed Grant the letter and prevailed upon him to let her go. The translation was finished and, had she not fallen ill, she would have left at once. As it was, another month passed before her departure. Early in 1854 she arrived in Rome with two assistants and lived with them in complete retirement, in which, for fear of Pierce, letters were sent to her under cover and those she wrote herself bore no address.

As she herself was ignorant of Propaganda's motive in sending for her, her hopes were high. But they were soon dashed. The discussions proved disturbingly inconclusive and moved at a cautious distance round the point. For there were other factors, unknown to Cornelia, which rendered Propaganda uneasy. Not only had Wiseman told them that, in his opinion, it would be better if Cornelia lived temporarily by another rule until her own was more clearly formulated, and that all her subsidiary houses should be separate from, and not subject to, the mother house, but Dr. Grant had intervened with another suggestion. Although he described Cornelia as "a woman of great talent and capacity," he emphasized the danger of Pierce's influence and proposed that "as in England there is always the danger of the raising of law by her husband . . . it might be better for her to be in America or elsewhere than in Rome or England." In addition, Propaganda was grappling with another difficulty, a grave and apparent discrepancy between the rule she had just presented and another, earlier, version which they had already circulated for consideration. That this was in fact Pierce's rule, sent in 1848, they had no idea. The correspondence had been lost and Asperti's and Cornelia's letters of repudiation at the time had apparently been overlooked in the flurry of Roman revolution. Acting in the circumstances with unsurprising caution, Propaganda advised Cornelia to return to England and produce a more detailed version of her rule. With vague encouragement, and the promise of a letter of confirmation, Cornelia returned to England.

But the letter never came.

Cornelia came back to the new struggle with Emily Bowles over Rupert House and to the old one with Dr. Duke over St. Leonards. To add to her distress, several of her young nuns, who had been struck by the prevalent disease of consumption, died. For ten long years she heard no more about her rule.

To an outsider, and especially to one who has become familiar with her quickness and decisiveness, her fearlessness of Bishops and her ability to argue, her silent acceptance of the situation is extraordinary. Throughout the many dealings over her rule this same acceptance, the same refusal to demand and insist, occurs again and again. It is as if, sure of herself on practical grounds, she would not hesitate to wage war but, in spiritual spheres, her humility silenced her, just as in interpreting the Fathers of the Church it prevented her from firing her imagination from theirs. This did not mean that she stopped trying for approbation. She never ceased, and again and again she wrote to Grant to beg for his support. But she never questioned him about what he had heard from Rome, she never asked the reason for his actions—which grew stranger towards her during the next ten years—merely his permission to persevere. The reverse side of humility has all the superficial appearances of pride.

What Grant never told Cornelia for ten years was that Propaganda had written to him to say that they could not give their formal approbation until the Society had gained more stability and that, for the time being at least, while Cornelia might be encouraged to strengthen her position, her novices should only be admitted "under the ordinaries with simple vows to be made once for all after noviceship which shall cease upon the retirement or dismissal of the sister." This would be an undermining which few orders could stand, for it would take away their perpetual vows and leave the nuns in a state of perplexed uncertainty.

The letter to Grant from Propaganda was not, however, an order, it was advice, and it left Grant the scope he detested. He had not the heart to tell Cornelia the truth of their decision (he, like Propaganda, was quite ignorant of the fact that the 1848 rule was Pierce's) nor the inclination to go against the advice and let the novices be fully professed. As usual he temporized. He did not forbid their profession but continually postponed the various dates suggested to him for their clothings, often at the very last minute and on the most insubstantial excuses. After a time he found this compromise as unsettling as did Cornelia and took a more definite step.

In September, 1859, he sent her word that for the future the nuns' vows were to be only annual. Against this Cornelia protested but to no avail. The blow was a bitter one, and although she did her best to reassure the nuns ("the yearly vow," she wrote, "is simply for safety, while the intention before

God is to live and die in the Society") she felt it as keenly as they did.

It is difficult to understand why Grant allowed the Holy Child order to continue at all in such a state of nebulous uncertainty, but probably he felt himself unable to decide about Cornelia's good faith. If she was, in fact, a good woman he had no wish to spoil her chances altogether; if she was not then he had at least protected her disciples from being carried too far in the wrong direction. It must have been his constant prayer that God would finally enlighten him.

In 1862, Cornelia wrote to Grant, sending him a further revision of the rule she had submitted unsuccessfully to Propaganda in 1854 and begging his help in achieving its approbation. Unfortunately, the year 1862 coincided with the disastrous ending to the affair of Annie McCave.

With the additional worry of Annie McCave and the training college, it was two years before Grant committed himself in answer to Cornelia's letter. At last, in 1864, encouraged by the spread and stability of the order in America, and by the way in which, in spite of every difficulty, it persevered in England, he wrote to Cornelia to tell her, for the first time, of Propaganda's letter of 1854 and to recommend that she should try once more for approbation.

For the first time Cornelia was made aware of the significance of Pierce's rule. She pencilled across the letter: "Rule presented in 1848 not known to us. C. C.," and thanked Grant for deciding to solicit the approval of the Holy See. She made no mention of the long, weary years of indecision and wasted energy which could have been avoided, or at any rate curtailed, if she had known of the letter earlier.

But Grant, having explained, started once more to hedge. Nothing was done. Suggestions and requests were turned aside. One privilege especially Cornelia begged to be allowed—that of convening the first General Chapter for the election of a Superior General and her Assistants. It was not in her power to do so without her Bishop, and she felt that the time had come for her to stabilize her position by general vote—the way in which, by her rule, Superiors were to be chosen. She also wished to provide a General Council from among the elected

Assistants through whom to legislate. But this the Bishop refused.

Hitherto, Cornelia had held office only by the implicit consent of the Bishop of the diocese on the one hand and of the nuns of the order on the other. She badly needed authority to make new appointments and, where necessary, alter old ones. For the order had spread beyond the simple practice of its foundation, when the appointment of a local Superior was a matter for her personal decision only. The organization now included twelve houses and demanded the proper formalities of Chapter and election.

Five more years passed. During them Cornelia visited her American convents, her old friend and enemy, Wiseman, died, and Grant himself began to show signs of the severe illness which was to kill him. Unwilling to distress him continually with her demands, and yet conscious that she herself was nearly sixty, Cornelia showed, for the first and only time, traces of nervous strain. The Bishop was still chary of admitting her nuns to permanent vows and the result, as perhaps he hoped, was to discourage postulants from entering. On this score the arguments between them continued. "My dear Lord," Cornelia wrote in 1864, in reply to some doubts he had expressed, "I should really not think it just, my Lord, to ask either your Lordship or any other Ecclesiastical Superior to guarantee the support of religious, under simple vows! The religious superiors are themselves bound to take the necessary measures to secure the support of the community and they have no right to ask for the services of sisters whose support they are unable to meet."

Ill and tired, the Bishop and the Reverend Mother wrote with more tact but no less vigor to each other. Among the many solicitations for each other's health and well-being, the current theme flows strongly still. On March 8, 1869, Cornelia wrote again:

MY DEAR LORD,

I am afraid that I shall only fret myself and get into a puzzle of uncertainty, and annoy your Lordship in your present too many sufferings, if I go on thinking or writing about the rule, etc., which really ought not to fall upon a woman in any responsible sense, even before revision.

Would it not be better and a great relief if I were to go to Rome with a letter to Cardinal Barnabo, expressive of your Lordship's wishes in all matters that you think necessary and desirable?

Grant was ill and there was no reply. A month later Cornelia wrote again. And this time the Bishop answered her appeal. She was to go to Rome to put the amended rule before the Sacred Congregation of Propaganda.

Overjoyed, she set out with two assistants and letters of sympathy and support from Grant and Manning, who had taken Wiseman's place as Archbishop of Westminster. She reached Rome in May and presented herself, as she had done fifteen years before, to Propaganda. A Franciscan, Padre Anselmo Knapper, was to act as Consulter. He informed her that her many careful revisions were inadequate and would have to be done all over again. Once more the earlier letters of Wiseman and Grant, and Pierce's intervention, proved the main stumbling block.

It was a blazing Roman summer. Throughout the heat and her great disappointment, Cornelia worked for two months to prevent the separation of her houses and to preserve as much as possible of her original rule—the first revised edition of which she had submitted in 1854. The former she managed to do, but over the latter she had to give way on certain points. These had mainly to do with her interpretation of the constitutions and the organization of her order. One of the clauses that Propaganda wanted abolished was the one which concerned a shared recreation between choir nuns and lay sisters. Unwillingly, and after much discussion, Cornelia submitted to the tradition of the Church. At the end of two months, Padre Anselmo intimated that there was little point in her remaining in Rome, and said he would have the revised revision printed and sent to her in England.

Worn out and disappointed, Cornelia returned to England, where her health, though not her spirit, broke down completely. Her doctors advised a winter in the South of France

as the only hope of restoring her. Grant and the nuns urged
her to go. A house was taken at Hyères and she went there in
November with a small party of nuns and children, who also
needed a gentler climate, and with the secondary intention of
finding a suitable place for a foundation in France. It was
from here that her plans reached out, at first unsuccessfully,
to Toul, and later to Paris.

It was to Hyères that the printed revision was sent from
Rome in February, 1870, accompanied by a letter from Cardinal Barnabo directing her to have it translated into English
and sent round to all her local Superiors and convents. The
translation was made, and a copy of this and the Cardinal's
letter was sent to every convent.

In this Cornelia made a fatal strategic mistake. She assumed
from her local Superiors the same unhesitating acceptance of
final authority that she herself had shown. She had suffered
fifteen years in preparation for Padre Anselmo's rejection of
so much of her rule. But her nuns had not. They had been
sustained throughout by Cornelia's firm faith in the ultimate
survival of her rule and the belief that one day all would be
well. She had told them so over and over again. Not only had
they been buoyed up by her strength but, in several instances,
they had become used to their own authority, their own powers
of decision. One of these last was Mother Lucy, who had
ratified Emily Bowles's purchase of Rupert House nearly sixteen years before. She had twenty years of administration and
responsibility behind her and her convent was run impeccably.
She shared the general horror at the new rule but, unlike the
rest, she did not write her protests. Instead, she signed the
rule, as she had been asked, and as all the others had done,
and sent a secret appeal to Rome both against it and against
Cornelia's government. Cornelia discovered this only when a
young nun of Mother Lucy's convent wrote to tell her, just
in time to prevent her from sending the fully signed document
to Rome.

Mother Lucy's influence was great, not only with her convent but with her neighborhood. When she found that her
course of action was known she abandoned all pretense and
openly criticized Cornelia. Cornelia herself had spent too

little time in the last years visiting her English convents. It was the inevitable result of being unable to call a Council and elect a local Superior for St. Leonards. She was herself the local Superior in charge of three schools and a novitiate, as well as Superior General, and the burden was too heavy. It was one of her strictest regulations in the rule that certain offices were mutually incompatible and should never be held by the same person. She was to prove by example how necessary the regulation was.

She was powerless to act without a Chapter, and Mother Lucy took full advantage of the fact. "No one has ever been equal to the position of acting in submission to those she was obliged to govern," Cornelia wrote to a priest who had professed astonishment at this lack of religious obedience. "Indeed, dear Father, I thought it would be impossible to keep the schools under these circumstances, and that we should be forced to give them up rather than encounter a continuance of such disorders in religious discipline." More than the discipline, it was the "want of trust" that hurt. "Regarding the Preston cabal," she wrote to one of her nuns, *what you tell me of their writing several letters asking me to explain matters about the rule, I am forced to tell you that it is absolutely false.* They never asked *any explanation* either by letter or message. The only complaint that I make is that they had the rules read to them eighteen months before they signed them and never made a single objection *to me,* but acted secretly against them and disapproved avowedly while they signed them to be sent to Propaganda."

The appeal had disastrous consequences. For one thing it slowed down, once more, the chances of approbation; for another it roused the rumors about Cornelia which had begun to die down. The wildest reports began to circulate once more —Cornelia was excommunicated, her Society to be suppressed. Priests and Bishops warned their parishioners against entering the order; some even urged those in it to leave. There was little point in adding ballast to a sinking ship. The sedition spread inwards. The nuns themselves, even the most loyal, began to regard Cornelia as a Jonah whose presence doomed

them to failure. Of her unhappy influence on fate Cornelia
was only too aware.

When she returned from Hyères it was to a new Bishop,
for Grant was dead. He had died agonizingly in June, 1870,
four months after he had advised Cornelia to go to France.
His place had been taken by Bishop Danell, a man whose rock-
like spirit was hidden beneath a soft and polished appearance.
It was to him, as Bishop of Southwark, that Propaganda sent
a request to make a special visit to the houses of the Holy
Child order to investigate the grievances about their rule.

This the Bishop did in 1872, and it was with surprise and
relief that the nuns learned they had won a reprieve. The
revised rule of 1870 was set aside and the old one of 1854
reinstated.

Peace and unity were restored, but the lull was only temporary and the Bishop's reasons for it not yet disclosed.

The first intimations came when he refused, as his predecessor had done, to allow Cornelia to convene a General Chapter. In vain she pleaded with him the urgency of her situation and that of her nuns, though the latter were, with the
exception of Mother Lucy's cabal, remarkably loyal: "I can
truly say, my Lord, that if there were not an almost unlimited
elasticity and simplicity of spirit amongst us, I should look
upon the faithfully loving confidence proved in our dear Community as an undeniable miracle of God."

For two more years the Bishop held out and then, quite
suddenly, in June of 1874, he sent out a circular letter ordering a General Chapter to meet on August 17. The Chapter
was held and Cornelia was elected Superior General with four
assistants. Mother Lucy was, by the same election, deprived
of her office. After the elections, the Council (composed of
the Reverend Mother of each convent and her assistants) re-
assembled to discuss the rule. They were expecting the Bishop
to want to hear their objections to the revised rule which had
only temporarily been set aside.

The Bishop had, however, a surprise in store. He had
guessed, he explained, how much they had suffered from the
revision and he had been given inspiration on this point. It
was a great consolation to him to be able to present them

with an entirely new rule, which he himself had written. They had been neatly conveyed from the frying pan to the fire. A little daunted by their reactions, the Bishop hastened to add that he would welcome any criticisms or emendations they had to make, after he had read it to them. But there was a hideous finality in the large, handsomely bound volumes which he handed round.

Of them all, Cornelia was the most silent. She said not one word either then or later, when the new rule had been read aloud, partly because she was never asked and the Bishop studiously ignored her in asking the opinion of her nuns and partly because, as her drawn, white face suggested, she was suffering from shock. In spite of her election as Superior General, her first Chapter was not a propitious one. She was suffering from an agonizing bout of rheumatic gout which swelled her legs and made her capable only of shuffling slowly forward. Bishop Danell was not a man to make allowances. He had heard enough about Cornelia's arrogance. When he arrived the nuns, according to custom, advanced to kneel and kiss his ring and to receive his blessing. Among them he noticed that Cornelia's obeisance was merely sketched, a travesty he considered of what it should be. He ordered her peremptorily upon her knees and immediately Cornelia obeyed, apologizing before her whole silent community, including Mother Lucy and her followers, for her apparent lack of respect. The Bishop, turning, left her and there she remained, unable to move, until one of her nuns, aware of her condition, helped her to her feet.

A Chapter that had opened so unpromisingly did not progress much better. After three weeks of endless discussion, in which Cornelia, "pale as death," took no part, and the only support for the Bishop came from the convent of Mother Lucy, the Bishop was forced to the unwelcome conclusion that his rule was not acceptable. He was sorry, however, to have to tell them that they were not at liberty to reject it. They were obliged to adopt it on trial for three years—after which he would return and hear their views.

The only reprieve Cornelia gained was that she was freed from her post as local Superior and was thus able to give more time to her duties as General. One of her first moves was to visit Mother Lucy's convent.

Mother Lucy, who had been relieved of her office of local Superior after the Chapter elections, had grown steadily more eccentric during the past months, and the first fascination her listeners felt for what she had to say had gradually turned to disapproval. Lately, she had sent Cornelia a letter veering towards reconciliation and Cornelia at once replied: "I am willing to believe that you mean what you say. Let bygones be bygones." It was one of her chief attractions that she knew how to accept an apology. But it was obvious that her removal from office had broken Mother Lucy's heart. She had never learned the art of religious obedience and was unprepared to face the strict rule of the order that rank, however high, is always, in the interests of humility and efficiency, temporary. A nun can be elected to the office of local, provincial, or General Superior, but at any stage, and at any election, she may be reduced once more to the level of an ordinary nun with no more demanding task than that of librarian. Finding herself so reduced, Mother Lucy could no longer bear religious life. Within a year she had been given a dispensation and left the order. Cornelia's visit to her convent, under her successor, showed that peace was restored.

But for all that, her position was an ambiguous and an upsetting one. For the Bishop's rule, as well as his manner to her, took power out of her hands and discouraged respect. Her loneliness had already been increased by the deaths of those nearest in age to her. She was now sixty-six and separated by a gap of twenty years from those next in age. Aware of the feeling that surrounded her, that she was responsible for the failure of the Society, and that only her weakness or death would give it back success, she must yet continue to lead and govern. There were even those among the community who felt she should either resign or live in retirement, with an attendant nun, in the unused presbytery at the bottom of the garden. Such feelings, although they were not voiced and remained behind the façade of community obedience, were none the less poignant for being hidden. Writing to comfort one of her Superiors, Cornelia reveals herself: "Do not allow your heart to be wounded, and if it is wounded in spite of your efforts, stitch up the wound with the love of God. . . . I very often have to remember this and then resign myself to endure more —very often—of late years, more than ever, not to allow one's poor heart to drop blood till it withers!"

The most recent thing to be endured was a misunderstanding with America.

When the two American delegates sent over to England for Danell's Chapter by their Superior, Mother Xavier, arrived back in America with a copy of Danell's rule and orders to obey it, Mother Xavier took no action whatsoever. She was ill at the time and found it easy to persuade herself that the rule was not intended outside Danell's own diocese. In thinking this she shared, though she did not know it, the opinion of several English Bishops who were in authority over various of Cornelia's subsidiary houses, including Mother Lucy's. But she had moved beyond the stage of opinion. Saying nothing to her nuns, or to her Bishop, she continued to live serenely by Cornelia's original rule.

The serenity did not continue long. One morning in 1875 a copy of Danell's rule, without letter or comment, reached the Archbishop of Philadelphia by post. Entirely ignorant of Danell's decision and of his rule, the Archbishop was both angry and indignant. Assuming, not unnaturally, that this was a high-handed innovation of Cornelia's, he wrote at once to England. Cornelia sent back a telegram to say that the rule had not been sent by her. She followed it with letters that showed she knew nothing about Danell posting a copy of his rule, or that her American nuns had failed to live by it. At the same time as she wrote in explanation to the Archbishop, she wrote to Mother Xavier to advise her immediate submission to Danell's rule. But Mother Xavier, roused by what seemed like indifference to her own rule on Cornelia's part, wrote angrily back. In vain one of Cornelia's assistants replied: "She has been blamed *here* for holding opinions like your own and for not wishing to change the rule. And now *you* turn and blame her as if *she* had caused the destruction of your peace and happiness."

The posts were at long and irregular intervals and communication was difficult. In addition, the Archbishop, who had now acquainted himself with Danell's rule, was dismayed and affronted by it. Like several of the English Bishops, he found it hard to approve of Danell's styling himself "Bishop Superior of the Institute." He refused to acknowledge the rule and to admit novices to profession, or postulants to the habit, until the affair should be settled by Rome. At the same time, shocked by Mother Xavier's suppression of the rule without his or Cornelia's authority, he wrote to Cornelia to say that he considered Mother Xavier incapacitated for office by her illness and wished her immediate recall. He also suggested a successor.

Mother Xavier's going was bitterly felt. She had been a beloved friend and leader to her community, and she left suffering from an illness that was to cause her death shortly after her arrival in England. Both her recall and her death were blamed by the American nuns entirely upon Cornelia. For, true to her own private practice of making no defense, Cornelia had never told them of the Archbishop's ultimatum. She took full responsibility for Mother Xavier's return and allowed no mark to be placed against the command of one who had been a brave, unselfish woman and had shown her loyalty to Cornelia's rule by her rejection, however misguided, of Danell's.

Although even before Mother Xavier's departure for England, the Archbishop relented about his decision not to profess novices, the American convents suffered for many years from the same uncertainty and lack of confidence that was spreading through the English houses of their order. Yet in spite of the suggestion, made to them constantly by friends and priests, that they should break off from England and become diocesan, they remained loyal to their founder and to their belief in the restoration of her rule.

In England, the three years under Danell's rule dragged slowly to their close. Everything had been done to obey. The complicated system of government, which made Cornelia practically a subject in her own house, was rigidly obeyed and so were the most minute instructions. The tradesmen's entrance was bricked up, at considerable expense and enormous inconvenience, since the Bishop's rule required that there should be only one entrance.

But the physical regulations were not so hard to bear as the change of spirit. Gaiety and lightheartedness had been resolutely crossed out. There were to be no flowers in the sickrooms and the whole tone was altered to one of slow pomp and solemn majesty. The simplicity of Cornelia's approach had given way to such grandiose conceptions as "Almighty God in His Incomprehensible Unity and Trinity." The Holy Child was never mentioned and the emphasis put, instead, upon loving God "in the Eucharist." It was clear that the Bishop shared, to a certain degree, the disparaging attitude to women that Pierce had shown. In Pierce's rule his opinion that the ambition of women should be small and well regulated was made clear by the frequency with which he prefixed the word "little" to the congregation and their activities. In the Bishop's rule it was laid down, as if daring rejoinder, that the nuns should "show special reverence to all priests" and remember that "their ministry is the holiest, the highest, and the most necessary and the most beneficial that can be conceived."

In November, 1876, the Bishop agreed to let Cornelia send two Assistants General to Rome to appeal against his rule. They went but their petition failed.

The following year he arrived to preside once more over the General Chapter, and Cornelia was once more elected Superior General. The nuns, with the exception of Cornelia, were all asked their opinion about the rule and expressed it unanimously. They wished it to end.

But this the Bishop would not allow. They were to work through it chapter by chapter, emending and reconsidering. For six days they worked with him. The result was the restoration of almost all the ascetical part of the rule; with the complicated system of government they were told they could not interfere. While waiting for the Bishop's final decision they drew up a formal list of their wishes:

First: That the new rule should be abrogated.

Secondly: That the old rule accepted by Propaganda in 1870, with the additions relating to the government of the Society, should be restored.

Thirdly: That an appeal should be made to Rome for an Apostolic Visitor to investigate all that had taken place, to clear away the misunderstanding which had arisen through the secret appeal, and to settle the serious difficulties with the Bishops, who would admit of no interference by the Bishop of Southwark, styled in the new rule the "Bishop Superior of the Order."

But they were doomed to disappointment. The Bishop insisted that, with certain amendments, his rule was to continue for another three years' trial.

Chapter 14

THE END

THE THREE years of extended trial for Danell's rule were to coincide with the last years of Cornelia's life, and to leave her on the shores of loneliness isolated by age, disapproval, and the deaths of many of her nuns and friends.

In 1877 she was sixty-eight. Many of her contemporaries had already died. In 1865 Wiseman had been the first to go, his good humor and cheerfulness returning in full spate with his last month of illness, his patience and consideration remarkable. "I have never cared for anything," he once said, "but the Church. My sole delight has been in everything connected with her. As people in the world would go to a ball for their recreation, so I have enjoyed a great function." His death was a tribute to his enjoyment. He demanded every rite the Church could offer and almost his last words were "Do not let a rubric be broken." Not one was. Full ceremonials attended every stage of his regal deathbed. On the morning of February 5 Canon Morris, his secretary, telegraphed Manning, who was in Rome, to come at his request. There was only one other person he wanted to see. "I asked him," wrote Canon Morris after a crisis in his condition a little before the end, "whether if he were to be again in serious danger there was anyone he would wish to be sent for. He said no one but Dr. Melia." His faith in Melia, who had become his private chaplain and confessor, remained unshaken to the end. On February 12 Manning arrived but Wiseman was too ill to recognize him. Three days later, early on the morning of the fifteenth, he died. Representatives of the various religious orders which he had helped to found or spread sang the Office of the Dead round him as he lay in state. For a week his coffin lay in the drawing room where he had asked to be carried before he died, and the Holy Child nuns who were in the London convent heard Mass beside him and, at the request of Canon Morris, made banners to go round the catafalque. On February 20 he was moved to the Procathedral at Moorfields. On the twenty-third his Requiem Mass was sung and the long procession that followed his body to its last resting place stretched for two miles until it dwindled and was dissolved by traffic and the London police.

It was a striking demonstration of the affection in which this "vivid, pliant, susceptible, but magnanimous" Cardinal was held after time had worn thin his early unpopularity. Wiseman himself had not been altogether unaware of it. "I think," he said to Canon Morris during his last days, "a good many will be sorry for me—Protestants, I mean. I don't think they will always think me such a monster." That they no longer did their newspapers made quite clear. His death was "a national loss." "The greatest among the present generation of England's great men has ceased to be numbered with the living." Their feeling was summed up by *The Patriot*, one of the leading organs of dissent: "Cardinal Wiseman, with all his faults, perhaps we might say *in* his faults, was a thorough Englishman." "Yesterday," commented *The Times* of February 24, "the body of Cardinal Wiseman was solemnly buried at the Roman Catholic cemetery of St. Mary's, Kensal Green, amid such circumstances of ritualisitc pomp as, since the Reformation at least, have never been seen in this country, and we add amid such tokens of public interest, and almost of sorrow, as do not often mark the funerals even of our most illustrious dead."

Three weeks later his place as Archbishop of Westminster was taken by Manning, who, at his consecration, looked, according to Sibthorp, who had returned to Roman Catholicism and his priesthood in time to witness it, "like Lazarus come out of the tomb in cope and miter—a richly vested corpse, but very dignified and placid." It was a new era with a central figure who was possibly more friendly to Cornelia, but who could never strike the imagination with the same force.

In 1870 Grant died, and in the next few years several of Cornelia's nuns, whose deaths she felt, as her letters showed, very deeply. Among those who remained, the Duchess still lingered, an incongruous figure becoming with age both more childish and more resolute. The two autocratic old ladies housed so strangely together and enjoying each other's company with respect tempered by wariness and, on Cornelia's part, with considerable amusement, played out a cautious game between them. The Duchess refused to confide her plans, promises, and changes of mind. Cornelia sought to beguile her confidence. The Duchess immediately took refuge in eccentricity. At the first sign of open combat she would retire into the solace of her absorbing and vivid imagination. Fond, irritated, amused, Cornelia never forgot her. "Much love to the Duchess," she scribbled as a postscript to her letters when she was away, and when her special guardian Mother Catharine had to leave for a few days, she wrote her conscientious reports on her charge: "The poor Duchess is better today and more reasonable but she assured me that she had not a farthing. This is the old song. She looked at me today when I came in as she was on the night stool. 'Ah! Connelly-Donnelly save Lane Fox's children, go quick, quick, they will all be murdered.' I asked her if she would like to see you but she always says 'no, don't want to see anybody.' Dr. Ady says there's something on her mind, something that has preyed on her. The day she went quite mad he had said to us that she was in perfect health. I hope she has not done anything wrong about the orphanage [which she had bequeathed by deed for a hundred children at Mark Cross] or tied them up. I do not think she would change the deed. She said to Sister Columbia, 'They will want to call the orphanage Mrs. Connelly's orphanage but they shan't.' Poor Duchess!" Whether or not it was the orphanage that preyed upon the Duchess's mind we shall never know, but she did manage to do something about it. On her death it transpired that she had left it only £80, and ordinary pupils had to be taken in to support the orphans until gradually the nature of the endowment changed.

The Duchess had never grown used to taking second place. Cornelia had had stone pillars in the chapel at Mayfield: she would have marble pillars at Mark Cross. It was in pursuing such delightful prospects of victory that her money went.

But there came a time when she escaped too far into her imagination and found the way back too difficult. Her mind began to cloud and she was no longer able to tell where fact ended and fantasy began. In February of 1874 Cornelia wrote to Mother Catharine: "The Duchess goes on as usual. Her mind goes and comes for a moment or so. And then runs off wildly upon the treachery of her enemies, etc. Today it is on the Russian Conspiracy and the Queen!" It was clear that the Duchess was getting worse. "The poor Duchess is gradually dying," wrote Cornelia to Sister Dunstan, "she is quite gone now in mind and we watch over her day and night." Two months later, on April 8, she died. She was eighty-one years old.

Her final gesture was in the tradition of the marble pillars and her last years. "Lady Stafford's funeral cost £800 and the Duchess's is to cost the same," Cornelia wrote to Mother Catharine, and added, with some weariness: "Oh! that all was over." But it was all over, in fact, too soon, and when her body, escorted by two Bishops and forty priests, had left the convent forever it left yet another gap behind.

Two months later, in June, 1874, the first Chapter, at which Danell presided and where Cornelia was elected Superior General amid such unfavorable conditions, was called. The same year, Cornelia went to France to see how her convent there was progressing and to relieve the embarrassment that her presence in England caused.

Her sufferings had destroyed none of Cornelia's natural buoyancy. To a nun who had tried to dissuade her she wrote: "Do not look on the black side. If we had not had more faith in God we should at this hour not have been beyond St. Leonards. Pray for the Paris foundation and it will be granted." She stayed to help with the removal from the house in the rue de Grenelle, where the nuns were temporarily lodged after leaving Toul, and then moved to the Petit Château in Neuilly to join the few nuns sent out from England who were there to meet her. Among them was Mother Maria Joseph Buckle, who had been one of the first to join the order in 1846. Mother Maria Joseph had not seen Cornelia for some years and she was appalled by the change in her appearance.

"My first impression when I saw our beloved foundress was very sad, and I was much struck with the change that her great trials had wrought in her exterior. Her eyes especially were sunken and had lost much of their brightness." But Mother Maria Joseph's powers of observation were allied with understanding. "When the first impression had worn off," she went on, "I began to admire the work of grace in her soul, manifest even to an exterior observer. If she had ever had too great an assumption of authority and too independent a spirit, all this had gone away, and she was yielding and gentle to everyone in a way that used to fill my eyes with tears." Mother Maria Joseph was not a sentimentalist. She was a woman of intelligence and intuition. It was she who had suffered so much from introspection and for whom, long ago, Cornelia had done so much to restore confidence. Her testimony is therefore of great interest. "That Mother Connelly," she said, "took all she had gone through as a trial especially sent to her from God, I can fully witness. And in all my intercourse with her at this time, which perhaps was the most intimate in my whole life, I never knew her to descend to merely human or lower views."

Danell's Chapter, and the view in which she was held after it, provided Cornelia with the hardest trial of her last years. To come through so much suffering, to have pitted her strength and her confidence in God's sanction of her efforts against so much disapproval and difficulty only now to meet with the abrogation of her rule and the prospect of total spiritual as well as physical failure, was a test of endurance that human strength alone could scarcely survive. Surely no ambition, however vast, that was not inspired by God could contemplate the destruction of all hope, all justification, with the calm with which Cornelia contemplated the ending of her rule—the rule she had urged herself and her nuns "to hold as dear as life itself."

But she neither faltered nor stumbled as the last nails of suffering pierced her spirit. There was nothing masochistic or egoistical in her acceptance. She neither indulged in nor greedily encouraged the refinements of her suffering. She accepted it quite simply both as something she deserved and as something she could offer up in return for the sufferings of our Lord. She was amazed at the power that suffering gave to console Him "for the ingratitude of mankind. Is it not a wonderful thought that He condescends to be consoled by the acts of His creatures."

Sometimes the struggle was hard. "Pray for me, my dear child," she wrote to Mother Maria Joseph, "that this trial may be blessed to my sanctification and that I may learn humility from what is well calculated to humble my pride." Cornelia was in no doubt about her pride. It was a sin she found easy to commit, and in a letter to Mother Maria Joseph which has been lost "she expressed herself as receiving only what she deserved and begged me to pray for her that she might be forgiven by God, and that He would spare the Society and accept her as its victim . . . the calmness and rectitude of her mind never left her, and though she deeply felt the destruction, as she thought, of what had cost her the labor of her religious life, she submitted without hesitation to all the commands of her ecclesiastical superiors." How far her pride went it is impossible to say. It is dangerous to trust her own statements. Holiness, meticulous by training and sensitive by inclination, has a tender reaction to sin. A confession of guilt is therefore intensely subjective and, though in God's eyes it may be a just assessment, to human judgment, formed by other standards, it often seems exaggerated.

To Cornelia, alone with her thoughts during the long hours of the night, the events that seemed to prove her wrong must have joined forces with the memory of those who had suffered through her, her children, and emphasized her failure. Yet there was no appearance of strain about her acceptance. It was almost a relaxation to be able to suffer instead of act—and Danell's decision had prevented the possibility of action.

Only a letter, to her niece Bella, suggests, by its changed attitude to marriage, how great the pressure of memory had become. Bella was the daughter of her brother Ralph, to whom, as to all members of her own family, she had written continuously during her life as a nun, responding with pleasure to their happiness and success, sympathizing with their disappointments, advising them with customary briskness on matters of finance, education, and ambition. Of Bella she was particularly fond and, because she was fond, not content with the second-rate. "If I were you," she had written in 1875, "I should rouse up from Texas and not get swamped there. Knowledge is power and there is no use in going to sleep when active energy would make us all the more useful and happy." But it is in a letter Cornelia wrote when she was embarking upon the most trying and exacting phase of her rule that the apprehension which is so foreign to everything else she has written breaks through the affection and spontaneity which accompanies it. It is, in every way, an exceptional letter, for in it Cornelia steps outside the role and sentiments with which one has learned to associate her. All her understanding of suffering, her joyfulness, and her approval of marriage and the happiness it can bring are swept away by sudden, unaccustomed feeling. For a moment she is weak, distraught. For a moment she is, rather shockingly, pathetic:

My Dearest Bella,

I do *not* like it dear [a photograph of Bella], it looks so sad and old, you might be thirty years of age and so worn and long-faced. I could almost cry to see you so changed as you must be. Oh! where has all your joy gone, my darling! Surely the thought of paradise is enough to give you joy under all the pains and sorrows of this life. This is only a little dream of sorrow . . . oh! what is life? To marry and die and leave children for others to be unkind to or something like this. You must come and be a nun my darling and bring Lizzie [her younger sister] over and do not give yourself to be any man's slave to die or leave a family. [Bella was having an unhappy love affair.] You are not strong enough to bear such a sad lot. And I do hope your mother sees this. My darling Bella you must be very lonely being without Corry but it is something to have Lizzie to teach and your brothers. . . . Write my Darling and if you have anything quite private to say to your loving aunt you have only to write private at the head of your letter and no one will see it but myself. My dear Bella I can only say that I love you as your own mother.

Now that the reins of government had slackened in her hands, Cornelia was able to give more time to her correspondence, and letters crept daily from her pen, though gout was beginning to cripple her hands as well as her feet. They were letters of spiritual direction and counsel, of spiritual books she had read and loved and wanted to pass on; letters about and to her nuns; little recipes of sulphur and nux vomica, of whipped-up eggs and brandy for the ailing; small unexpected enthusiasms: "Do you know that Father Baron gets beautiful muscatel wine at 12s. per dozen! It is delicious wine and pure grape juice."

But she had one weakness that grew on her with old age: she loved getting letters in return. "You must not always expect long letters from me," she wrote to Mother Dunstan, "though I always expect to hear from you, about once a month." The plea was a frequent one, to her nuns and to her family, although she herself had often to provide the excuse: "Though I force myself to do the utmost possible in the way of writing, still the pen will not go quite like the needle of the sewing machine."

Age never impaired Cornelia's judgment. She remained as objective and as fair-minded as ever, and was still sometimes amazed that feminine judgment could be so often a thing of emotion. "Try to be just in your judgments my dear one," she wrote to one of her Superiors, "and do not fancy that I act without advice, or that I would encourage anyone to do so." It was, perhaps, this quality that drew back the trust of those who had deserted her. It had drawn back Emily Bowles and now it drew back Mother Lucy. For it was to Cornelia that Mother Lucy confided her bewilderment and the bitterness of her feelings when she was deprived of her office. Cornelia wrote to her, a letter of great warmth, and comforted her for much that lay outside the disagreement between them, but she begged her to remain on good terms with her successor, whose authority Mother Lucy found particularly galling. "I do not think," Cornelia ended her letter, "that Mother de Britto acts under instructions from others . . . perhaps you may have misunderstood . . . why not be frank with her and tell her the substance of what you have mentioned to me."

Mother Lucy's resentment had grown too deep. It was impossible for her to stay. But she left emptied of much of her gall.

In March, 1877, Cornelia left the convent at Neuilly, which had started well, and returned to St. Leonards. Frequent attacks of bronchitis now added to the paralyzing effects of her rheumatic gout. She did not often mention her health in her letters, but on one occasion she wrote: "The gout flies through my system. The foot and ankle would be nothing (if it would remain there) but when your heart is either palpitating or stopping you do not know where you will be the next half hour." Much of her time had to be spent in a Bath chair, for her limbs were no longer the servants of her will. It was from this high wicker chair that much of her work was done. In it she would join the children and nuns at recreation, and, with it drawn up beside her desk, she wrote her letters and conducted her affairs.

But the appearance of a calm old age spent in the midst of gentle consideration is a misleading one. The consideration and gentleness were there, but they were in response to duty and not affection. The atmosphere was full of depression and doubts of the future, of sidelong inferences that without Cornelia the prospects would be different. The nuns listened to, and sought, Cornelia's spiritual advice, which in all honesty they followed and found good, but they waited with quiet and folded hands for her death.

It would be inaccurate to suggest that Cornelia tried to die, but she certainly made no effort to live. For a woman who had fought so strongly all her life against every circumstance, including her own constitution, she settled down to her last illness with surprisingly little resistance. It was as if by consenting to her Bath chair she consented to her death.

She spent long hours in prayer and meditation and seems, in those last months, to have enjoyed a mystical union with God that softened the impact of the practical world and her reactions to it, which her abilities had previously kept so keen. "Doing the will of God," she told a nun, not as advice but as a reflection on personal experience, "is the only happiness and the only thing worth living for." Nothing had the power to disturb her. She became curiously remote from the rule and correspondingly optimistic: "Our rule will be given back to us one day to the letter." It was the casual certainty with which she spoke that made the remark memorable. "No," she said one day, "I have begun it but others will bring it to perfection." It was as if with the relaxation from authority came another—a relaxation of personality. With the disappearance of the need for executive and sole responsibility, with the situation stilled by Danell's interference and the regulation of the vote, Cornelia retracted within her shell of discipline to a softer, sweeter core. She lost some of the stiffness, though not all of the brusqueness, that characterized her business dealings and which made her, in company with her intelligence and her determination, so formidable an opponent. It was this second relaxation rather than the first which freed her gaiety and gentleness from restraint and allowed her to seem, in those last few years, less invulnerable, more human, than before.

She had always loved Mayfield, and in the summer she went to live there and be near her novitiate, which had been moved there for the quietness she had always wished for it. The novices were young and innocent. They knew nothing of the troubles that were running beneath the surface of the order, and they listened to and enjoyed Cornelia's gaiety and laughed at her stories and were made happy by her sympathy, that powerful intuitive sympathy she had with loneliness and fear. She had become very fond of chess in her old age, and both novices and children came in the evenings to try to beat her in the game. They were not successful.

But by Christmas she was back in St. Leonards, as if in preparation for the last phase. She was almost at once confined to her room. By the middle of January she was seriously ill, and on the twenty-ninth the doctor announced that she was in danger of death. Her oldest nuns, Mother Maria Joseph and Mother Ignatia Bridges, were summoned from Neuilly. Cornelia was given the Last Sacraments and prepared herself, in peace and prayer, to die.

But the stage had been too carefully set. It was not time for the curtain to come down. When Mother Maria Joseph arrived in England she found that Cornelia was better and was struck with the life that had flowed back into her face. "All her beauty had returned, and she looked as she used to look many years ago . . . immediately she interested herself about my health and seemed as much concerned at my ill looks as if she had not been ill herself."

Perhaps there was still something of the old imperiousness in Cornelia's desire to die, to go out in her own time to meet her God. Perhaps in those long hours of illness and prayer, when her spirit reached out and touched the hem of death, she came to understand this. For, after receiving the Last Sacraments, she began, with greater strength, to rally her spent forces and start the slow, weary struggle back to vigor. Her mind and senses responded, but her body never recovered. For a few hours, or sometimes a day, she was able to leave her bed for her Bath chair, but she was seldom free from pain. The days turned into weeks and then into months. All the time she was writing and taking an interest in all her convents. Of Neuilly, her last and favorite foundation, she thought often. One of the nuns there had died and the thought of her replacement worried her: "I trust all the sisters will try to make up her loss to the school as far as in them lies. The children expect to find mothers in the sisters, and indeed we cannot expect them to be attached to the place unless they find this motherly care." America seemed to her distressingly far away and she wrote to a nun there: "You know I am oftener with you in spirit than you can well imagine. Our window looks to the West, and the sunset takes me directly across the great ocean where you are, no doubt, fast asleep and not thinking of me." There was no lack of effort now in her response to life. "I am going to take again the water of Lourdes that if God wills me to be of any use I may regain my strength and go to America to see you all, for which I must get leave, being now nearly seventy years of age."

This was her consent, the evidence that her will was lying straight upon her Maker's. No more was asked of her. A few days later she fell seriously ill. It was January, 1879, exactly a year since she had last received Extreme Unction. For three months she lay in bed and, as if the diseases active in her were not strong enough to do the work alone, a third disease attacked her, a particularly virulent form of eczema. It grew, spreading out from the first ungainly patches until it covered her whole body, and penetrating inwards so that it caused her to vomit continually. The irritation was intense, but she did not complain. After Communion in the morning she could be heard singing the "Adoro Te" and her favorite hymns. It was as if the joy of possessing Him could not be contained. On April 14 she again received the Last Sacraments. A few hours later she was unconscious.

For four days those round her were unable to tell whether or not she regained consciousness, except for a brief moment on the seventeenth when, as if to subdue the irritation, she pressed one doubled hand against the other three times, saying, "In this flesh I shall see my God." But the rash broke through her unconsciousness, twitching the muscles of her face and giving off a dry, still heat. It added to the horror of death, depriving her of all comeliness and repelling those who came to help her. On the morning of the eighteenth the discoloration grew worse, a bright sickening red. She looked as if she had been scalded from head to foot—a terrible reminder, had there been any there to remember it, of another January, thirty-nine years ago, when her small son lay dying.

At a quarter to one on Friday, April 18, without regaining consciousness, she died. And as she died the rash faded into the clean white pallor of death. It was a strange dramatic moment, for as it went Cornelia's beauty returned, swept back, it seemed to those who watched, as if by the hand of God. It was exactly thirty-three years since the day on which she had set out from Rome to begin her order. Cornelia had always felt a peculiar attraction to the number thirty-three. At first she assumed that it was her destiny to found thirty-three houses, but later she imagined it must be a subconscious reaction to the years of Christ's life on earth. Perhaps it was.

There was little pageantry to see Cornelia to her grave, and only the tears of a few. Even her funeral was a matter for indifference outside her convent. "I am most grieved," wrote Danell, "that you have lost your good mother foundress. If she had many troubles she has had great consolations. . . .

Let me know the day of the funeral as I propose to come to it—Tuesday or Wednesday next would be the most convenient for me. If you have it on Monday I should have to come fasting, as I cannot come on Sunday evening." Cornelia, however, won the last round with the Bishop. She was buried on the Monday and the Bishop had to come fasting.

Her body had been brought to Mayfield, where she often said she wished to be buried, and on a mild spring day she was lowered into the earth. It was not her final resting place. In 1935 her remains were removed to the Mayfield chapel, where, beneath a stone image, crusaderlike and white, she lies today—inscribed above her the words she would have chosen: "Love knoweth no measure, feareth no labor, maketh sweet all that is bitter, findeth rest in God Alone."

A year after Cornelia's death her successor, whom Cornelia herself had designated and in whom she had complete faith, Mother Angelica Croft, was elected Superior General. It was her decision to wait before appealing to Rome once more about the rule. It was her decision also, it is said, that forbade Cornelia's name being mentioned and destroyed all her papers. But here there is a discrepancy. For Mother Angelica Croft's first action on replacing Cornelia, under whom she had worked as a devoted and efficient assistant, was to write to all friends and members of her family to ask if they had kept letters from her which might prove useful additions to the material she was already collecting for Cornelia's biography. (It is in fact from her efforts that such descriptions as we have of Cornelia come.) This is not the gesture of a woman who dislikes the memory of her predecessor. It seems, in the circumstances, more likely that pressure was soon brought to bear on Mother Angelica by other nuns and members of the clergy whose advice was sought and who thought that the Society's best chance of success was to keep as far as possible from the name Connelly, whose other bearer, Pierce, was in any case still living heartily and, judging by his pamphlets, vociferously in Florence. It is altogether unlikely that Mother Angelica Croft, who had made so definite an effort to gather material about Cornelia's life, should have deliberately destroyed her papers. It is far more likely either that Cornelia, whose reticence about her private emotions and thoughts was outstanding, should have destroyed them herself before her death or that they were put away out of sight and mind shortly afterwards, and only later, and inadvertently, destroyed. Those few scraps that remain—her spiritual diaries and notes—turned up many years later on the top of an old cupboard.

But whatever the explanation, the effect was the same. Cornelia's name was never mentioned and her memory banished. It is curious that this sudden overwhelming banishment had its counterpart outside the convent. The name of Cornelia Connelly, which for a short time during the 1850s was on everybody's lips and in the columns of every newspaper, is not to be found in the index of any biography of the men with whom she was so bound up—Shrewsbury, Wiseman, Grant, or Danell. The incredible dramatic story might, except for its effect on various members of the Connelly family, never have happened.

Two years after Cornelia, Bishop Danell died. His death put down the first barricade. Pierce's in 1883 put down the second. After it, the Society received formal notice from Propaganda that a renewed request for the approbation of the rule would now be considered. Two Assistants General went, accordingly, to Rome, but difficulties again arose and they were told that once more the rule must be remodelled. History was repeating itself. There seemed no way out. And then, quite suddenly, a Jesuit Cardinal, Mazella, who had known and sympathized with the Holy Child nuns in America, took up their cause and put one of his priests, Father Cardella, on the Committee of Consulters with orders to carry the rule through for approbation.

Father Cardella faced, undaunted, the task of working backwards through the many revisions and counterrevisions of the rule. He came eventually to its source and, on doing so, he wrote to Mother Angelica Croft. What, he wished to know, were the present wishes of the Society? They coincided exactly with Cornelia's original rule. The answer to Father Cardella seemed obvious. He therefore presented Cornelia's original rule, in its entirety, for approval. His boldness was rewarded. Not a single sentence was rejected.

On August 7, 1887, the news that the Pope had given his formal approbation was telegraphed to the Society in England. Father Cardella followed it with a letter in which he said: "Your rule was praised unanimously by the Committee as one of the very best proposed for approbation."

The confirmation of their rule restored peace to the community, but, with startling incongruity, it failed to restore confidence in the name of their founder. It was many years before the incongruity struck Cornelia's spiritual descendants and an interest in her revived. By that time the order had grown and spread "to meet the wants of the age," as she had hoped. But the problems about her remain the same, only the perspective has changed, and Cornelia herself does little to help our knowledge for she had learned well the lesson she considered so important, "the value of a suffering and a hidden life."

Her letters to her family, though warmhearted, reveal nothing of her real opinions and motives throughout her personal struggle. Those to her nuns are the kindly, authoritative letters of an older woman to her disciples. Intimacy, in the sense of a mutual exchange of confidences, is unthinkable. And in the carefully remembered descriptions of her left by nuns writing, for the most part, after her death, much of the warmth and naturalness is left out and a sense of awe and dignity creeps in, for they are essentially the memories of much younger women who saw in her a pattern of perfection or of an overwhelming authority.

By any standards Cornelia was a woman of outstanding talent. But when she founded an order she abandoned the personality, as well as the habits, of one woman for that of another. She was pressed out of her original form by the will of God and the strain was great, not only the strain of sacrifice but the strain of constant authority, the responsibility for other people's souls, their bodies, their welfare, their property; the strain of foundation and of persevering against the wishes of her ecclesiastical superiors, who were themselves endeavoring to do God's will but whose decisions seemed so often to contradict the conviction she had got from God. It accounts perhaps for the forthrightness that priests disliked in her and for the formidable stiffness that quelled so many of her detractors and which she came to recognize and regret in herself. If there were elements of pride in Cornelia's resolution and the tactlessness that helped to prolong several disagreements—as at times, if Cornelia herself is to be believed, there were—there is also evidence of a personality overreaching itself in an unfamiliar role on God's behalf.

When Cornelia was asked by Pierce to become first a Catholic and later a nun she was, as Pierce wrote after their separation, a woman "loved more than it is given to most women to be loved." Her sense of duty made her agree to the first, a reluctant submission to God's will to the second. But in the next few years she learned the full meaning of love—the ability to give without question, to act without doubt. She had come to realize that "it is a great thing to know God's will and to be ready to do it generously." At that time, when she was still at the Trinità dei Monti, she made the vow of which part was oddly prophetic of her future: "I offer myself to Thee to suffer in my heart with Thee and for Thee, not to do my will but Thine in the will of my superiors. I offer myself to Thee to suffer the loss of any esteem whatever and to be despised without any exception. I offer myself to Thee to suffer in my body by all my senses, by cold, by hunger, by thirst and in any manner whatever (and without reserves) that may the most contribute to the glory and the good of souls."

In fulfilling her vow, Cornelia's talent and capacities were increased and widened until they grew to surprising strength. Her system of education spread over England and America, and later to Europe and Africa; her spiritual manifesto, her rule, survived every disaster to become the handbook of a growing order, and remains a wholehearted dedication fashioned within the mold of common sense and bearing the grace and attraction of its founder.

But in fulfilling it she opened herself to two criticisms: indifference to her children and arrogance towards authority.

The evidence is all against the first, for there can be little doubt that Cornelia was a woman strongly devoted to her children. The only two times she is known to have wept after she became a nun were on Frank's visits and Mercer's death. What private tears she shed we do not know. But it was the thought of Pierce's efforts to use her children against her that finally hardened her towards him. She refused to be black-mailed. She would not see or speak to him, as she wrote to Lord Shrewsbury, until he returned Adeline to her. Three years later when she heard Mercer was going to America away from Pierce, it was her first reaction to follow and plead with him. Only the firm advice of the Archbishop of New Orleans prevented her. There was a moment at this time when her agony of mind seemed to burst from her and she wrote to this same Archbishop of her longing to go to Japan as a missionary to lose herself in a selfless, wholehearted zeal and, possibly, martyrdom. But this, too, was forbidden her.

It is unlikely that a woman whose early letters reveal, as hers do, so much absorption in her children, and who found it a colossal effort of will not to go to Adeline before six in the evening when she had measles at Grand Coteau, should be-come as indifferent to them as her enemies suggested. The sight and sound of other children always round her must have been an unbearable reminder. It is a measure of the discipline she imposed upon herself that no one guessed her suffering and most condemned her for her apparent lack of it. It was possible only because of her attitude of mind, and though this was conditioned by the desire to do God's will, which seemed to demand the loss of her children, it was conditioned also by the attitude of an age in which the concept of mother-hood was sterner than today, although often overlaid by in-tense demonstrations of affection. It was considered a mother's duty to lead her child to uprightness and God, to give him a sense of destiny and responsibility, not, as today, to protect him from a sense of inferiority, to act as an insurance against emotional insecurity. Within this concept it is easier to un-derstand Cornelia's initial agreement to enter a convent and forgo a natural relationship with her children whose material well-being was, in any case, guaranteed by Shrewsbury and Borghese. It was not in her power to see into the future and realize how wrongly it would all turn out in fact, and she failed entirely to see the psychological dangers inherent in the plan. Of these she seems always to have been oddly unaware, and yet out of the mistakes she unwittingly inflicted on her own children she learned the intuitive sympathetic understanding of others which is the keynote of her educational system. It was a sacrifice whose cost we cannot reckon, but it was not a sacrifice in vain.

Its effect, though superficially unapparent, was great. The human soul, like the body, cannot undergo great pressure and remain the same. It must become, like steel that is tempered, strong, or, like spirit that is diluted, weak. With Cornelia the change is clearly marked. It is, moreover, shadowed in her handwriting. Before 1850, the loss of her children, and the trial, Cornelia's writing was leisurely and large and flowing, an ideal medium for the gentle truths, French pieties, and high aspirations it revealed. Afterwards the calligraphy shrank, the letters sloped more forwards and were more firmly formed. It was a concise brisk hand with no room for French quotation or high-flown sentiment, and it is significant that these no longer existed. They were replaced by the taut comprehensive reflections of the early Fathers or by the practical exciting imagery of St. Theresa.

Until then she had listened and obeyed. From then on she took counsel only from God and reserved her obedience for the direct commands of the Church. The docility that so delighted Pierce became the authority that so annoyed Wiseman. She listened neither to Emily Bowles nor to Lady Shrewsbury. She would not see Pierce until and unless he sent her Adeline. He did not and the course was set.

She had opened herself to the second criticism levelled against her by so many of her contemporaries—that she was arrogant and bold. Bold she undoubtedly was, for it was her belief that she was called by God to act a part, and the thought contained her. In His cause she became a pioneer and a fighter and when she thought herself in the right she gave no quarter. She was unhesitant and unyielding for, as she wrote: "I cannot give up what He has given me to do," and on another occasion: "I belong all to God. There is nothing that I would not leave to do His holy will and satisfy Him."

Her arrogance opens a larger issue—for if it exists it implies a thread of personal ambition, a flaw in the nature of her spirituality. There are only three witnesses for both her prosecution and her defense—her words, her actions, and the opinion of those who knew her. Her words deny the possibility. They exhort her and her followers constantly to preserve love and humility, to give everything to God. "Remember that you all have three superiors—God, your religious superior, and your conscience," she wrote to a nun, and again to another one of them: "I would grind myself to powder if by that I could accomplish God's will." She had, too, no fear of death, whose "taper in the outer room" would surely light up pretense unbearably, but longed for it as a means of enjoying "the ecstatic delight of loving God without interruption."

Words can be false witnesses. Without action they are nothing. Yet followed through the labyrinthine ways of argument, dissent, and disapproval, Cornelia's actions do support her words. In every instance she tried, without spite or pettiness, to interpret her "three superiors" and, when the three appeared irreconcilable, to interpret the first by means of the third.

She made mistakes. It was not in keeping for a Reverend Mother to send Pierce envelopes to post back addressed "in a feigned hand"*; it was foolish to trust Emily Bowles to the extent she did; it was unwise to send round the emendations to her rule suggested by Rome in 1870 without an explanation. But throughout the many administrative quarrels that dogged her it would be mistaken to think her wrong because she fought. In this respect she was no more than a pioneer who, in any circumstance in any age, encounters opposition. She was hampered, too, by being in Victorian England, where women in administrative capacities did not recommend themselves to public approval. Her ideas were in advance of her

---

* If it is true she did so, for the evidence is Pierce's and against its publication in one of his pamphlets Cornelia has pencilled, "I do not know what this means. No one ever opened any of his letters but myself, nor did anyone ever attempt such a thing that I know of." Pierce's point, however, was that it was done not so much to prevent other people from reading his letters as to avoid their knowing how often he wrote.

time, and had she lived a hundred, even fifty, years later many
of the things she fought for, or insisted on, would be looked
upon as the commonplace aspects of her duty as head of a
religious teaching order.

Yet the fact remains that apart from her business transac-
tions, her sturdy rebuttals of criticism and astringent pioneering efforts at expansion and creation, many who should have
been her friends became her enemies.

The explanation may lie in her manner, which was often
cold and reserved, or in the unfeminine and unpopular role
she still continued to play in spite of the repercussions of the
scandal which she had caused, but it may also lie in the fact,
a simple one to those who believe in God, that only by adversity and trial can sanctity be achieved.

Whatever the reason why the opinion of those outside her
convent remained so long against her, the loyalty within was,
in the circumstances, exceptional. And public opinion is in-
variably fickle. Alone, it cannot judge sanctity.

Was Cornelia a saint in her determination to do God's will
and attain perfection for His sake? It was certainly her ambition to become one, as it must be of all those who seek the
love of God. And though to an outsider such an ambition
seems based in pride, and may in fact at any stage become
so, it is in essence as far removed from pride as love is from
vanity, or charity from self-interest. There is no room for pride
in the love of God as there is no room for it in human love.
And sanctity is a dedication of love—a careful, deliberate,
wholehearted desire to meet perfection with perfection, to
gain virtue for God so that through it the soul can acquire
the possibility of identification with Him. It is this longing
to be at one with the beloved, a familiar one in the context
of human love, which makes all sacrifice, self-discipline, and
self-denial on God's behalf seem nothing. For to those who
love God only sin is unbearable, for only sin can hurt Him.

It is impossible to doubt Cornelia's love of God. But it is
possible to wonder whether her will was sufficiently subject
to Him to purify and strengthen her love till it became magnified to the heroic proportions of a saint.

It is with this matter of comparison and degree that canonization is concerned, and it is only for the purposes of canonization that it arises.

Today, Cornelia's case is being investigated, and her letters and documents are being collected for examination, by the tribunal set up to debate it by the Bishop of the diocese in which she died. The tribunal will listen to evidence for and against the alleged sanctity of this "Servant of God," as, in the initial stages, a candidate for canonization is called, and will be composed of three judges, a notary, and the Promoter of the Faith, more commonly known as the Devil's Advocate. When the evidence is complete a full report of the diocesan process will be sent to Rome, to the Sacred Congregation of Rites, which will subject it to a very close scrutiny before approving it for the "apostolic process," the next step in this careful and lengthy procedure. If, in time, Cornelia's cause is formally introduced it will be the business of the Devil's Advocate to produce the arguments used against her in her lifetime. It is tempting to wonder whether he will succeed or whether it will be proved that she "practiced in the heroic degree chiefly the three theological virtues, Faith, Hope, and Charity, and the four cardinal virtues, Justice, Prudence, Courage, and Temperance, with all these suppose and involve," and that she practiced them not "under certain circumstances" but supported by "numerous acts. A permanent and habitual practice, principally of charity, is required; and with regard to the cardinal virtues, the habit of that virtue which is the proper and distinguishing excellence of a person's calling."

This is the definition by which Cornelia will be judged, and in wondering whether she has attained that degree of heroic virtue we must divest ourselves of a natural prejudice against the scandals that attended her, and of our astonishment at the strange steps by which she was led to her vocation, for the ways of God are strange, and look to her rule for a guide to her intentions. To read it is to find the calm center of the fast-revolving wheel, and to discover so much that made Cornelia great, her practical resolution, her tranquillity, her faith, and her simplicity.

But however one decides in her regard, and one must do so

without pity, for she had none for herself, and with humor, for she had a great deal, one thing stands out—that in this altogether astonishing case perhaps the most astonishing thing of all is that Cornelia, if she is a saint, belongs not to that great and glorious band who, from the first, find their vocation in God, but to those few, brave, incalculable spirits who stumble, almost by accident, into sanctity and thereafter find it their vocation.

BIBLIOGRAPHY

GENERAL WORKS

T. W. ALLIES, *A Life's Decision*, Burns & Oates, 1913

LADY MARY ARUNDELL OF WARDOUR (edited by), *Arundell Papers*, Longmans

EDWARD BELLASIS, *Memorial of Sergeant Edward Bellasis*, Burns & Oates, 1893

CUTHBERT BUTLER, *The Life and Times of Bishop Ullathorne*, Burns & Oates, 1926

B. CHAMPNEYS, *The Memoirs of Adelaide Drummond*, Smith & Elder, 1915

L. E. O. CHARLTON, *Recollections of a Northumbrian Lady*, Jonathan Cape, 1949

WILLIAM FABER, *Lives of the Saints*, Burns & Oates, collected edition, 1900

DENIS GWYNN, *Cardinal Wiseman*, Burns & Oates, 1929
   Shrewsbury, Pugin and the Catholic Revival, Hollis & Carter, 1949

E. E. Y. HALES, *Pio Nono, A Study in European Politics and Religion in the 19th Century*, P. J. Kenedy & Sons, 1954

B. HOWE, *A Galaxy of Governesses*, Verschoyle, 1954

SHANE LESLIE, *Henry Edward Manning: His Life and Labours*, Burns & Oates, 1921

BASIL LUBBOCK, *Colonial Clippers*, Brown, Son & Ferguson, 1921
   Western Ocean Packets, Brown, Son & Ferguson, 1925

DAVID MATHEW, *Acton, The Formative Years*, Eyre & Spottiswoode, 1946

V. L. PARRINGTON, *Main Currents in American Thought*, Harcourt, Brace, 3 vols., 1927

ALISON PEERS, *The Collected Works of St. Teresa*, 3 vols., Sheed & Ward
  Mother of Carmel, S.C.M. Press Ltd., 1945
E. RAIKES, *Dorothea Beale of Cheltenham*, Constable, 1908
GRACE RAMSEY, *Thomas Grant, First Bishop of Southwark*, Smith & Elder
SHEILA KAYE-SMITH, *Quartet in Heaven*, Harper & Brothers, 1952
CECIL WOODHAM SMITH, *Florence Nightingale*, McGraw-Hill, 1951
SOCIETY OF THE HOLY CHILD JESUS, A Member of, *The Life of Cornelia Connelly 1809–1879*, Longmans, 1922, 4th edition, 1950
SPALDING, *The Life of Bishop Flaget*, Webb & Levering, Kentucky
CHRISTOPHER SYKES, *Two Studies in Virtue*, Alfred A. Knopf, 1953
WILFRID WARD, *The Life and Times of Cardinal Wiseman*, Longmans, 1897
NICHOLAS WISEMAN, *Recollections of the Four Popes*, Burns & Oates, 1858 (Pius VII, Leo XII, Pius VIII, Gregory XVI)
ZILONI, *Life of Princess Borghese (née Gwendoline Talbot)*, Burns & Oates, 1894

PAMPHLETS AND PRINTED PUBLICATIONS

CORNELIA CONNELLY, "The Book of Studies," 1863
  "The Book of the Rule," S.H.C.J. Several editions
PIERCE CONNELLY, An Address Delivered at the Anniversary Meeting of the Managers of the Female Orphan Asylum (Natchez), March, 1833. *Andrew Marschalk*, Washington, 1833
  "The Coming Struggle with Rome, Not Religious but Political," *T. Hatchard*, 1852
  "Domestic Emancipation from Roman Rule in England," *T. Hatchard*, 1852
  "Reasons for Abjuring Allegiance to the See of Rome," *T. Hatchard*, 1852

"Petition of Pierce Connelly, Clerk (Requesting that the House of Commons order the suppression of convents. With special reference to Cardinal Wiseman and Cornelia Augusta Connelly)," *Parliamentary Debates*, 1852

"The Madiai," a letter to the Rt. Hon. Earl of Aberdeen, *T. Hatchard*, 1853

"Case of the Reverend Pierce Connelly," *T. Hatchard*, 1853

"Supplement to the Case of the Reverend Pierce Connelly," *T. Hatchard*, 1853

"Oaths of Allegiance, A Security for National Independence," *T. Hatchard*, 1854

"Cardinal Newman versus the Apostles' Creed" (a sermon), *T. Hatchard*, 1880

UNDER THE PSEUDONYM OF JOCELYN: "The Pope in England and Who Shall Turn Him Out?" Three Letters to Sir W. Broadlands, London, 1853

"The Pro-Popery Conspiracy," A Fourth and Fifth Letter to Sir W. Broadlands, London, 1853

UNDER THE PSEUDONYM OF PASCAL THE YOUNGER: "Cases of Conscience," Thomas Bosworth, 1852

HOBART SEYMOUR, "A Lecture in Reply to Cardinal Wiseman," Bath, June 7, 1852

"A Review of Convents and Nunneries," June 7, 1853

ESSAYS AND ARTICLES

GORDON ALBION, "Restoration of the Hierarchy," published in *The English Catholics*, Burns & Oates, 1950

J. BATTERSBY, "Educational Work of the Religious Orders of Women," published in *The English Catholics*, Burns & Oates, 1950

PHILIP HUGHES, "The Bishops of the Century," published in *The English Catholics*, Burns & Oates, 1950

SHANE LESLIE, "Unpublished Letters of Wiseman to Manning," published in *Dublin Review*, No. 339, October, 1921

DAVID MATHEW, "Old Catholics and Converts," published in *The English Catholics*, Burns & Oates, 1950

MORGAN SWEENY, "Diocesan Organisation and Administration," published in *The English Catholics*, Burns & Oates, 1950

NICHOLAS CARDINAL WISEMAN, "The Hierarchy," published in *Dublin Review*, No. 58, December, 1850

"The Catholic Hierarchy," published in *Dublin Review*, No. 59, March, 1851

"The Madiai," published in *Dublin Review*, No. 67, March, 1853

And various articles in: *Dolman's Magazine*, 1845; *Dublin Review*, passim (see *Dublin Review*, 1836–1936, A Complete List of Articles Published between May 1836 and April 1936); *The Tablet*, passim (see especially January 8, 1848; May 12–19, 1849); *The Times*, passim (see especially the years 1848–1853); *Bills Weekly Messenger, Britannica, John Bull, Herald, The Morning Advertiser, Morning Herald, Punch, Rambler, St. James's Chronicle, Standard*, for the years 1849–1853

UNPUBLISHED SOURCES

Private Papers and Letters in the possession of Princess Marina Borghese

Private Papers and Letters in the possession of Miss Mary Ann Noonan, Cornelia Connelly's great-niece

Society of the Holy Child Jesus Archives. Nearly all the unpublished material I have used is contained in these archives. They contain many letters from various members of the Connelly family and from Lord and Lady Shrewsbury, Cardinal Wiseman, Bishop Ullathorne, Bishop Grant, and Bishop Danell, as well as Cornelia's spiritual notebooks, her conventual records, and her school and housekeeping accounts. They also include duplicates of many relevant documents contained in the Vatican and Westminster Archives, among them Pierce Connelly's proposed rule for the Society of the

Holy Child Jesus and papers to do with the St. Leonards dispute.

The relevant documents in the Southwark Archives have been sealed off pending investigation into Cornelia Connelly's cause.

INDEX

Image Books

. . . making the world's finest
Catholic literature available to all

THE WORLD'S FIRST LOVE
By Fulton J. Sheen

The whole story of Mary, Mother of God, lovingly and reverently portrayed in the inimitable style of the great Bishop.

D30—75¢

THE SIGN OF JONAS
By Thomas Merton

The absorbing day-by-day account of life in a Trappist monastery by one of the great spiritual writers of our times.

D31—95¢

PARENTS, CHILDREN AND THE FACTS OF LIFE
By Henry V. Sattler, C.Ss.R.

An invaluable guide for parents and teachers for sex instruction of children, based on tested and approved Catholic methods and principles.

D32—75¢

LIGHT ON THE MOUNTAIN
The Story of LaSalette
By John S. Kennedy

The miraculous appearance of the Blessed Virgin Mary at LaSalette in 1846 dramatically and inspiringly portrayed.

D33—65¢

EDMUND CAMPION
By Evelyn Waugh

The heroic life of the great English Jesuit and martyr told in the matchless prose of one of England's greatest authors.

D34—75¢

HUMBLE POWERS
By Paul Horgan

Three beautifully told novelettes which magnificently emphasize the eternal power of faith, love and sacrifice.

D35—75¢

SAINT THOMAS AQUINAS
By G. K. Chesterton

A superb introduction to the work and personality of the Angelic Doctor by the scintillating and irresistible G.K.C.

D36—75¢

ON THE TRUTH OF THE CATHOLIC FAITH (SUMMA CONTRA GENTILES) BOOK TWO: CREATION
By St. Thomas Aquinas, newly translated, with an Introduction and notes, by James F. Anderson.

The second volume of the new translation of St. Thomas Aquinas' great classic *Summa Contra Gentiles.*

D27—95¢

If your bookseller is unable to supply certain titles, write to Image Books, Department MIB, Garden City, New York, stating the titles you desire and enclosing the price of each book (plus 5¢ per book to cover cost of postage and handling). Prices are subject to change without notice.

8

Image Books

... making the world's finest Catholic literature available to all ...

THE PILLAR OF FIRE
by Karl Stern
Absorbing story of an eminent psychiatrist's spiritual journey from Judaism to Catholicism.
D83—85¢

ORTHODOXY
by G. K. Chesterton
One of the most enduring masterpieces of 20th-century Catholicism's outstanding literary figure.
D84—75¢

THIS IS CATHOLICISM
by John J. Walsh, S.J.
Comprehensive and authoritative question-and-answer explanation of the Catholic religion.
D85—$1.25

MEDIEVAL ESSAYS
by Christopher Dawson
Brilliant study of Christian culture, its origins and its influence.
D86—95¢

VESSEL OF CLAY
by Leo Trese
Informal, informative revelations of a parish priest's daily life.
D87—65¢

SAINTS FOR SINNERS
by Alban Goodier, S.J.
Nine saints whose varied roads to sanctity have deep significance for modern men and women.
D88—65¢

THE LONG LONELINESS
by Dorothy Day
Stirring autobiography of an unusual and dedicated woman.
D89—85¢

THIS IS THE MASS
by Henri Daniel-Rops
Introduction by Fulton J. Sheen
Illustrations by Karsh
The Mass eloquently described by Daniel-Rops and graphically illustrated by Karsh photographs of Bishop Sheen.
D90—95¢

If your bookseller is unable to supply certain titles, write to Image Books, Department MIB, Garden City, New York, stating the titles you desire and enclosing the price of each book (plus 5¢ per book to cover cost of postage and handling). Prices are subject to change without notice.

23

Image Books

THE ORIGIN OF THE JESUITS
by James Brodrick, S.J.
An absorbing chronicle of the events and characters involved in the founding of one of the Church's greatest orders, the Society of Jesus. **D91–85¢**

A POPULAR HISTORY OF THE REFORMATION
by Philip Hughes
A popular and comprehensive presentation of the characters and events of the Reformation, told by an outstanding Catholic historian. **D92–95¢**

THE RESTLESS FLAME
by Louis de Wohl
An exciting novel of St. Augustine and his times. **D93–85¢**

PROGRESS AND RELIGION
by Christopher Dawson
A thorough analysis of the concept of progress in world history, its development through the centuries, gradual decline, and position today. **D94–85¢**

SCHOLASTICISM AND POLITICS
by Jacques Maritain
Thought-provoking reflections of the world-famed philosopher on the human person—what he is, the basis for his innate dignity, what is true human freedom, and the meaning and ultimate destiny of human life. **D98–95¢**

THE CATHOLIC CHURCH IN THE MODERN WORLD
by E. E. Y. Hales
A panoramic survey of the Catholic Church and her role in world affairs from the French Revolution to the Hungarian uprising in 1956. **D95–95¢**

THE LIFE of Teresa of Jesus
by St. Teresa of Avila
Trans. by E. Allison Peers
One of the great spiritual classics of all times—the autobiography of the renowned mystic and saint—in the definitive English translation. **D96–$1.25**

GIANTS OF THE FAITH
by John A. O'Brien
Revealing portraits of six great figures and their far-reaching effects on the history of Christianity. **D97–95¢**

THE SON OF GOD
by Karl Adam
A brilliant dissertation on the proofs of the divinity of Christ and a searching analysis of the belief that He is true man and true God. **D99–85¢**

THE MAN WHO WAS CHESTERTON
Ed. Raymond T. Bond
A superb collection from the writings of the inimitable G.K. presenting the brilliant literary genius at his scintillating best. **D100–$1.45**

If your bookseller is unable to supply certain titles, write to Image Books, Department MIB, Garden City, New York, stating the titles you desire and enclosing the price of each book (plus 5¢ per book to cover cost of postage and handling). Prices are subject to change without notice.